The Bristol Sessions

CONTRIBUTIONS TO SOUTHERN APPALACHIAN STUDIES

1. *Memoirs of Grassy Creek:*
Growing Up in the Mountains on the Virginia–North Carolina Line.
Zetta Barker Hamby. 1997

2. *The Pond Mountain Chronicle:*
Self-Portrait of a Southern Appalachian Community.
Leland R. Cooper and Mary Lee Cooper. 1997

3. *Traditional Musicians of the Central Blue Ridge:*
Old Time, Early Country, Folk and
Bluegrass Label Recording Artists, with Discographies.
Marty McGee. 2000

4. *W.R. Trivett, Appalachian Pictureman:*
Photographs of a Bygone Time.
Ralph E. Lentz. 2001

5. *The People of the New River:*
Oral Histories from the Ashe, Alleghany and
Watauga Counties of North Carolina.
Leland R. Cooper and Mary Lee Cooper. 2001

6. *John Fox, Jr., Appalachian Author.*
Bill York. 2003

7. *The Thistle and the Brier:*
Historical Links and Cultural Parallels Between Scotland and Appalachia.
Richard Blaustein. 2003

8. *Tales from Sacred Wind:*
Coming of Age in Appalachia. The Cratis Williams Chronicles.
Cratis D. Williams. 2003

9. *Willard Gayheart, Appalachian Artist.*
Willard Gayheart and Donia S. Eley. 2003

10. *The Forest City Lynching of 1900:*
Populism, Racism, and White Supremacy in Rutherford County, North Carolina.
J. Timothy Cole. 2003

11. *The Brevard Rosenwald School:*
Black Edcuation and Community Building
in a Southern Appalachian Town, 1920–1966
Betty Jamerson Reed. 2004

12. *The Bristol Sessions:*
Writings About the Big Bag of Country Music
Edited by Charles K. Wolfe and Ted Olson. 2005

Bill Hartley - 276-645-0111 (Repres)

Greg Wallace - 423-538-5758 (P.fn.)

The Bristol Sessions

Writings About the Big Bang of Country Music

Edited by
CHARLES K. WOLFE *and*
TED OLSON

CONTRIBUTIONS TO SOUTHERN APPALACHIAN STUDIES, 12

McFarland & Company, Inc., Publishers
Jefferson, North Carolina, and London

The editors thank the rights holders for permission to reprint these lyrics:

"I Am Bound for the Promised Land" by Alfred G. Karnes ©1928 by Peer
International Corporation (renewed). International copyright secured. All
rights reserved.
"The Longest Train I Ever Saw" by Claude Grant ©1927 by Peer International
Corporation (renewed). International copyright secured. All rights reserved.
"Sleep Baby Sleep" by Jimmie Rodgers ©1953 by Peer International Corporation
(renewed). International copyright secured. All rights reserved.
"The Soldier's Sweetheart" by Jimmie Rodgers ©1927 by Peer International
Corporation (renewed). International copyright secured. All rights reserved.
"Song of the South," by Bob McDill ©1980 Songs of Polygram International,
Inc. All rights reserved. Used by permission. Warner Bros. Publications
U.S. Inc., Miami, FL 33014.
"We Shall All Be Reunited" by Alfred Karnes and B. Bateman ©1929 by
Southern Music Pub. Co. Inc. (renewed). International copyright secured.
All rights reserved.
"The Wreck of the Virginian" by Alfred Reed ©1927 by Peer International
Corporation (renewed). International copyright secured. All rights reserved.

Library of Congress Cataloguing-in-Publication Data

The Bristol sessions: writings about the big bang of country
music / edited by Charles K. Wolfe and Ted Olson.
    p.   cm — (Contributions to southern Appalachian
studies ; 12)
    Includes bibliographical references and index.

    ISBN 0-7864-1945-8 (softcover : 50# alkaline paper)

    1. Country music — History and criticism.   2. Sound
recordings — Tennessee — Bristol.   I. Olson, Ted.   II. Wolfe,
Charles K.   III. Series.
    ML3524.B73   2005
    781.642'09768'96 — dc22   2005002558

British Library cataloguing data are available

On the front cover: A mural celebrating the Bristol sessions,
located on State Street in Bristol, painted by Tim White.
Photographed by John Maeder.

Manufactured in the United States of America

McFarland & Company, Inc., Publishers
  Box 611, Jefferson, North Carolina 28640
  www.mcfarlandpub.com

To Ralph Peer, the producer of the historic Bristol sessions, without whom many of the musicians that recorded in Bristol, Tennessee/Virginia, during 1927 and 1928 might never have been heard outside their home communities; to the Stoneman Family, whose members not only helped Peer realize the Bristol sessions in the 1920s but also more recently helped in the realization of this book by generously cooperating with every stage of research; and to Ralph Blizard, master fiddler of the nearby community of Blountville, Tennessee, who kept the music of the Bristol area alive for new generations to enjoy.

Contents

Part III: Remembering the Bristol Sessions

Part IV: Musicological Studies of the Bristol Sessions

Part V: After the Bristol Sessions

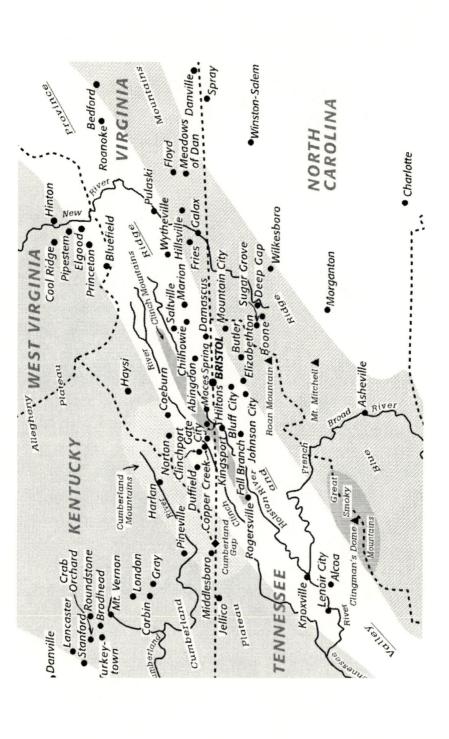

Introduction

Country music, which has attained international success and popularity, was forged from a variety of American musics, including Southern gospel, blues, Western music, Cajun music, and Tin Pan Alley. Arguably, though, the predominant regional music to influence country music was from Appalachia. When new technologies, introduced after World War I, allowed for the permanent preservation of sounds in reasonably life-like form, commercially distributed recordings of various genres of music became widely popular. By the mid-1920s, the first recording sessions of country music were occurring in such major cities as Atlanta and New York, attracting musicians from across the southern United States, including from Appalachia. Soon, the kind of music preserved at these studios — essentially the same music that was being performed on front porches and at community events in the South — sold far more copies when commercially released as records than producers and their companies had originally anticipated, creating a widespread demand for more records containing "hillbilly" music (a catch-all term encompassing much of the white folk music performed in the South during that era). Before long, producers looking for additional musical talent to make more hillbilly records brought their equipment into the countryside where most of the musicians who performed that type of music lived.

Opposite: Map of Bristol, Tennessee/Virginia, and the Tri-Cities Area, showing the locations from which musicians had to travel in order to record in Bristol in July/August 1927. Courtesy Nancy Fischman, Center for Appalachian Studies and Services, East Tennessee State University.

By 1927, two of the major record companies of the 1920s, Columbia and OKeh, had successfully released hillbilly records, while another important early label, the Victor Talking Machine Company (later renamed RCA Victor), was seeking to tap more deeply into the new market. That year, Victor's newly hired producer Ralph S. Peer identified an ideal place in which to make such records: Bristol, a small city straddling the Tennessee-Virginia state line and near several Appalachian areas known for distinctive musical heritages. A pioneering producer responsible for the first commercially released recording of Southern white music (a 1923 78 rpm record made in Atlanta containing two performances by Fiddlin' John Carson), Peer knew that a number of the musicians who had heretofore made hillbilly records resided near Bristol, including Ernest V. Stoneman and Henry Whitter. So, on Friday, July 22, 1927, Peer and two Victor engineers, Edward Eckhardt and Fred Lynch, set up a temporary studio in a building on the Tennessee side of downtown Bristol's State Street — a studio that incorporated the latest recording technology. On Monday, July 25, Peer recorded Stoneman, at that time the best-known among the local musicians (Stoneman already had several hillbilly hits to his credit). Between that day and August 5, 1927, Peer presided over the now-famous "Bristol sessions," recording 19 separate acts and obtaining 76 acceptable takes. Utilizing state-of-the-art equipment (most notably, new Western Electric microphones), Peer and his engineers ensured that the sound quality of the recordings they made in Bristol exceeded that of virtually all previous hillbilly recordings. Equally significant was the high quality of the performances recorded during the Bristol sessions. Today, many of the Bristol recordings — even those by now-obscure musicians — are appraised as having been technically and aesthetically ahead of their time. Additionally, some of the finest acts in country music history (especially Jimmie Rodgers, of Meridian, Mississippi, and the Carter Family, from nearby Maces Spring, Virginia) made their first records during the Bristol sessions. Peer went to great lengths to produce definitive recordings, and they continue to influence musicians, not only in contemporary country music but also in such genres as bluegrass, revivalist folk music, and rock music.

Charles K. Wolfe and I first discussed the creation of this book in the spring of 2001, at the International Country Music Conference held annually at Belmont University, in a meeting room with a stunning view of Nashville. From that vantage point, overlooking the city that purports to be the capital of country music but that in fact assumed that position rather late in country music history, Dr. Wolfe and I talked about the importance of disseminating the story of the Bristol sessions in order to encourage a more balanced view of the evolution of country music. While the Bristol sessions had recently received romanticized attention from music aficionados disgruntled with mainstream Nashville country and excited by the music of such legendary performers as Jimmie Rodgers and the Carter Family, Dr. Wolfe and I decided that the Bristol sessions and the movement behind the field recording sessions of the era were still not widely understood. Another reason for our undertaking the book was the imminent celebration of the 75th anniversary of the Bristol sessions, a fact duly noted around Bristol (especially by the Bristol-based organization the Birthplace of Country Music Alliance, which had planned for a series of concerts commemorating the Bristol sessions). As the music community in and around Bristol prepared to celebrate that anniversary, it soon became clear that Dr. Wolfe's pioneering article on the Bristol sessions ("The Legend That Peer Built: Reappraising the Bristol Sessions," included in this book) was virtually the only reliable source of information on what actually happened in Bristol from late July to early August in 1927. It became apparent that, while people around the world are familiar with the Bristol sessions because they launched the careers of Jimmie Rodgers and the Carter Family, relatively few articles had been published that insightfully interpreted the Bristol sessions' influence on later music and musicians. For this project, Dr. Wolfe and I sought to compile already published articles that explored aspects of the Bristol sessions story, as well as newly written articles on heretofore neglected aspects of the story. Articles from several music scholars were commissioned to fill in the gaps in the story, while Dr. Wolfe contributed an important new article illuminating the 1928 Bristol sessions and the previously overlooked 1928 and 1929 sessions in nearby Johnson City, Tennessee. In many respects, those sessions are companion field recording sessions to the 1927 Bristol sessions in that they help round out the picture of the music scene in the heart of Appalachia at the dawn of the recorded sound industry. In an effort to underscore the fact that the area around Bristol remains a vital music scene today, Ajay Kalra and I added an essay tracing musical developments in the area since the Bristol sessions. Any doubts that those sessions were as significant as local music boosters had claimed were allayed in 2003 when the Bristol sessions were placed by the Library of Congress on its inaugural list of fifty most significant historical recordings (compiled for the National Recording Registry program).

As the person responsible for creating a coherent manuscript about the Bristol sessions out of valuable yet disparate parts, I'd like to gratefully acknowledge the following people for their significant help with this project: Charles Wolfe, for his expertise, his invaluable suggestions, and his dedication to sharing his knowledge of the Bristol sessions; Nolan Porterfield, for his pioneering scholarship and for allowing us to borrow from his now much-quoted phrase about the Bristol sessions for the title of this book; Bill Hartley, executive director of the Birthplace of Country Music Alliance, for his ongoing interest in this book project; Kathy Hawthorne Olson, for her familiarity with the people and places in and around Bristol; Ajay Kalra, for his computer skills; and Ned Irwin, Nancy Fischman, Troy Gowen, and Brad Reeves, all staff members of East Tennessee State University's Center for Appalachian Studies and Services, for their technical assistance.

Dr. Wolfe and I both wish to express thanks to the authors who have written articles especially intended for this book; thanks also to a number of people — writers, photographers, editors of periodicals, and representatives of organizations (archives and song publishers, primarily) — who have generously granted us permission to include in this book other documents that will help increase general understanding of the Bristol sessions (credit information is provided). We are especially indebted to Stacey Wolfe, who compiled the detailed index for the book. Equally vital has been the encouragement from descendents of several musicians who recorded in Bristol in 1927 (specifically, members of the Carter Family and the Stoneman Family); these descendents share the goal of everyone involved in this project: to ensure that a new generation will hear and more fully appreciate the music and the musicians that Ralph Peer recorded in Bristol more than 75 years ago ... during the field recording sessions that shook the world.

Ted Olson
Spring 2005

PART I

Before the Bristol Sessions

1. Early Sound Recording Technology and the Bristol Sessions

Eric Morritt

In July 1927, Ralph Peer, a talent scout and producer for the Victor Talking Machine Company, came to Bristol, Tennessee, looking for new "hillbilly music" performers to record. He brought with him what at the time was still a very new technology. Prior to 1925, making field recordings at remote locations was only possible with bulky equipment, and the resulting recordings were of limited quality and were not pressed for public enjoyment. Recordings made outside of a studio were used primarily for folkloristic study or for experimental purposes. Since the discovery of recorded sound in 1877, recording technology had evolved significantly; the equipment used at the Bristol sessions made it possible to release to the public recorded music of a much higher quality.

The history of successful sound recording began with Alexander Graham Bell, the inventor of the telephone. In 1875, Bell was attempting to transmit the human voice over telegraph lines. Having studied hearing and acoustics, Bell was familiar with a device from the 1850s, developed by a Frenchman named Leon Scott, called the *phonautograph*. Recording sound patterns on a soot-covered paper, the phonautograph revealed that sound existed in wave form and that sound waves could be traced on paper and studied. Bell developed the telephone based upon ideas culled from both the telegraph and the phonautograph. For the telephone, he used a metal diaphragm that converted sound vibrations into mechanical vibrations when one spoke into the sender; depression of the diaphragm in response to a compression in the sound wave pattern caused a wire attached to the diaphragm to touch the surface of a liquid that filled a cup at the bottom of the sender, closing an electrical circuit. The wire dipping in the solution — under the action of the diaphragm being vibrated by the voice — opened and closed the circuit, mimicking the switching action of a telegraph key. Instead of sending dots and dashes, Bell's device set up a pulsating current in the line that represented the sounds being spoken into the sender.

Shortly after the invention of the telephone, another inventor active in advancing telegraph technology, Thomas Alva Edison, experimented with a telegraph recording device that could send, receive, and store messages on an embossed paper disc, recorded by a sharp stylus that captured sound vibrations in a fashion similar to the movement of the wire in Bell's telephone. Familiar with Bell's work, Edison discovered a method for actually playing back sound when he ran one of his telegraph recordings at high speed. Edison later described the sound that this device made as "light and musical — almost like human speech heard indistinctly." Edison began to seriously experiment with recording speech in July 1877, and in December of that year, his machinist, John Kreusi, finished a prototype of a recording machine. Edison succeeded in making a sound recording on a strip of tinfoil, and, for the first time in history, actual recorded sounds were reproduced.

A prolific professional inventor, Edison, satisfied with his invention of the first sound recording machine, turned his attention to other projects. Other inventors, including Alexander Graham Bell's cousin Chichester Bell and the latter's associate, Charles Sumner Tainter, began to develop sound recorders based on Edison's ideas. Chichester Bell and Tainter made changes in recording technology, eliminating the tinfoil, which could not be saved or re-played many times, and substituting a wax-coated cardboard tube that could be played repeatedly, or even shaved and reused for a new recording. The two inventors also changed the design of the machine, introducing a motor to spin the tube, which resulted in a clearer, steadier sound and solved the problem of speed variations caused by rotations from an uncoiling hand-wound spring. In 1886, Bell and Tainter introduced the graphophone.

Edison realized that others were taking interest in his invention and that he needed a better machine if he was to make his *phonograph* marketable on a large scale. Calling his staff together, Edison and his team worked without interruption for three days and emerged with a significantly improved phonograph — one that featured a better motor, substituted a solid wax cylinder for the unstable coated cardboard of Bell and Tainter's machine, and contained an improved recorder and reproducer.

It is interesting to note that neither Bell and Tainter nor Edison thought of using the phonograph for entertainment purposes: the machine's intended use was for office dictation and business communications. The 1880s and 1890s saw numerous lawsuits between the two teams of inventors over patents, but agreements were finally reached, and both of the teams' companies began leasing their phonographs to businesses for use as dictation equipment. Both companies experimented with recordings of entertainment material, and soon "coin-in-the-slot" phonographs started showing up in hotel lobbies, restaurants, train stations, and other public places. By the mid–1890s, as superior recording and record duplication techniques emerged, small and affordable cylinder phonographs meant for use in the home appeared on the market.

As wax cylinder recording was being developed, another inventor, Emile Berliner, attempted a disc-based system of recording. Berliner noted that wax cylinders were very fragile, required considerable storage space, and could only hold two minutes of recorded material. Berliner's recording device traced the sound on a zinc plate coated with beeswax. The recording was then sprayed with acid to etch the grooves into the zinc plate, forming a master record. The master was then electroplated, and the metal negative peeled away from the master plate was used to press copies in Duranoid–a hard plastic material that had previously been used to make buttons and telephone receivers.

In 1887, Berliner began marketing a simple hand-cranked device he called the *gramophone*, along with Duranoid records. The device was initially viewed as a toy, and the quality of the reproduced sound it delivered was inferior to that produced by cylinder phonographs, largely because of the acid etching involved in Berliner's process. Berliner hired machinist Eldridge Johnson to develop a spring motor for his gramophone. Fascinated by Berliner's machine, Johnson developed a better process for recording and duplicating records. Forming his own company, the Consolidated Talking Machine Company, located in his hometown of Camden, New Jersey, Johnson developed and marketed an improved gramophone and higher quality records. In 1900, Berliner filed suit against Johnson over the sale of the latter's gramophone, claiming patent infringement; Berliner, however, lost the lawsuit. In 1901, to commemorate his court victory, Johnson renamed his improved gramophone the "Victor," and adopted Francis Barraud's now famous painting, "His Master's Voice," as his official trademark. He also changed the name of his company to the Victor Talking Machine Company.

At the turn of the twentieth century, three major companies were competing in the phonograph industry: Edison's company; Bell and Tainter's company, American Graphophone (better known by their distribution company name of Columbia); and Victor. Over the next twenty years, the phonograph would become a popular source of entertainment. Commercial recordings during this period primarily showcased marching bands, popular singers and comedians, dance music, and opera. Few recordings were made of stringed instruments, or of other instruments that did not produce significant volume, the reason for this being that in the early days of recorded sound, recording was accomplished without electricity. Records were made with raw sound energy through a process called acoustic recording.

In the early days of recording, a typical session took place in a sparsely equipped "recording room" or unsophisticated "recording laboratory"—a very different environment from the elaborate sound studios of today. Although simple carbon microphones had been developed for the telephone, they were useless for recording; telephones worked on battery power, and the signal was transmitted without amplification. Amplifiers had not yet been invented, and the unamplified signal from a microphone was no better than that captured acoustically by the horn. Early recordings incorporated the raw energy of the sound produced by the musicians, employing large horns to direct the sound and focus it on a thin glass or metal diaphragm. The cutting stylus, attached to the diaphragm, made contact with the rotating cylinder or disc. The musicians performed before the horn, and the sound waves traveled down the horn, creating a corresponding vibration pattern in the diaphragm. The pattern was then transmitted to the recording stylus, cutting a groove in a soft wax blank.

An acoustic recording session was often described by those involved as an ordeal. Musicians, singers, conductors, and other personnel were placed in peculiar locations. If there was a conductor, he was usually relegated to a corner of the room, instead of in front of the group as at a public performance. Instrumentalists would be crowded behind a singer, with some sitting on bleachers. This unusual arrangement was employed in an effort to direct as much sound as possible from the voices and instruments into the recording horn. Sometimes modified instruments, such as the Stroh violin, were utilized at early recording sessions; a diaphragm and horn attached to the bridge of some modified stringed instruments lent the sound produced by the instruments better direction, resulting in improved clarity of the recorded sound.

Refinements in acoustic recording technique over time led to an improvement in the quality of recordings, chiefly a result of the better placement of instrumentalists, discovered through trial and error. Audio mixers had not been invented, so if an instrument was not heard distinctly or was inordinately loud in the resultant recording, that instrument had to be moved closer or farther away from the horn, and the recording was tried again.

Opera singers had to be physically repositioned in relation to the horn during certain passages in order to balance their voices with the orchestra.

In addition to marching band music, dance music, and singing and talking records, another category of recordings emerged around 1918: "ethnic" or "race" recordings. Improvement in radio broadcast quality and competition from live music broadcasts on the radio prompted recording companies to seek additional niche markets as well as regional and ethnic musics to increase listening audiences; previously unrecorded musics also held novelty appeal to mainstream audiences. Early musical performances marketed as ethnic or race recordings featured musicians mimicking Irish, Jewish, Negro, and various rural or "rube" accents. The market expanded to include hillbilly music when two enterprising musicians from Texas, fiddlers Eck Robertson and Henry Gilliland, recorded sides for the Victor Talking Machine Company in New York City on June 30, 1922. On June 14, 1923, Fiddlin' John Carson recorded two numbers in Atlanta for the OKeh label. Although not big sellers by later standards, partly because the limitations of the acoustic recording process made stringed instruments sound thin and weak, Carson's recordings sold in surprisingly substantial numbers, leading the northern-based recording companies to sense a significant untapped market for music from the rural American South.

Acoustic recording lasted through the mid–1920s. In 1906, Lee De Forest had developed the audion, a three-element vacuum tube that made radio possible. Spurred by a technical paper presented in 1919 by A. G. Webster on the theory of matched impedance, the Western Electric Company's J. P. Maxfield and H. C. Harrison began work on an electronic recording system that would be capable of making more dynamic records than those made using the acoustic process. Their system, introduced in 1924, employed the newly designed microphone, an electronic amplifier in the studio, and an electromagnetic cutter on the lathe in the control room. The new electronic recording process captured sound more faithfully than did acoustic recording, and allowed musicians to be placed in a comfortable formation around the microphone while ensuring that they would be heard distinctly. This electronic system recorded soft sounds and subtle instrumentation with a clarity approaching what theretofore had been only possible with very loud sounds. The electronic equipment's portability also made it possible to record in locations other than a record company's studio, since the equipment could be set up almost anywhere. An acoustic recording setup was usually built into a recording room and could not be moved.

The Victor Talking Machine Company and the Columbia Phonograph Company began issuing electronically produced recordings to the public in mid-1925, and Victor's Orthophonic Victrola and Columbia's Viva-Tonal

Advertisement for Victor, the recording company that hired Ralph Peer and that released the recordings from Peer's 1927 and 1928 Bristol sessions. The ad reflects the transition from the acoustic to the electronic recording process during the 1920s. In using the phrase "Electrically Recorded," Victor was accurately representing its embrace of the improved recording process, and at Bristol the company utilized state-of-the-art recording technology, including a new type of microphone made by Western Electric. Some other recording companies of that era, as a ploy to sell more records, bragged in their ads about offering "electrically recorded" releases yet continued to use the inferior acoustic recording process. Courtesy Eric Morritt.

phonographs became available later that year. Both machines were specially designed *acoustic* phonographs created to play back the new electronic recordings. The electronic recording equipment initially used by the studios was very expensive, and electrical playback systems were far too costly for the average consumer. Maxfield and Harrison designed an affordable acoustic phonograph that contained a six-foot-long folded horn, the taper and shape of which followed a logarithmic formula, unlike the horns used in earlier acoustic phonographs. This design gave an acoustic phonograph the frequency response necessary to faithfully reproduce electronically recorded music. Together, the higher fidelity of the electronic recording process and the improved acoustic phonographs displaced the acoustic recording process from the recording industry.

Electronic recording dramatically influenced musical styles. For example, the use of the new microphones on early recordings and in early radio was directly responsible for the increasing popularity of the soft, crooning style of singing practiced by such popular artists as Rudy Vallee. This more relaxed vocal style was already in evidence in the singing of Jimmie Rodgers on the Bristol sessions recordings. Additionally, the electronic process rendered possible higher quality recording of stringed instruments, and thus led to an increase in the number of recordings of string bands, a favored format in the early years of country music.

The popularity of new commercial discs containing recorded music increased during the 1920s, and soon stores began to specialize in the sale of a wide variety of these "records." Collection of Charles K. Wolfe.

These developments in recording technology during the mid-1920s had a major impact on the record industry and on the business of commercial music. With this new technology, Ralph Peer nurtured a music that would grow into a top-selling genre of recorded music — initially nationally, but eventually internationally.

PART II

The Bristol Sessions

2. The Legend That Peer Built: Reappraising the Bristol Sessions

Charles K. Wolfe

In the summer of 1927, RCA Victor Records — then known as the Victor Talking Machine Company — set up a temporary recording studio in Bristol, Tennessee. Over two weeks, seventy-six performances by nineteen different acts were recorded at that studio; among the performers were such country music pioneers as Ernest V. "Pop" Stoneman and his family, guitarist-singer-harmonica player Henry Whitter, and protest singer Blind Alfred Reed. The most historically important of the recordings, however, were made by two theretofore unknown acts. The first act was a solo performer named Jimmie Rodgers, who was then living in Asheville, North Carolina, but was originally from Meridian, Mississippi. The second act was a family trio from nearby Maces Spring, Virginia, who called themselves the Carter Family. These recordings have imbued the Bristol sessions with a legendary quality and have ensured that the sessions are mentioned in virtually every history written about country music. Bill Malone, in his definitive book *Country Music USA*, has referred to the Bristol sessions as "one of country music's most seminal events"; Johnny Cash, whose wife's mother was one of the original Carter Family members, has said, "These recordings in Bristol in 1927 are the single most important event in the history of country music." In 1972, I published the first attempt to document the entire session (in *Old Time Music* magazine), and since then numerous other schol-

Reprinted from *The Journal of Country Music*, 1989. Used by permission of the Country Music Foundation, Inc.

ars and collectors have contributed to the effort to reconstruct the Bristol sessions. With new research generated by the Country Music Foundation Records reissue album *The Bristol Sessions,* by recently uncovered discographical data, and by previously unavailable interviews, it seems an appropriate time to take a fresh look at the event, and to try once again to understand just what went on in Bristol during the summer of 1927 and how those field recording sessions made such an impact on country music.

Almost from the start, the Bristol sessions were viewed through stereotyped and romantic lenses. Some of these perceptions were generated by Victor itself, or by its sessions supervisor, Ralph S. Peer. In 1928, barely a year after the 1927 Bristol sessions, Peer gave an interview in which he recalled that Jimmie Rodgers had been "running around in the mountains" before his session in Bristol, and that when he tried out "he was laughed at." In the 1930 Victor Records catalogue, the biographical sketch of Rodgers describes the session as "a Victor recording expedition into the mountains of Tennessee." Peer later claimed that when the Carter Family first appeared at the

Downtown Bristol: The 1927 Bristol sessions took place in late July and early August of 1927, on the second and third floors of the building used by the Taylor-Christian Hat Company. Courtesy Birthplace of Country Music Alliance.

temporary Bristol studio, they looked like they had "come through a lot of mud" either by "horse and buggy or an old car.... He [A. P.] was dressed in overalls and the women are country women from way back there — calico clothes on.... They looked like hillbillies." Local tales in Bristol depicted the Carters as never having worn shoes and as never having been in town before; such tales even characterized the Carters as having climbed into the studio via the fire escape because they were too embarrassed to be seen in public.

None of these images is accurate, and many of them have no basis in fact. Jimmie Rodgers had been working on radio in Asheville before the sessions, and Peer spent more time than usual with him, suggesting that Rodgers was respected upon his arrival at the studio. A "recording expedition" (with the connotations of a jungle safari) was a fairly routine activity by 1927, and Bristol, a good-sized city, was hardly a mountain camp. The Carters routinely came into Bristol, and while they may have been modestly dressed, none of the Carters remembered recording barefoot. So why did Peer and Victor distort the representation of the Bristol sessions? One possible reason was that they perceived that the commercial appeal of this "old-time" music lay in its rural, mountain character. It was Peer, after all, who had first recorded Fiddlin' John Carson in 1923, thus sparking wider interest in such music; and it was Peer who, in 1925, coined the name "Hill Billies" to describe a popular Virginia string band. Record jackets and catalogues featured rural or mountain iconography: fiddlers at old-time dances, mules coming down mountain trails, singers sitting on cabin porches. Just as early country music radio program directors like George D. Hay and John Lair would create a hayseed image for the music they promoted, Peer and other early record company publicists sought to authenticate their product by emphasizing its rural origins.

Another reason for a distorted image of the Bristol sessions is our modern naïveté regarding the early recording industry, particularly its relation to country music. Doubtless, the recording industry as represented in Bristol during the summer of 1927 was a lot less complex than the industry of today; still, by no means did Peer merely saunter into town, make some primitive wax masters, pay everyone a flat rate, and head back to New York. Indeed, the trip was carefully planned — Victor had appropriated some $60,000 for Peer's trip to Bristol, Charlotte, and Savannah. Peer knew pretty much what he wanted: Victor, though the world's largest record company, was lagging far behind its arch-rivals OKeh and Columbia in capitalizing on the emerging country music market, and had hired Peer to build up its catalogue. "I had what they wanted," Peer later recalled. "They couldn't get into the hillbilly business, and I knew how to do it." Peer actively sought cover versions of songs that were hits on other labels, and signed most of his artists to three separate contracts: a recording contract with Victor that generally paid them $50 per side up front, as well as a modest royalty on each record sold; a song publishing contract with Peer's newly formed Southern Music publishing company; and a personal management contract with Peer himself. The recordings themselves were not primitive — the original Victor sessions sheets show that Peer and his two engineers, Edward Eckhardt and Fred Lynch, would often spend hours on a recording, doing three or even four takes, trying to get the best possible balance with their new Western Electric microphones. In a 1958 interview, recalling the equipment used in the 1927 Bristol sessions, Peer said that it "was very much like that used today." Although the studio was makeshift, the equipment was state-of-the-art, and the commercial recording industry in general was already fairly sophisticated, complex, and responsive to its market.

Years later, when asked why he chose Bristol for his first Victor sessions, Peer would admit: "I can't tell you why I picked Bristol, Tennessee — it just seemed to be a likely spot." In fact, there were good reasons for choosing Bristol. Flanked on the south by Johnson City, Tennessee, and on the west by the new "planned" city of Kingsport, Tennessee, Bristol was part of an urban area called the Tri-Cities, which in the 1920s boasted a collective population of over 32,000 people. This made it one of the largest urban areas in Appalachia, bigger even than Asheville. It was on the Tennessee-Virginia border and within easy driving distance from three other states: Kentucky, North Carolina, and West Virginia. Peer told a Bristol newspaper upon his arrival in that city for the 1927 sessions: "In no section of the South have the pre-war melodies and old mountaineer songs been better preserved than in the mountains of East Tennessee and southwest Virginia, experts declare, and it was primarily for this reason that the Victor Company chose Bristol as its operating base." It would be tempting to conclude that Peer's "experts" were in fact such pioneer folk song collectors as Cecil Sharp and John Harrington Cox, whose published collections of Appalachian songs had appeared in 1917 and 1925, respectively. There is only slim evidence, however, that Peer knew of them. One of the musicians Peer knew before his stint with Victor, Ernest Stoneman, had learned songs from Cox's *Folk Songs of the South,* and during one of Cecil Sharp's visits to America, the Victor company had engaged Stoneman to supervise a well-publicized series of recordings of English country dances which were, as the Victor catalogue put it, "gathered from the peasantry through years of search by Mr. Sharp himself." This was well before Peer joined Victor, but it is possible that someone in the Victor front office informed Peer about Sharp's work.

Most likely, Peer's experts were talent scouts from the other commercial record companies, men who had been going into the field across the South since 1924 to collect old songs on fragile wax masters. No talent scout had actually gone into Appalachia before, however, except for Peer himself: he had supervised a field recording session for OKeh in Asheville, North Carolina, during the summer of 1925. He also knew, from his participation in the small but competitive world of hillbilly music, that the area around Bristol was becoming known in the record trade as a hotbed for old-time music. By the middle of 1927, at least thirteen acts from that area had already recorded at various studios in the South, Midwest, and New York City: Fiddlin' Cowan Powers and Family (Victor, Edison), Henry Whitter (OKeh, Gennett), G. B. Grayson (Gennett), Ernest Stoneman (OKeh, Victor), Dedrick Harris (Broadway), the Roe Brothers (Columbia), Charlie Bowman with the Hill Billies (OKeh, Vocalion), the Avoca Quartet (OKeh), George Reneau (Vocalion), the Johnson Brothers (Victor), Uncle Am Stuart (Vocalion), John Dykes (Brunswick), and Dudley Vance (OKeh).

Far from being embarrassed over the hillbilly image their town was acquiring, the Bristol newspapers viewed the recording activity in Bristol with an attitude of boosterism, covering the events fully and sympathetically. Nearly two months after Peer's sessions, for instance, an article appeared in the *Bristol Herald Courier* (September 25, 1927) that summed up the year's record-making:

MANY PHONOGRAPH RECORDS MADE OF
LOCAL TALENT DURING PAST SUMMER

Musical talent from this section is rapidly winning favor with the leading phonograph record producing companies. Three times since the first of January companies who are recognized as leaders in the recording field have utilized talent from this section in the production of their records. The latest company to secure the services of talent from this section is the Okay [*sic*] Record Company of New York City, recognized along with Columbia and Victor as the biggest record producer in the world.

Tobe S. McNeil, local dealer for the Okay Company, induced F. B. Brockman ... to come here early in August to hear local talent in a tryout arranged at the McNeil Furniture Company. Approximately 30 persons tried out before Mr. Brockman and after hearing them he finally selected the male quartet of Avoca Tennessee Methodist Church. Composed of O. M. Hunt, K. T. Hunt, W. R. Stidman, and W. H. Bowers, the quartet went to Asheville, North Carolina, on September 12 and made six records for world distribution and probably 100,000 of them will be made.

Columbia was first to utilize local talent, H. W. Dolton coming here early in the year to hear talent recommended by Miss Margaret Owen, in charge of the Music Dept. at Boggs-Rice Company. Among those heard were Fred and Henry Roe, with Lewis Morrell. Dutton sent this trio to Atlanta in April, where they made three records, with Morrell doing the vocals.

Following this, Peer, Eckhart [*sic*], and Lynch of Victor came here in July and set up a regular recording station on State Street in the building at one time occupied by the Buchanan Furniture Company. The record station was kept open for approximately two weeks, during which time talent from all parts of these sections had try-outs.

Among the talent was: The Tennessee Mountaineers, Tenneva Ramblers, West Virginia Coon Hunters, Blue Ridge Corn Shuckers, Ernest Phipps, Ernest Stoneman, B. F. Shelton, Mr. and Mrs. Baker, and Mr. and Mrs. Carter of Gate City, Virginia.

The article was prophetic: Ralph Peer would return to Bristol to record again in the fall of 1928, while rival Columbia Records would set up shop in nearby Johnson City in 1928 and 1929. Brunswick, a latecomer to the country music recording industry, settled for field sessions in Knoxville during 1929 and 1930. Just as Peer had good reasons for choosing Bristol, so too did he lay his plans carefully. Part of the Bristol legend implies that Peer just wandered into town, improvising and relying on serendipity for his discoveries. Yet, even this early in the history of commercial recordings, Peer was in the habit of making a preliminary trip to scout for talent. "I made two trips," he said in discussing his field techniques in general. "I had learned all of this at OKeh. The preliminary trip is to stir up local interest and find out if there actually is anything." His planning trip to Bristol took place in late June, though Cecil McLister, the local Victor dealer and Peer's contact in Bristol, recalled that Peer had been there "two or three times before he made any recordings." McLister put him in touch with a local musical group who had recently auditioned for Brunswick, the Carter Family, and Peer corresponded with A. P. Carter, setting up a recording date. Another recommendation was Blind Alfred Reed, from Princeton, West Virginia, who had recently written a popular topical ballad about a train accident, "The Wreck of the Virginian." Locally, Peer contacted Charles and Paul Johnson, duet singers who accompanied themselves with a Hawaiian steel guitar, and who had already recorded for him in New York City. Peer also contacted Ernest Stoneman, who lived over the mountains in Galax, Virginia, and asked for Stoneman's help in locating local musical talent. Stoneman recalled:

> I remember when Mr. Peer wrote me a letter, and wanted me to find a place in town, in Galax, rent an empty room, so he could hold auditions. And he asked me to go around over the country and find some string bands and singers that could come for an audition, and he could find

which ones he wanted to record for Victor. I rented some rooms and went upon the mountain to the Lowes and Hankses, and I don't know how many places I did go, and I'd listen at them, and let them rehearse, so I could kind of tell whether he'd want to hear them or not. I took ever so many of them down there, but he didn't care about any except old Uncle Eck Dunford and Iver Edwards, a young boy from Ward's Mill who played harmonica and ukelele.

Through such efforts, Peer probably had over 60 percent of his time already booked when he arrived in Bristol. He knew many of the acts he was going to record, and in a few instances, he knew what he was going to record. Much like Stoneman, other individuals held auditions for Peer. These included a Victor dealer named Walter Howlette in Hillsville, Virginia, who found for Peer the Shelor Family–Dad Blackard band, as well as the group led by J. P. Nestor.

All of the aforementioned highlights another problematic aspect of the Bristol legend: Peer's efforts to publicize his work so as to attract new talent. From diverse sources, it now seems apparent that only nine of

An advertisement for "The New Orthographic Victrola," published in a Bristol newspaper on July 24, 1927, containing the only official public notice announcing the beginning of the 1927 Bristol sessions. Courtesy Birthplace of Country Music Alliance.

the nineteen acts recorded at Bristol in 1927 had not already been enlisted to record before the start of the sessions, and of these, only Jimmie Rodgers, the Tenneva Ramblers (Rodgers' former band), gospel singer Alfred Karnes, and banjoist B. F. Shelton were to have any significant success. Yet Peer did endeavor to spread the word about the sessions. For years, scholars looked in vain for the "newspaper advertisement" that Sara Carter thought she remembered seeing, but the only advertisement that actually appeared was a small box in a routine Victrola advertisement for the Clark-Jones-Sheeler Company, the local Victrola dealer. The ad ran in the *Bristol Herald Courier* on Sunday, July 24, the day before the sessions began, and stated, "The Victor Co. will have a recording machine in Bristol for 10 days beginning Monday to record records — Inquire at our store."

This was hardly an invitation to make records and become a recording star, but instead seemed designed to appeal to the curiosity of Victrola customers, or perhaps even to solicit custom recordings by parents who wanted to preserve their children's voices.

The newspaper piece that attracted so much attention was not a paid ad, but a cleverly planted story that appeared on Wednesday, the third day of the 1927 sessions. Peer recalled years later in a *Billboard* article:

> In Bristol, the problem [of finding talent and repertoire] was not easy because of the relatively small population in that area. The local broadcasting stations, music stores, record dealers, etc., helped me as much as possible, but few candidates appeared.
>
> I then appealed to the editor of a local paper explaining to him the great advantages to the community of my enterprise. He thought that I had a good idea and ran a half a column on his front page.

Peer's memory serves him wrong in one respect: the first "local broadcasting station," Bristol's radio station WOPI, did not go on the air until 1929. Nevertheless, his account of the newspaper story is indeed accurate. The story described in detail the recording of "Skip to Ma Lou, My Darling" with Eck Dunford and the Stoneman Family, which took place that morning. The ringer, though, was the last paragraph:

> The quartette costs the Victor company close to $200 per day — Stoneman receiving $100, and each of his assistants $25. Stoneman is regarded as one of the finest banjoists in the country, his numbers selling rapidly. He is a carpenter and song leader at Galax. He received from the company $3,600 last year as his share of the proceeds on his records.

Mention of the amount of money that one musician made from records had a more powerful effect on nearby poverty-stricken Appalachian communities than did any advertisement. In Peer's own words, "the story worked like dynamite and the very next day I was deluged with long-distance telephone calls from the surrounding mountain region. Groups of singers who had not visited Bristol during their entire lifetime arrived by bus, horse and buggy, trains or on foot." Peer wrote these words in 1953, long after he was hailed as the discoverer of modern country music, and he understandably might have dramatized events. Nevertheless, there were a few acts who were almost certainly drawn in by this news story: the Bull Mountain Moonshiners, led by fiddler Charles McReynolds, from Coeburn, Virginia; the Alcoa Quartet, a gospel group from the town of Alcoa, Tennessee, near Knoxville; Mr. and Mrs. J. W. Baker (cousins of the Carters), who lived near Fall Branch, Tennessee; the West Virginia Coon Hunters, a string band from Bluefield, West Virginia; and the Tenneva Ramblers, from Bristol. The story possibly drew in Jimmie Rodgers, the biggest star discovered at the sessions. We cannot be sure how many acts Peer auditioned and turned down, but he was apparently so busy during the second week that he had to resort to scheduling night sessions.

Another aspect of the Bristol sessions legend is the debate among scholars regarding the extent to which the Bristol recordings reflected traditional Appalachian music. A resolution to this debate hinges upon the degree to which musicians saw themselves as professional — either on the vaudeville circuit and theatrical venues, or through regular performances at dances, clubs, resorts, circuses, and the like. While we do not have detailed biographical information on all of the acts, we know that at least some of the musicians considered themselves professional entertainers: Jimmie Rodgers, the Tenneva Ramblers, Ernest Stoneman, Henry Whitter, the Johnson Brothers (who had perhaps the strongest vaudeville repertoire), and Red Snodgrass, a jazz band leader who worked at a Bristol hotel. Another group of musicians at the Bristol sessions would have to be classified as gospel performers: Alfred Karnes, Blind Alfred Reed, the Alcoa Quartet, the Tennessee Mountaineers, Ernest Phipps and His Holiness Quartet, and the Dixie Mountaineers (which included members of the Stoneman Family). All in all, 31 of the 76 performances recorded for Victor were gospel songs — about 40 percent, testifying to Peer's interest in gospel music and to his confidence that it formed a significant and popular part of the repertoire of old-time music. About 35 of the 76 performances were traditional (by most folkloric definitions), including songs recorded by such professional musicians as Ernest Stoneman and the Tenneva Ramblers. Among those 35 were some first recordings of songs that would become popular favorites: Eck Dunford's "Skip to Ma Lou, My Darling," the first Southern recording of this song later known to every school child; B. F. Shelton's haunting "Pretty

The Dixie Mountaineers recorded a number of sacred songs during the Bristol sessions. When the 1927 sessions began, the group's leader, Ernest V. Stoneman, was the best-known musician in the band, having already recorded for the OKeh, Edison, and Gennett recording companies. Seated left-to-right in this 1928 photograph are George Stoneman, Ernest Stoneman, and Bolen Frost; standing left-to-right: Iver Edwards, "Uncle Eck" Dunford, and Hattie Stoneman (Ernest's wife). Collection of Charles K. Wolfe.

Polly," the famed murder ballad, issued in a rare 12-inch format that gave the song over four minutes of playing time; Henry Whitter's harmonica showcase, "Henry Whitter's Fox Chase," which remained in the Victor catalogue until World War II; Mr. and Mrs. Baker's driving rendition of "The Newmarket Wreck," a train accident ballad that influenced a generation of folksingers; the Tenneva Ramblers' "The Longest Train I Ever Saw," the most popular early recorded version of a song later known as "In the Pines"; J. P. Nestor's "Train on the Island," featuring Norman Edmonds' exceptional fiddling, which found new favor during the urban folk revival of the 1960s after being included on compiler Harry Smith's *Anthology of American Folk Music*; and the Carter Family's "Bury Me Under the Weeping Willow" and "The Storms Are on the Ocean," both soon to become country and bluegrass standards. Peer did not just take whatever his performers had worked up for him: he left no doubt that he was seeking a specific type of music. His famous comment about Jimmie Rodgers—"we ran into a snag almost immediately because, in order to earn a living in Asheville, he was singing mostly songs originated by the New York publishers"—testifies to Peer's interest in old songs, both because the market demanded it, and because he wanted them for his publishing company. By the same token, Peer also wanted songs—vocal performances—as opposed to instrumentals, and he wasn't above pushing his artists in that direction. Clarice Shelor, who recorded with a group known as the Shelor Family or Dad Blackard's Moonshiners, recalled the process her band went through:

> They had Pa name over some old pieces and they'd say, "We got that, we've got that, we've got that," and Pa said, "Well, I'm about named out"; and he knew a lot of old pieces. But he finally mentioned some pieces they didn't have. They had all the tunes they already had in a big book. And they had more instrumental than singing records and said that singing helped sell the records.... I had to sit down over there and write out the words to that "Big Bend Gal." Lots of times I would sing just a verse here and there but I never had tried to sing it all. They wanted it all sung....

Ernest Stoneman told a similar story about Peer's reluctance to record some of the Galax area string bands that he had scouted up for the pre-session audition in Galax: "He turned down some pretty good music. But they didn't seem to be interested—they were bands. The trouble of it is, they couldn't none of them sing, and he [Peer] wanted songs. And Uncle Eck Dunford had a whole bunch of old songs, and that's what he was interested in."

Of the seventy-six recordings finally made, only seven (or about 9 percent) could really be called instrumentals, and four of these were harmonica novelty items. Four other sides (two by the Shelors and two by J. P. Nestor) were string band recordings with only incidental singing—possibly inserted at Peer's insistence.

The fact that such veteran Appalachian musicians as Clarice Shelor and Ernest Stoneman were surprised at the kind of music Peer wanted casts some doubt on the accuracy with which Peer was judging the actual nature of the region's music. Fiddlers and string bands were certainly integral components of Appalachian music in the 1920s, and in fact had been featured on most of the earlier recordings of the region's music on such labels as OKeh, Columbia, and Vocalion. Yet, Peer hesitated about recording fiddles and string bands for his new series on Victor, or if he did he tried to convert them into singing groups with instrumental accompaniment. One reason was that Peer sensed he was developing a new commercial art form—the genre of music eventually called country music—and that this art form was to be derived from, though not fully reflective of, traditional mountain music. In spite of all his public relations posturing about "pre-war melodies" and "old mountaineer tunes," Peer did not hesitate to tinker with his acts' styles and their repertoires. Songs, of course, had greater profit potential than instrumental tunes, as they were more distinctive and were more likely to be interpreted as unique rather than as variants of traditional tunes. If Peer could copyright songs with his new publishing company, upon each subsequent recording they would reap an additional harvest in royalties. "My policy was always to try to expand each artist by adding accompaniment or adding a vocalist," Peer recalled in 1958. An incentive to do so was a technological advantage he enjoyed over his earlier counterparts among field recording producers: Peer had the new electrical recording equipment recently designed by Western Electric. "I had all my experience, of course, from handling the OKeh situation," he remembered, "but now I had electronic equipment and two engineers instead of one." In spite of some limitations with the new microphones — certain vowel sounds for instance, did not "take" through them — the equipment was far more sensitive than the equipment in the old acoustic process, and this made possible the kind of balance needed to clearly hear a singer over the loud backing of a string band. In summary, songs were now easier to record, were more copyrightable, more profitable, and had an appeal to audiences far beyond the confines of Appalachia. The Bristol sessions thus became the first major field recording sessions to emphasize vocal music — which, in the end, was possibly the most important contribution of all.

Peer's success with his new recording style was not immediate. In spite of popular legends about sudden, spectacular success of the Jimmie Rodgers and Carter Family records, neither actually proved to be instant smashes; nor were either act's records issued in the first batch of releases from the session — Rodgers' record was buried in the middle of the second bunch of releases, ranking number 8 or 9 in the releases, while the Carter Family's debut was held up until the third batch, and then was released only at the request of Bristol's Victor dealer. The Rodgers coupling ("Sleep, Baby, Sleep" and "The Soldier's Sweetheart") apparently sold adequately, but not so much that Peer scrambled to get Rodgers back into the studio, as he did with the Carter Family. Rodgers' second series of recordings were, on the contrary, done when Rodgers turned up at Peer's office in New York City, where Rodgers had gone at his own expense.

What did Peer think would sell? As early as September 23, 1927, barely a month after he had returned to New York from the field trip to Bristol, Charlotte, and Savannah, Peer released the first two records from the Bristol session. Their "electrical" qualities were hailed by the *Bristol Herald Courier* in a story announcing the release of the records:

More than fifty mountain singers and entertainers were brought to Bristol in July and August by the Victor company for the making of phonograph records. The recording was made by the microphone method and was in charge of Ralph S. Peer. Those who heard the actual recording and the new records that are out say that the reproduction is actually better than the original rendition.

The first two records were Victor 20834, two songs by Ernest Phipps' "holy roller" gospel group, and Victor 20835, a skit by Ernest Stoneman's group (the Blue Ridge Corn Shuckers) called "Old-time Corn Shuckin'," parts 1 and 2. Peer probably rushed out the latter because Victor's arch-rival Columbia had struck paydirt a few months earlier with a similar sketch of rural comedy about a Georgia fiddling contest (by the Skillet Lickers). The former record reflected Peer's confidence in gospel music as a strong seller: of the first six records issued from Bristol, five were gospel records. Advertised as "New Orthophonic Victor Southern Series Records," 16 Bristol records — 32 songs — were issued by the end of 1927. Eventually all but seven of the 1927 Bristol sides were issued, and sold well enough that most of the performers would be invited back into the studios to record again. Indeed, only six of the acts did not return to the studios for further recordings.

How do the intervening years add to our understanding of the 1927 Bristol sessions? First, time has not diminished the impact and importance of those recordings; if anything, they loom larger in the annals of American cultural history. Yet, several aspects of the "Bristol legend" can be challenged. For one, it is now clear that the 1927 Bristol sessions were much better planned than previously thought, and the "advertising" Peer used was low-key and considerably less effective than popular myth suggests. Additionally, the event was by no means a capturing of pure Appalachian folk music performed by barefoot hillbillies at a remote mountain hamlet, but rather a calculated exercise in recording and marketing an emerging commercial art form within a bustling Southern city. The Victor label was not attempting to document traditional Southern musics but was making a sophisticated response to a perceived market demand. Gospel music played a large and significant role in the music of the Bristol sessions, and while many of the performers were bona fide traditional musicians, others were fully experienced professionals with vaudeville or stage backgrounds. Although not the first hillbilly music recording sessions, the 1927 Bristol sessions were among the first to be held within the Appalachian region, and the first in the history of country music to take advantage of the new electric recording technology. They were the first recording sessions to emphasize vocal music and songs, and the first to capture a broad cross-section of Southern music for a major recording company. Finally, the 1927 Bristol sessions yielded key debut

When he recorded at the 1927 Bristol sessions, singer, guitarist, and harmonica player Henry Whitter had just begun his historic collaboration with fiddler G. B. Grayson. Whitter recorded alone at Bristol, performing harmonica solos. Courtesy the JEMF Collection in the Southern Folklife Collection, Wilson Library, University of North Carolina at Chapel Hill.

recordings by two of the most influential acts in country music history, as well as initial recordings of numerous individual songs that would become important standards in the mainstream American music repertoire.

All in all, the 1927 Bristol sessions constituted an almost perfect representation of early country music: fiddle and banjo tunes, old traditional ballads, gospel music, old popular and vaudeville songs, rustic comedy, and instrumental showcases. The performers and their music also had an impact on later country and other roots-based musics. Jimmie Rodgers and the Carter Family are two obvious examples, but Ernest Stoneman — one of the greatest of the unsung pioneers whose family musical dynasty extends to present-day country music — did some of his best work at the 1927 Bristol sessions. The Bull Mountain Moonshiners were led by Charles McReynolds, who was the grandfather of modern bluegrass greats Jim and Jesse McReynolds. The Alcoa Quartet later performed on Knoxville radio with a young Roy Acuff. Jack Pierce, of the Tenneva Ramblers, eventually formed a western swing band, the Oklahoma Cowboys, which recorded for the Bluebird label. Blind Alfred Reed's songs became popular during the urban folk revival when performed by the New Lost City Ramblers and, later, by Ry Cooder and Linda Ronstadt. Henry Whitter, a year after the 1927 Bristol sessions, teamed up with famed fiddler and singer G. B. Grayson and became the first to record classics like "Train 45" and "Tom Dooley." The 1927 Bristol sessions would reverberate far beyond their time, sending ripples through the years, touching all kinds of people and their musics, and finally emerging as the legend they deserve to be. Those particular field recording sessions may not have ushered in a new type of music, but they did usher in a new musical era as well as a new way of perceiving and merchandising rural Southern white music.

The Bristol Sessions: A Chronology

The following is derived from the original Victor 1927 Bristol sessions sheets, as well as from the author's research.

Friday, July 22, 1927 Peer, his two engineers (Edward Eckhardt and Fred Lynch), and Peer's wife, arrive in Bristol and start setting up a studio at 408 State Street, 2nd and 3rd floors.

Saturday, July 23 Peer gives an interview to a reporter from the *Bristol Herald Courier* about the purpose of his visit.

Sunday, July 24 The *Herald Courier* publishes an initial story about the sessions in its morning edition, as well as a notice within a small box advertisement in the local Victrola advertisement.

Monday, July 25 The recording sessions begin, according to the following schedule:

8:30–10:00—Ernest Stoneman, Kahle Brewer, and Ralph Mooney
          Dying Girl's Farewell (2 takes)   Victor 21129
          Tell Mother I Will Meet Her (3)   Victor 21129
10:00–11:00—Ernest Stoneman, Irma Frost, and Eck Dunford
          The Mountaineer's Courtship (2)   Victor 20880
11:00–12:00—Ernest Stoneman and Irma Frost
          Midnight on the Stormy Deep (3)   Unissued*
1:30–5:00— Stoneman's Dixie Mountaineers
          Sweeping Through the Gates (3)   Victor 20844
          I Know My Name Is There (2)   Victor 21186
          Are You Washed in the Blood (3)   Victor 20844
          No More Goodbyes (2)   Victor 21186
          The Resurrection (2)   Victor 21071
          I Am Resolved (2)   Victor 21071

Tuesday, July 26

9:00–12:00 and *1:30–3:50*—Ernest Phipps and His Holiness Quartet
          I Want to Go Where Jesus Is (2)   Victor 20834
                                   Bluebird 5273
          Do, Lord, Remember Me (3)   Victor 20927
          Old Ship of Zion (2)   Victor 21186
          Jesus Is Getting Us Ready
             for That Great Day (3)   Victor 21192
          Happy in Prison (2)   Victor 21192
          Don't You Grieve After Me (2)   Victor 20834

Wednesday, July 27   An editor from a local newspaper, the *Bristol News Bulletin*, attends the morning session, and later that afternoon publishes a long description in the evening paper.

9:00–10:00—Uncle Eck Dunford and Mrs. Hattie Stoneman
          What Will I Do, for My Money's
             All Gone (3)   Victor 21578
10:00–11:00—Uncle Eck Dunford
          The Whip-Poor-Will's Song (2)   Victor 20880
          Skip to Ma Lou, My Darling (3)   Victor 20938
11:00–12:00— Uncle Eck Dunford and Ernest Stoneman
          Barney McCoy (2)   Victor 20938
1:30–4:00—The Blue Ridge Corn Shuckers
          Old-Time Corn Shuckin'
             Parts 1 & 2 (2/4)   Victor 20835

*Issued in 1987 on CMF-011

Thursday, July 28 According to Peer, phone calls and inquiries start pouring in. Nonetheless, he completes a very full schedule.

9:00–12:00—The Johnson Brothers (Charles and Paul)

The Jealous Sweetheart (2)	Victor 21243
A Passing Policeman (2)	Unissued*
Just a Message from Carolina (2)	Victor 20891

12:00–1:00—Peer takes the Johnson Brothers and his two engineers (Eckhardt and Lynch) to a noon luncheon at the local Kiwanis Club: he talks about making records, and the Johnson Brothers perform "My Carolina Home," "Alacazander," "Turkey in the Straw," "New River Train," "Old Happy Valley," and a Hawaiian march.

1:30–4:00—Blind Alfred Reed

Wreck of the Virginian (Train No. 3) (2)	Victor 20836
I Mean to Live for Jesus (2)	Victor 20939
You Must Unload (2)	Victor 20939
Walking in the Way with Jesus (2)	Victor 20836

4:00–5:30—The Johnson Brothers

Two Brothers Are We (from East Tennessee) (3)	Victor 21243
The Soldier's Poor Little Boy (3)	Victor 20891
I Want to See My Mother (2)	Victor 20940

5:30–6:40—El Watson

Pot Licker Blues (2)	Victor 20951
Narrow Gauge Blues (2)	Victor 20951

Friday, July 29 Two musicians from Corbin, Kentucky — B. F. Shelton and Alfred Karnes — arrive at the studio, traveling together, lured by the newspaper stories. Shelton performs solo with banjo, while Karnes accompanies himself on guitar; on some selections, it sounds as if Shelton plays a second guitar behind Karnes.

9:00–12:30—B. F. Shelton

Cold Penitentiary Blues (2)	Victor 40107
O Molly Dear (2)	Victor 40107
Pretty Polly (2)	Victor 35838†
Darling Cora (2)	Victor 35838†

1:30–5:10—Alfred Karnes

*Issued in 1987 on CMF-011
†These represent 12-inch masters, running four minutes each.

Called to the Foreign Field (2)	Victor 40327
I Am Bound for the Promised Land (2)	Victor 20840
Where We'll Never Grow Old (2)	Victor 20840
When I See the Blood (2)	Unissued
When They Ring the Golden Bells (2)	Victor 20933
To the Work (2)	Victor 20933

Saturday, July 30–Sunday, July 31   Peer spent part of the weekend auditioning new acts, and part driving into the mountains with his wife. No recording was done.

Monday, August 1   Logs show no recording activity in the morning, and it is likely that the time was devoted to auditions.

9:00–11:00—Auditions
12:00–2:30—J. P. Nestor and Norman Edmonds

Train on the Island (3)	Victor 21070
Georgia (1)	Unissued
John My Lover (1)	Unissued
Black-Eyed Susie (1)	Victor 21070

2:30–4:45—The Bull Mountain Moonshiners

Sweet Marie (2)	Unissued
Johnny Goodwin (2)	Victor 21141

6:30–9:30—The Carter Family

Bury Me Under the Weeping Willow (2)	Victor 21074
Little Log Cabin by the Sea (2)	Victor 21074
The Poor Orphan Child (2)	Victor 20877
The Storms Are on the Ocean (2)	Victor 20937

Tuesday, August 2

9:00–10:45—The Carter Family (minus A. P. Carter)

Single Girl, Married Girl (2)	Victor 20937
The Wandering Boy (2)	Victor 20877

11:00–12:30—The Alcoa Quartet

Remember Me, O Mighty One (2)	Victor 20879
I'm Redeemed (2)	Victor 20879

1:30–4:30—Henry Whitter

Henry Whitter's Fox Chase (3)	Victor 20878
Rain Crow Bill (2)	Victor 20878

Wednesday, August 3

9:00–12:00—Auditions

1:30–5:00—The Shelor Family

Big Bend Gal (3)	Victor 20865
Suzanna Gal (3)	Victor 21130*
Sandy River Belle (2)	Victor 21130*
Billy Grimes, the Rover (2)	Victor 20865

6:30–8:30—Mr. and Mrs. J. W. Baker

The Newmarket Wreck (2)	Victor 20863
On the Banks of the Sunny Tennessee	Victor 20863

Thursday, August 4

8:00–11:00—The Tenneva Ramblers (Jack Pierce, Claude Grant, and Jack Grant)

The Longest Train I Ever Saw (2)	Victor 20861
Sweet Heaven, When I Die (2)	Victor 20861
Miss Liza, Poor Gal (2)	Victor 21141

11:00–12:00—Red Snodgrass and His Alabamians

Weary Blues (3)	Unissued

2:00–4:20—Jimmie Rodgers

The Soldier's Sweetheart (4)	Victor 20864
Sleep, Baby, Sleep (3)	Victor 20864

Friday, August 5

10:00–1:00—The West Virginia Coon Hunters

Greasy String (2)	Victor 20862
Your Blue Eyes Run Me Crazy (2)	Victor 20862

3:00–3:30—The Tennessee Mountaineers

Standing on the Promises (3)	Victor 20860
Beautiful River (2)	Victor 20860

1927–1928 Releases from the Bristol Sessions

Released September 16, 1927

Victor #	*Artist*	*Title*
20834	Ernest Phipps and His Holiness Quartet	Don't You Grieve After Me

*These sides released under the name Dad Blackard's Moonshiners

20835	The Blue Ridge Corn Shuckers	I Want to Go Where Jesus Is Old Time Corn Shuckin'— Part I Old Time Corn Shuckin'— Part II
20836	Blind Alfred Reed	Walking in the Way with Jesus The Wreck of the Virginian
20840	Alfred G. Karnes	I Am Bound for the Promised Land Where We'll Never Grow Old
20844	Ernest V. Stoneman and His Dixie Mountaineers	Are You Washed in the Blood
35838	B. F. Shelton	Sweeping Through the Gates Pretty Polly Darling Cora

Released October 7, 1927

20860	The Tennessee Mountaineers	Standing on the Promises At the River (Beautiful River)
20861	The Tenneva Ramblers	The Longest Train I Ever Saw Sweet Heaven When I Die
20862	The West Virginia Coon Hunters	Greasy String Your Blue Eyes Run Me Crazy
20863	Mr. & Mrs. J. W. Baker	The Newmarket Wreck On the Banks of the Sunny Tennessee
20864	Jimmie Rodgers	Sleep Baby Sleep The Soldier's Sweetheart
20865	The Shelor Family	Billy Grimes, the Rover Big Bend Gal

Released November 4, 1927

20877	The Carter Family	The Poor Orphan Child The Wandering Boy
20878	Henry Whitter	Henry Whitter's Fox Chase Rain Crow Bill
20879	The Alcoa Quartet	Remember Me, O Mighty One I'm Redeemed
20880	E. Stoneman, Miss I. Frost, E. Dunford	Mountaineer's Courtship The Whip-Poor-Will's Song
20891	The Johnson Brothers	The Soldier's Poor Little Boy Just a Message from Carolina

Released November 18, 1927

20927	Ernest Phipps and His Holiness Quartet	Do, Lord, Remember Me
20951	El Watson	Old Ship of Zion Pot Licker Blues Narrow Gauge Blues

Released December 2, 1927

20933	Alfred G. Karnes	When They Ring the Golden Bells
		To the Work
20937	The Carter Family	The Storms Are on the Ocean
		Single Girl, Married Girl

Released December 16, 1927

20938	Uncle Eck Dunford	Skip to Ma Lou, My Darling
		Barney McCoy
20939	Blind Alfred Reed	I Mean to Live for Jesus
		You Must Unload

Released January 20, 1928

21070	J. P. Nestor	Train on the Island
		Black-Eyed Susie
21071	Stoneman's Dixie Mountaineers	The Resurrection
		I Am Resolved
21074	The Carter Family	Bury Me Under the
		Weeping Willow
		Little Log Cabin by the Sea

Released February 17, 1928

21129	E. Stoneman, E. K. Brewer,	Dying Girl's Farewell
	M. Mooney	
		Tell Mother I Will Meet Her
21130	Dad Blackard's Moonshiners	Suzanna Gal
		Sandy River Belle

Released c. February 28, 1928

| 21141 | The Bull Mountain Moonshiners | Johnny Goodwin |
| | The Tenneva Ramblers | Miss Liza, Poor Gal |

Released March 2, 1928

21192	Ernest Phipps	Jesus Is Getting Us Ready
	and His Holiness Quartet	for That Great Day
		Happy in Prison

Released March 16, 1928

| 21186 | Stoneman's Dixie Mountaineers | I Know My Name Is There |

Released April 6, 1928

21243	The Johnson Brothers	The Jealous Sweetheart
		Two Brothers Are We
		(from East Tennessee)

Released October 5, 1928

21578	Uncle Eck Dunford	What Will I Do, for My Money's
		All Gone

Remaining issues were Victor 40107 ("Cold Penitentiary Blues"/"O Molly Dear" by B. F. Shelton, released on September 6, 1929) and 40327 ("Called to the Foreign Field" by Alfred Karnes, released on December 5, 1930). Some of the 21000 series were out of print as early as March 1928, months before Peer's return to Bristol.

A Note on Sources

My earlier study of the 1927 Bristol sessions is "Ralph Peer at Work: The Victor 1927 Bristol Session," in *Old Time Music* 5 (Summer 1972): 10–15, supplemented by "The Discovery of Jimmie Rodgers: A Further Note" (which contains the 1928 newspaper interview with Peer) in *Old Time Music* 9 (Summer 1973): 24. The definitive account of Rodgers' role in the 1927 Bristol sessions is in Nolan Porterfield's *Jimmie Rodgers: The Life and Times of America's Blue Yodeler* (Urbana: University of Illinois Press, 1979). Peer's statements are taken from an unpublished interview with Lillian Borgeson, January and May 1958, in the files of the John Edwards Memorial Foundation, and in my own files; other comments about the 1927 sessions are taken from Peer's article "Discovery of the First Hillbilly Great" in *Billboard LXV*, no. 20 (May 16, 1953): 20–21. Material regarding Cecil Sharp's interaction with the Victor label is drawn from a company supplement dated November 1915, entitled *New Victor Record*. Material on Peer's Asheville sessions and early Bristol recording artists is taken from my own files and unpublished research. Comments by Cecil McLister are culled from an unpublished interview conducted on November 23, 1973, by Elizabeth Justus. Ernest Stoneman's quotes are taken from an unpublished interview, dated May 24, 1962, by Mike Seeger, while material involving the Shelor Family comes from Tom Carter's "The Blackard-Shelor Story," published in *Old Time Music* 24 (Spring 1977): 4–7. I am also indebted to Richard Blaustein, who shared with me his memories of his talks with Claude Grant; to Ed Kahn, an eminent Carter Family scholar; to Bob Pinson, for sharing discographical and copyright research;

to Carl Wells, for information about his father's Alcoa Quartet; to Edd Ward and Donald Lee Nelson, for their information about Karnes and Phipps; to Ivan Tribe, for his research on Ernest Stoneman; to Mrs. J. B. Hatcher for her help in Bristol; to L. S. Freeze; to Steve Davis; and to Richard Weize.

3. The Bristol Sessions: The Cast of Characters

Charles K. Wolfe

The Alcoa Quartet

This unaccompanied white gospel singing group was, as their name suggests, from Alcoa, Tennessee, south of Knoxville. It was headed by John "Lennie" Wells, who sang baritone, along with first tenor J. E. Thomas, J. H. Thomas as the second tenor, and W. B. Hitch on bass vocals. Hardly an amateur group fresh from the hills, in 1925 the quartet had recorded for Columbia (an early version of "Shall We Gather at the River") and was a favorite group to sing at a major funeral or religious gathering in East Tennessee. Later, the Alcoa Quartet would be heard with a young Roy Acuff over Knoxville radio.

The two songs they recorded in Bristol, "I'm Redeemed" and "Remember Me, O Mighty One," were, according to the session notes, sung directly from the seven-shape "convention" songbooks so much in vogue then.

Another set of recordings was made in late August 1927 in Winston-Salem for the OKeh label by "The Alcoa Quartet," featuring fiddle and guitar accompaniment. Family members feel, and audio clues support, that this was a different Alcoa Quartet.

Mr. and Mrs. J. W. Baker

At the time that Mr. and Mrs. James Wylie Baker recorded in Bristol, on August 3, 1927, they listed their address as Fall Branch, Tennessee, but

Mr. and Mrs. J. W. Baker: Like their relatives the Carters, the Bakers were a family group who recorded in Bristol in 1927; unlike the Carters, who went on to achieve worldwide fame as country music stars, the Bakers never recorded again. The men seated in front are believed to be the Bakers' sons (names unknown). Collection of Charles K. Wolfe.

later interviews with family members indicated that the two were from Coeburn, Virginia. Mrs. Baker was fond of singing old ballads, and her husband played the fiddle and guitar; they were cousins to the Carter Family.

On their recording made in Bristol, Mrs. Baker played the autoharp, and the Bakers were accompanied by J. E. Green on fiddle and J. H. Holbrook on banjo.

The Bakers recorded only two songs, but one of them was a fascinating ballad about a local train accident, "The Newmarket Wreck." The wreck was hardly news at the time; it had occurred September 24, 1904, when two passenger trains from the Southern Railway met head-on near Hodge's Station, a mile and a half from New Market, about 16 miles northeast of Knoxville, Tennessee. Sixty-two people died in the disaster, which was the result of a switching error by a railroad employee; the Southern Railway later even tried to suppress pictures of the wreck. Soon at least two ballads emerged; the one the Bakers used was first printed as a "broadside"—a single sheet of paper containing song lyrics, a tradition dating back hundreds of years to England and Ireland. "The Newmarket Wreck," credited to R. H. Brooks of Whitesburg, Tennessee, was printed on a sheet that had a drawing of the wreck on the front and the words on the back; this explains the reference in stanza 3 of the ballad, "You'll see a picture of the wreck, / Just over on the back."

The Blue Ridge Corn Shuckers

The Blue Ridge Corn Shuckers was a *nom de plume* used by Ernest "Pop" Stoneman and his group, based in Galax, Virginia, when they recorded a comedy skit called "Old Time Corn Shuckin'," parts 1 and 2. Included were Stoneman, Eck Dunford on guitar, Hattie Stoneman (Ernest's wife) on fiddle, and Ivor Edwards on ukelele. The remarkable success of recordings of such skits by the Georgia band the Skillet Lickers ushered in a fad for that type of record, and it was almost certainly Peer's idea to try to tap into that market. Among Ernest Stoneman's papers are the typed scripts for the skits.

The Bull Mountain Moonshiners

This square dance band from the town of Coeburn in Wise County, Virginia, was composed of members from two separate families. The leader was fiddler Charles M. McReynolds (1873–1952); his son William McReynolds played banjo. The senior McReynolds was the grandfather of two stars of bluegrass music, Jim and Jesse McReynolds. Also in the band were two brothers, Howard and Charles Greer, who both played guitars. A fifth member, Bill Deane, was the singer on the session.

According to Howard Greer, it was Bill Deane who heard of Peer's activities in Bristol, and the members of the band convinced a friend named Hughes to drive them over to Bristol on August 1. The band did not really have a name at this time, and on the trip over the men began worrying about what to call themselves. It was Hughes who suggested "Bull Mountain Moonshiners," and the name stuck. The band auditioned for Peer that morning, and that afternoon they recorded two sides, "Johnny Goodwin" and "Sweet Marie." The former, a version of the song "The Girl I Left Behind Me," was the only one released. Howard Greer recalled the engineers had to put a pillow under Charles McReynolds's foot because he could not play without stomping; they also moved Howard further away from the microphone because his guitar was "too loud." No one is sure why the other side was not released, but there is some evidence that the wax master was damaged when it was shipped to the Victor pressing plant in Camden, New Jersey.

The band had hoped to make more recordings later, but plans fell apart when Bill McReynolds died of appendicitis; soon afterward, Charles McReynolds stopped playing the fiddle.

(Howard Greer was interviewed in 1999 by David Winship and Tim White, and this is the source of much of this information.)

The Carter Family

Probably the best-known story to come out of the 1927 Bristol sessions is that of the Carter Family: A. P., his wife Sara, and Sara's teenaged cousin Maybelle, all of whom lived in nearby Maces Spring, Virginia. The six songs they recorded on August 1 and 2 in Bristol not only launched their own career as the most important singing group in country music history, but went a long way toward defining the sound of modern country music. Several accounts of their participation in the Bristol sessions appear in this collection, and dozens — if not hundreds — of articles have chronicled the career of the Carter Family.

In many ways, the first Carter session at Bristol was a harbinger to the kind of songs they would record in many later studio sessions: traditional Appalachian songs alongside older nineteenth-century sentimental and gospel songs rearranged and even rewritten by A. P. The Carter Family's very first recording was "Bury Me Under the Weeping Willow," a major hit that later became a country and bluegrass music standard (though often mistitled "Bury Me *Beneath* the Weeping Willow"). Both Sara and Maybelle had known the song since childhood, and it had been recorded by other singers before the Bristol sessions. "Little Log Cabin by the Sea" was a song A. P.

and Sara had featured as a duet long before they began recording; A. P. learned the song from a seven-shape shape note hymn book (the notation of which he could readily read). The song was a 1903 song penned by a Tennessee writer named W. C. Hafley, who originally named it "The Bible in the Cabin by the Sea."

The third song, featuring all three musicians, was "The Poor Orphan Child," a sentimental song copyrighted in 1899 by H. W. Elliot and rearranged by A. P. as a duet with Sara. "The Storms Are on the Ocean" is steeped in Appalachian tradition, yet has its roots in Scottish balladry.

The following morning Sara and Maybelle by themselves recorded two more songs, "Single Girl, Married Girl" and "The Wandering Boy." According to both Sara and Peer, it was Sara's high, driving version of "Single Girl, Married Girl" that convinced Peer the Carters were something special. Sara had learned the song from a friend back in Russell County, Virginia, some twenty years earlier.

The Carter records were, surprisingly, not among the first from the session to be released to the public. Eleven other pairings were released on Victor before the first of the Carter recordings — Victor 20877, "The Wandering Boy," backed with "The Poor Little Orphan Child" — came out on November 4, 1927. It was not until December 2 that the company issued "The Storms Are on the Ocean" and "Single Girl, Married Girl." The third Carter Family pairing was made available on January 20, 1928.

Uncle Eck Dunford

Although he appeared at the Bristol sessions as a member of Ernest Stoneman's assembly of musicians, Alex Dunford (1878–1953) was a remarkable fiddler, singer, and comedian in his own right. A native of Ballard Branch in Carroll County, Virginia, Dunford became part of the Stoneman family about 1908, when he married Callie Frost, a relative of Ernest's wife Hattie. According to Stoneman biographer Ivan Tribe, people who knew Dunford recalled him as an odd person who spoke an unusual drawl that some believed was derived from a Scots-Irish dialect. Little is known about his early life — some thought he was born out of wedlock. After his wife's death in 1921, Dunford remained alone until his own death in 1953.

Apparently, the Bristol sessions were Dunford's first recordings, and while he performed on many of them, only three were issued under his own name. The best known was "The Whip-Poor-Will Song," which Peer copyrighted in Dunford's name, though it was based on an earlier song called "The Call of the Whippoorwill" from 1889. The second Dunford recording was "Skip to Ma Lou, My Darling," which he sang solo, the first commercial recording of this well-known American play-party classic. "What Will I Do for My Money's All Gone" was a duet with Hattie, the actual recording of which was described at some length in the Bristol newspaper article about the sessions. Another duet credited to Dunford and Hattie was "Barney McCoy," a familiar nineteenth-century ballad that has appeared in numerous folksong collections.

Peer seemed fascinated with Dunford, and was especially intrigued by his comic monologues. Although the latter recorded none of these at Bristol, Peer invited Dunford to come to a session in October 1927 in Atlanta, where he recorded four bizarre monologues in his distinctive accent: "Sleeping Late," "My First Bicycle Ride," "The Taffy Pulling Party," and "The Savingest Man on Earth." When Peer returned to Bristol in 1928, Dunford, again with the Stoneman Family, made two influential recordings under his own name, "Angeline the Baker"

Eck Dunford

Eck Dunford: A multitalented performer who made records as a singer, a fiddler, and a comedian, Alex "Uncle Eck" Dunford appeared at Bristol with Ernest Stoneman, with Stoneman's wife Hattie, and as a solo performer. In the latter configuration, Dunford was the first person to record what has become an American classic folk song: "Skip to Ma Lou, My Darling." Courtesy JEMF Collection, in the Southern Folklife Collection, Wilson Library, University of North Carolina at Chapel Hill.

and "Old Shoes and Leggins"— the latter becoming known through its inclusion in the famed 1952 collection, *Anthology of American Folk Music.* In 1937 Dunford also recorded for the Library of Congress on fiddle as part of Galax's Bogtrotters Band.

The Johnson Brothers

Although they were popular in the 1920s, very little is known today about the background of the Johnson Brothers, Paul and Charles. Evidence and repertoire suggest that they were professional musicians and that they probably had worked in vaudeville before coming to Bristol. A 1925 newspaper story lists their home then as Boone, North Carolina. Ralph Peer already knew the Johnson Brothers, having recorded them at the Victor studio in Camden, New Jersey, three months earlier in May 1927. This is probably also why Peer invited the duo to join him at the Bristol Kiwanis luncheon on July 28, where the Johnsons performed a half-dozen musical numbers, including "My Carolina Home" and "New River Train," both songs they never recorded. At that first Victor session in May 1927, the duo recorded a distinctly urban vaudeville piece called "Alacazander." But they also recorded more traditional fare like "Careless Love," "Down in Happy Valley," and "Wings of an Eagle."

At Bristol, the Johnson Brothers made six more recordings on their own, while one of the brothers backed harmonica player El Watson on another piece. Their recordings included the first recording of a familiar sentimental song "I Want to See My Mother" (often known as "Aged Mother"), the only commercial recording of the British ballad "The Soldier's Poor Little Boy," and "A Passing Policeman," one of the more popular vaudeville songs. Later, in May 1928, Peer would invite the brothers back to Camden to do seven more songs, including the only recording of a topical event ballad, "The Crime of the D'Autremont Brothers," about a 1923 train robbery on the Southern Pacific Railroad that left four trainmen dead. In 1932, the Johnson Brothers did a final, though not very successful, session for the Gennett Company.

In many ways, the Johnson Brothers were harbingers of the new country music scene starting to develop in the late 1920s. The duo mixed old songs with pop songs, and apparently wrote a good deal of their material — a fact that certainly would have endeared them to Peer. The brothers were versatile, and could play guitar, steel guitar, mandolin, bones, and possibly even the instrument known as the tiple. It is quite possible that they came from East Tennessee; one of their songs speaks of Happy Valley, and though the phrase is a cliché, there was a real community called Happy Valley on the very edge of what is now the Great Smoky Mountains National Park, in Blount County. An original song by the duo, "Two Brothers Are We (from East Tennessee)," reinforces that conjecture. Nevertheless, leads on their later careers are slim to none. Researcher Gus Meade found a 1932 song copyright in the Library of Congress that bore the address of "Tuco, Kentucky," but such a place has not yet been located; it may have been a company town near Lexington, Kentucky, belonging to the Tuco manufacturing company.

Possibly because they were somewhat slick and professional sounding, very few of the 20 recordings made by the Johnson Brothers for Victor have

Johnson Brothers

The Johnson Brothers: A popular vaudeville duo during the 1920s who have since been overshadowed by other Bristol sessions recording acts, Paul and Charles Johnson recorded for Ralph Peer at Victor's Camden, New Jersey, studio shortly before traveling to Bristol to make additional records for Peer. Courtesy Guthrie T. Meade Collection, in the Southern Folklife Collection, University of North Carolina at Chapel Hill.

been reissued on modern LP and compact disc. They remain among the least known and recognized musicians who recorded at the 1927 Bristol sessions.

Alfred G. Karnes

This preacher and gospel singer who lived in Corbin, Kentucky, proved to be one of Peer's favorite singers, though most of the recordings he made at the 1927 sessions were familiar gospel standards like "Where We'll Never Grow Old" and "To the Work." His one original song, "Called to the Foreign Field," was his best-known recording. Included in this book are articles on Karnes's personal life, written by Donald Lee Nelson, and on Karnes's progressive singing style, written by Thomas Townsend.

Karnes's complete recorded work is currently available on the Document CD entitled *Kentucky Gospel.*

J. P. Nestor

The banjo and fiddle duo of J. Preston Nestor and Norman Edmonds had only two recordings released from the Bristol sessions, but for many fans and critics the two sides represent the apogee of Appalachian string band music. "Train on the Island" and "Black-Eyed Susie" summon up an earlier time when the fiddle and banjo constituted the customary string band, before the guitar made its way into Appalachia. "Train on the Island," especially, has become a favorite of string bands in modern times, and has been repeatedly reissued since 1952, when compiler Harry Smith included the tune on the *Anthology of American Folk Music.*

Not much is known today about J. P. Nestor, other than that he was probably from Hillsville, Virginia. It is thought that Nestor died in the late 1960s. We do know quite a bit about his musical partner at Bristol, Norman Edmonds. Born in Wythe County, Virginia, in 1889, Edmonds learned fiddle tunes and his fiddling style from his father, who in turn had learned it from his father. Norman held the fiddle on his chest rather than under the chin, again reflecting an archaic Appalachian style. In later years, starting in 1970, Norman came out of retirement and performed as a guest at the Galax Old Fiddler's Convention, and proved that he still had a firm command of his distinctive repertoire and style. He later appeared on several Galax compilation LPs, had his own show over Galax radio (*The Old Timers*), and recorded an entire LP for the independent Davis Unlimited label in 1970.

The other two sides recorded by Nestor and Edmonds at Bristol were "Georgia" and "John, My Lover," but these were for some reason never released, and the masters no longer survive in the Victor vaults. Several months after the Bristol sessions, the duo received an offer for an expense-paid trip to New York City to make more records, but Nestor refused to go.

Ernest Phipps and His Holiness Quartet

This group of religious singers from the Corbin, Kentucky, vicinity is noteworthy for being one of the very few acts to record the surging, unbridled Pentecostal singing styles during the early years of the recording industry. Details of their leader, Ernest Phipps (originally of Gray, Kentucky), are presented within this book in a newly researched article by Brandon Story.

Blind Alfred Reed

A remarkable singer, songwriter, and fiddler, Blind Alfred Reed made his living busking on the streets in and around Princeton, West Virginia. His original songs have emerged as some of the most acclaimed protest songs from the early years of the hillbilly music industry. The research conducted by the owners of Rounder Records (for that label's 1972 LP reissue of Reed's recordings) form the basis for the article included in this book.

Jimmie Rodgers

By far the best known and most famous of all the Bristol "discoveries" (along with the Carter Family) was Meridian, Mississippi native Jimmie Rodgers, who later gained fame as "America's Blue Yodeler." Included in this book are two important first-hand accounts of Rodgers' discovery, one written by Ralph Peer and one by Rodgers' wife Carrie Rodgers, as well as a new essay by John Lilly. The definitive Rodgers biography is Nolan Porterfield's *Jimmie Rodgers: The Life and Times of America's Blue Yodeler* (Urbana: Illinois Press, 1979).

The Shelor Family

The Shelors, a family string band from Meadows of Dan, Virginia, are the subject of an article by Tom Carter included in this book.

B. F. Shelton

One of the most remarkable banjo players to record at Bristol, or for that matter at any of the other early field recording sessions, was Benjamin Frank Shelton (1902–1963), a barber from Corbin, Kentucky. His four recordings from Bristol are considered by many experts to represent the epitome of the eastern Kentucky song style. Ralph Peer was impressed enough that he requested the Victor label to put two of Shelton's songs on twelve-inch discs — the type of disc usually reserved for classical music, allowing up to four and a half minutes of playing time per side as opposed to the usual three. Shelton's two longer sides contained the minor key ballads "Pretty Polly" and "Darling Cora," delivered in his eerie nasal voice. Shelton's other two recordings were of stark mountain blues: "O Molly Dear" is a version

B. F. Shelton: Probably lured to Bristol from his home in Corbin, Kentucky, in late July 1927, by newspaper articles chronicling Victor's recording sessions, Shelton was a masterful clawhammer banjo player; his recording of the traditional Appalachian ballad "Pretty Polly" remains one of the more moving performances from the 1927 Bristol sessions. Collection of Charles K. Wolfe.

of the piece that came to be known as "East Virginia Blues," while "Cold Penitentiary Blues" (which Shelton may have learned in prison) featured a steel slide on the banjo.

Born in Clay County, Kentucky, Shelton came from a family of musicians; he played the harmonica and guitar in addition to the banjo. Friends remember that in the 1920s Shelton operated a barber shop in downtown Corbin. Across the street from the shop was a restaurant that played the latest old-time records out on the sidewalk; Shelton was often seen running outside with a scrap of paper to write down the words to a new song. He knew Alfred Karnes, and the two musicians probably traveled to the Bristol sessions together.

Although Shelton made no more commercial recordings, his classic 1927 sides have been reissued numerous times since the 1960s.

Red Snodgrass and His Alabamians

This small dance band recorded one selection at the 1927 Bristol sessions, the jazz standard "Weary Blues," which was never released. Consisting of several instruments — a cornet, two clarinets, a trombone, a piano, a banjo, and drums — the band worked in a Bristol hotel (probably the one at which Ralph Peer was staying). Peer possibly recorded the band as a favor to the band leader — or perhaps "Weary Blues" was made for a fee as a vanity recording.

Ernest Stoneman

The musician who was the original reason Peer set up the 1927 Bristol sessions, Ernest V. "Pop" Stoneman was already a recording veteran when he showed up in Bristol. A native of Monarat, Virginia, Stoneman (1893–1968) was a carpenter by trade and was working in the Galax area in the 1920s. After hearing some of the early recordings by such other Blue Ridge singers as Henry Whitter, Stoneman felt he could sing better, so he traveled to New York City in 1924 to record his version of "The Titanic," which became a hit. This led to a plethora of other recording invitations for companies like OKeh, Edison, and Gennett. Stoneman first met Peer at his initial recording session in 1924, when Peer was working for OKeh, and a friendship ensued. When Peer joined the Victor Talking Machine Company in 1926, he signed Stoneman, encouraged him to organize a larger band, and paid the band's way to Camden for more recordings. By the time of the 1927 Bristol sessions, Stoneman had already recorded some two dozen sides for Victor alone, and over 100 sides for other labels.

Further details on the musical arrangements of some of Stoneman's Bristol sessions are in Jocelyn Neal's article, included in this book. A definitive biography of Stoneman and his family is *The Stonemans: An Appalachian Family and the Music that Shaped Their Lives* by Ivan Tribe (University of Illinois Press, 1993).

The Tennessee Mountaineers

The last group to record at the 1927 Bristol sessions — as a sort of benediction — was a church group from nearby Bluff City, Tennessee. One of the members of this group, named by Peer the Tennessee Mountaineers, was Roy Hobbs, a brother-in-law of A. P. Carter. One of the last surviving members of the group, Mabel Phelps Morrell, contributed a brief account of the session to this book.

The Tenneva Ramblers

Best known as the band that came to Bristol with Jimmie Rodgers, the Tenneva Ramblers featured three musicians from Bristol, Jack Pierce and brothers Claude and Jack Grant. Splitting from Rodgers the night before the auditions, the Ramblers were a well-known local band that kept busy playing for fairs and dances. Richard Blaustein's interview with Claude Grant provides details of the band's career and presents an interesting perspective on Jimmie Rodgers.

The Ramblers recorded three sides at Bristol in 1927, then traveled to Atlanta in February 1928 to record an additional six sides for Peer. These included "Darling, Where Have You Been So Long," "If I Die a Railroad Man," "I'm Goin' to Georgia," "The Curtains of Night," "The Lonely Grave," and "Seven Long Years in Prison." The band also recorded for Columbia later that year in Johnson City as the Grant Brothers.

In 1936, fiddler Jack Pierce recorded some sides for the Bluebird label after he organized a more modern string band called the Oklahoma Cowboys.

El Watson

Little is known about the harmonica soloist El Watson, who was the only African American participant in the 1927 Bristol sessions. A person with a similar name appears in the Johnson City directory for 1927, where he is listed as a laborer, but there is no certainty that that person was the Bristol sessions musician. His two sides, "Pot Liquor Blues" and "Narrow Gauge Blues," featured guitar accompaniment from Charles Johnson. The Johnson Brothers had recorded just before Watson, and Watson's harmonica is heard on their version of "The Soldier's Poor Little Boy." Those sides qualify as among the very first integrated country music or blues recordings.

An impressed Peer invited Watson to Victor's New York City studio in May 1928 to record four more numbers, including such old-time favorites as "Fox Chase" and "Sweet Bunch of Daisies," as well as "Bay Rum Blues" and "One Sock Blues." It seems likely that Watson also recorded at the 1928 Columbia sessions in Johnson City under the name Ellis Williams.

The West Virginia Coon Hunters

John Lilly discusses this remarkable string band from Bluefield, West Virginia, in some detail in Chapter 10.

Henry Whitter

A versatile musician from Fries, Virginia, Henry Whitter (1892–1941) came to Bristol in 1927 with a substantial discography behind him. He was a major figure for OKeh Records and would later win fame as the performing partner of the legendary Appalachian fiddler G. B. Grayson. Both of the harmonica solos that Whitter recorded in Bristol, "Rain Crow Bill" and "Henry Whitter's Fox Chase," he had recorded earlier for Peer when the latter was an OKeh producer.

4. Jimmie Rodgers and the Bristol Sessions

John Lilly

Folks everywhere knew about Jimmie Rodgers, and although some of them were reluctant at first to believe that he was really there in person, playing their own town, they soon learned that he was as much at home in Sweetwater or O'Donnell as in front of a Victor microphone or on the stage of some fancy big-city theater. Vernon Dalhart and Gene Austin might make a lot of records, but they didn't come out into the boondocks to rub shoulders and tell bawdy jokes and laugh with the plain folks who bought them. The effects of the Blue Yodeler's tours had been apparent for some time. Just when the first baby was named after Jimmie Rodgers isn't known, but there would be many to follow; and everyone had a personal story to tell about him — what Jimmie had said the time he played Wetumpka or Conroe, how he'd given his guitar to a blind newsboy in McAlester, the way he sang his way out of jail after killing his girlfriend, the time he invented the yodel, ran off with the mayor's wife, threw beer bottles off the hotel balcony, shot up the city square, or paid off the mortgage for a destitute widow. Most of the stories were pure fabrication, a few had some basis in fact, but all were derived from the simple, eloquent circumstance that Jimmie Rodgers was a genuine hero to those who needed one most — the plain, ordinary people across the land.

This account, taken from Nolan Porterfield's masterful biography *Jimmie Rodgers: The Life and Times of America's Blue Yodeler* (Urbana: University of Illinois Press, 1979), depicts the far-flung effects of Jimmie Rodgers' short recording and performing career. The long-term effects are played out

54

on a daily basis over country music radio stations, in recording studios, in live performances, and on front porches, more than 75 years after "America's Blue Yodeler" made his historic first recordings in Bristol, Tennessee, on August 4, 1927.

Born James Charles Rodgers on September 8, 1897, in the east Mississippi town of Pine Springs, Jimmie was the youngest of three boys born to Eliza and Aaron Rodgers. Aaron was a section foreman on the Mobile & Ohio Railroad, and his work kept him away from home much of the time. Eliza was a frail woman for much of her life. She died during childbirth when Jimmie was five years old. In 1904, Aaron remarried, and the family moved to nearby Meridian, Mississippi.

At odds with his stepmother, Jimmie Rodgers was brought up in a series of foster homes in Mississippi and Alabama, occasionally tagging along with his dad on railroad runs. His education was sporadic, mostly coming from the streets and railyards where he and his buddies loafed and hustled their time away. Living by his wits and constantly on the move, Rodgers' "rough and rowdy ways" were established early. He grew to be a clever, self-reliant individualist, happy-go-lucky and carefree on the one hand, lonely and disaffected on the other.

Rodgers' musical upbringing was as checkered as his home life. He had a grandfather and a preacher uncle who both fiddled, an aunt who was trained in "serious" music, and an early personal fascination with medicine shows and cylinder recordings. Drawn to the fun, excitement, and potential financial rewards of show business, young Jimmie organized neighborhood shows, entered talent contests, and even ran away with a traveling troupe. He learned blackface comedy; he also learned to sing in various styles and to play the banjo, mandolin, ukulele, and guitar.

Whatever his musical ambitions might have been at that time, Rodgers kept coming back to Meridian, and, like his father and older brother, he worked on the railroad. He labored alongside his father on the Mobile & Ohio Railroad and, at various times, held full-time positions as a call boy, a flagman, a baggage master, or a brakeman. He also worked for the New Orleans & Northeastern Railroad, the Florida East Coast Railroad, the Southern Pacific Railroad, and probably other railroad companies. Raised in a railroading family and growing up in a railroading town, it was natural that Jimmie Rodgers looked to the rails for income as well as for diversion.

Between railroad excursions, during long hours spent in the yards "waiting for a train," Rodgers learned how the yardmen, switchers, and hoboes amused and expressed themselves. During the 1920s, Mississippi was a haven for black blues artists, and Rodgers had extensive contact with these musicians and singers through his work and travel on the railroad. The simplicity, directness, and depth of feeling inherent in the blues also became essential elements in Rodgers' music, and his incorporation of the blues played a huge part in defining commercial country music as distinct from European-American traditional musics of the southeastern United States.

When he was 19 years old, Rodgers married Stella Kelley, a young college student from Louisville, Mississippi. This marriage did not last long, as Rodgers' irregular habits and sporadic earnings clashed sharply with Stella's expectations. The couple separated in less than a year, and divorced within two. The failed marriage left in its wake a sadder but wiser Jimmie Rodgers, and an infant daughter named Kathryn. Rodgers apparently did not realize that his estranged wife was pregnant, and he knew nothing of the child until meeting her unexpectedly, ten years later, after a show in Oklahoma, where Stella and Kathryn had settled.

In 1920, Rodgers courted and married Carrie Williamson, who was also from Meridian and was the daughter of a local Methodist minister. In 1921, the couple had a daughter who they named Anita. To Rodgers, his young family was a source of tremendous pride and inspiration, probably his first experience with domestic stability. Carrie and Anita Rodgers would stay with him through many highs and lows over the next 12 years.

In his early efforts to provide for his family, Rodgers combined occasional railroad assignments and sputtering forays into show business in which he scratched together pick-up bands and signed on with traveling tent shows. This pattern might have continued indefinitely except for an act of fate. In 1924, Rodgers was diagnosed with tuberculosis; hospitalized, he nearly died. At the time, a cure for T.B. had not yet been found, and the disease was a leading cause of death in the United States. Despite its burden on his spirits and on his family's prospects, the disease served to challenge and to drive Rodgers to pursue his dream of a musical career, since the physical rigors of railroading proved too great a strain for him.

While Rodgers aspired to break into professional music, his transition was not immediate. He never learned to read sheet music, and he had difficulty keeping even time. In her 1935 book about Jimmie Rodgers, Carrie Rodgers notes that her husband initially was not a very confident guitarist; for many years, he considered the banjo to be his main instrument. Musical limitations, combined with the attractiveness of a relatively reliable income from railroad work, repeatedly drew Rodgers back to the railroad yards. His health would inevitably fail him and he would lose his job; he would then perform music until another railroading job came along, beginning the cycle anew.

Several times, Rodgers and his wife sought new opportunities in Florida, New Orleans, Arizona, and Texas, but they always returned to Mississippi, with Rodgers sick and exhausted and without much money. In early 1927, Jimmie decided to try his luck in Asheville, a mountain resort town in western North Carolina. It is generally thought that he chose this destination for health reasons, believing that the fresh air and lofty altitude would be beneficial to his ailing lungs. Carrie Rodgers, however, wrote that her husband went to Asheville looking for railroad work, a prospect that worried her a great deal. She was pleased when he found other jobs — first working as a "special detective," then stoking a furnace at an apartment building. He soon sent for his wife and daughter to join him.

The move to Asheville provided Rodgers with the fresh start he needed. Nearly thirty years old and battling a terminal illness, he now approached his musical ambitions with a new sense of urgency and determination. Once he and his family had settled into a rent-free cottage, Rodgers began making the rounds and ingratiating himself to the local musicians. He was generally well-liked, found other musicians with whom he could perform, and soon secured a few bookings.

On February 21, 1927, the first radio station in Asheville — WWNC — was established. The call letters of the station stood for "Wonderful Western North Carolina," and the popular station continues to broadcast today. Rodgers was excited about this opportunity. On April 18 of that same year, he made his radio debut over WWNC with duet partner Otis Kuykendall on a thirty-minute program, which was received with little fanfare.

The following week, Rodgers traveled 60 miles over the mountains to Johnson City, Tennessee, where a large Rotary Club convention was taking place. He hoped to talk his way into a performance slot on one of the entertainment programs being offered there. Among the many other musicians at the event was a group from nearby Bristol, which straddled the border of Tennessee and Virginia. Called the Tenneva Ramblers, they took their name from a combination of the two states' names and played an impressive style of traditional string band music. The group consisted of guitar player and vocalist Claude Grant, his mandolin-playing brother Jack Grant, and 19-year-old fiddler Jack Pierce. Impressed with their music, Rodgers asked the trio to return to Asheville with him and become his "hillbilly ork" (i.e., his orchestra). Carrie Rodgers attested that her husband had already decided that he needed to find a full-time backup band, so he was on the lookout for such an ensemble. True to form, Rodgers was charming and persuasive, tempting the young musicians with the chance to join him on his radio broadcasts and offering them an opportunity to make money. It is doubtful that he disclosed the fact that his WWNC radio career, to that point, had consisted of one brief performance.

The Grant brothers and Jack Pierce were duly impressed, but they declined Rodgers' offer, as they were already committed to playing a full schedule of their own bookings. They kept Rodgers' phone number, however, and called him several weeks later to see if his offer was still good. Informed that it was, the trio came to Asheville, and debuted as the Jimmie Rodgers Entertainers on May 30, 1927, on WWNC.

The new act's repertoire consisted of traditional string band material, popular and Hawaiian songs, blues, comedy, and original numbers that Rodgers put together. The entire group stayed in the small cottage with Rodgers and his family, where they spent their first days together in rehearsal. According to his wife, Rodgers sometimes struggled during rehearsals to get his new team of musicians to play music with sufficient emotion. "Listen, fellas," she quoted him as saying. "Let's put more feeling in this. This is supposed to be pathetic."

The group was willing to play whatever music Rodgers required, anywhere they could find an audience. However, things were not going their way. The weekly radio program over WWNC was cancelled after a few weeks, and other bookings were hard to find. Money was tight, and Rodgers reportedly used what little money the group did generate to cover their living expenses and pay for publicity, with nothing left to pay the band members' salaries.

The Grant brothers were understandably disappointed. The group persisted for another few weeks, however, scraping together a few odd bookings in various mountain communities during the busy summer tourist season. Rodgers and the Tenneva Ramblers finally landed a substantial regular booking at the luxurious North Fork Mountain Resort outside of Marion, North Carolina, about 40 miles east of Asheville. At last, the group had steady work. The men stayed in comfortable tourist cabins during the day and played dinner music for well-heeled resort guests each evening.

In late July of 1927, Rodgers and Jack Pierce traveled over the mountains from North Fork back to Bristol to persuade Pierce's father to buy the musicians a new car. The trip proved fortuitous for Rodgers in more ways than one. Mr. Pierce was a successful barber, and Mrs. Pierce operated a boardinghouse in downtown Bristol on State Street, the main road through town that ran right along the Tennessee-Virginia state line. The Pierces' boardinghouse was on the Virginia side, directly across from a vacant storage building on the Tennessee side. An unusual number of musicians were staying at the boardinghouse that evening, and Rodgers soon learned that the Victor Talking Machine Company was in Bristol to record local artists. Musicians from across southern Appalachia had gathered in town for their chance to make records.

This was precisely the kind of opportunity that Rodgers had been seeking. He had already set his sights on becoming a recording star and had personally written letters earlier that year to both Victor and their competitor, Brunswick-Balke-Collender, requesting an audition. He was determined to make the most of this lucky break. The morning after securing the car deal and before driving the newly acquired 1925 Dodge back to North Fork, Rodgers and Jack Pierce crossed the street and introduced themselves to Victor recording representative, Ralph Peer. Mr. Peer greeted them cordially and showed polite interest when he heard that Rodgers and Pierce were members of a string band. "Bring the whole bunch in," Peer told them. Although Peer made no promises other than to give them a listen, Rodgers headed back to North Carolina filled with renewed hope and enthusiasm.

In North Fork, the Grant brothers were not so sure. Claude Grant later recounted that he and Jack did not feel that they had any material suitable for recording. Rodgers replied that he had already made up his mind to leave the group and to try his luck as a solo artist in Washington, D.C. The musicians might as well make a few recordings since they were going to be passing through Bristol anyway, he reasoned. The Grant brothers and Jack Pierce were convinced by Rodgers' argument. Serving notice at the resort and driving the Dodge to Asheville to pick up Rodgers' family and all of his worldly possessions, the group arrived in Bristol on the afternoon of August 3, 1927.

The events leading up to Rodgers' first recording session are unclear today, a result of 75 years of retelling and imperfect memory. In short, Rodgers and the other three musicians parted ways and recorded separately — he as a solo artist, and they as the Tenneva Ramblers.

According to Carrie Rodgers' account, the three other musicians went behind Jimmie's back and arranged to make their own Victor recording without him. "My thoughts were wild," she wrote. "How could they? O — how could they treat him so?"

Claude Grant, in a 1975 interview with Richard Blaustein of East Tennessee State University, claimed that an argument between Jimmie Rodgers and Claude's brother Jack was the cause of the split. Jack Grant and Rodgers had apparently had their differences for some time concerning the group's finances and Rodgers' unconventional business methods. These differences came to a head in Bristol, Claude said, and after an argument, Jack announced, "Claude, I'm not going to make any records with him."

In the liner notes to a 1972 reissue LP recording of the Tenneva Ramblers on Puritan Records (Puritan 3001), researcher Dave Samuelson offers a different version of the events leading up to the split. Samuelson claimed that the group actually arrived in Bristol on the evening of August 2 and auditioned several numbers together on the morning of August 3, including Rodgers' soon-to-be-famous song "T For Texas (Blue Yodel)." After a

Jimmie Rodgers and the Tenneva Ramblers (from left to right: Jack Grant, Rodgers, Jack Pierce, and Claude Grant): Accounts differ regarding the reasons Jimmie Rodgers left his former group, the Bristol-based Tenneva Ramblers, immediately before his participation in the Bristol sessions. Rodgers would quickly become a country music star, while the Grants and Pierce achieved far more modest, and primarily local, recognition. Courtesy Richard Blaustein Collection, Archives of Appalachia, East Tennessee State University.

successful audition, Samuelson wrote, the group set about rehearsing for the upcoming recording session. According to this account, an argument broke out among the musicians concerning what name they would use for the recording session. Rodgers wanted the group to be listed as the Jimmie Rodgers Entertainers; the others preferred their old name, the Tenneva Ramblers, with credit given to the vocalist for each song. When the group rejected his compromise offer of "Jimmie Rodgers and the Grant Brothers," Samuelson wrote, "Rodgers immediately went across the street to ask Peer if he could record alone."

Peer, interviewed in 1953 by the *Meridian Star* newspaper, offered a third version of the story, claiming that it was he who engineered the split. According to Peer, Rodgers and the group did audition together, but the music was not satisfactory to his ear. "The records," Peer said, "would have been no good if Jimmie had sung with this group because he was singing ... blues and they were doing old-time fiddle music. Oil and water, ... they don't mix." Peer conveyed that he decided to allow the string band to record some numbers "in order that nobody's feelings would be hurt," then he later brought Rodgers back to record as a solo artist.

Nolan Porterfield goes into considerable detail about these events in his biography of Rodgers, assembling a most-likely-case scenario. According to this version of the story, the four musicians arrived in Bristol and auditioned on August 3. Although Peer had reservations about the quality of their music, he scheduled the group to record together the following day. The musicians quarreled over their billing during a rehearsal that evening, and split up by mutual consent. Rodgers then showed up to record by himself the next day, to Peer's considerable relief.

Rodgers stood in front of a recording microphone for the first time around 2:00 P.M. on Wednesday, August 4, 1927, in a vacant storage building at 408 State Street in Bristol, Tennessee. It took him until 4:20 P.M. that day to record two songs: "The Soldier's Sweetheart" and "Sleep, Baby, Sleep."

The first number, "The Soldier's Sweetheart," was a sentimental ballad about a young man killed in World War I. Sung to the tune of "Where the River Shannon Flows," it was a song that Rodgers had put together about a boyhood friend who was a casualty in the war. "Sleep, Baby, Sleep" was a popular old lullaby that Rodgers had sung over WWNC. The songs were released as two sides of Victor recording number Vi 20864, on October 7, 1927.

The combination of ease and intensity in his singing voice and guitar work, his relaxed phrasing and clear articulation, and his strange and beautiful yodeling are all present in these earliest of Rodgers' recordings. Peer apparently recognized these qualities and sensed Rodgers' potential as a recording artist. Even though Rodgers' Bristol session did not initially yield tremendous sales for Victor, Peer arranged for a follow-up recording session on November 30, 1927, in Camden, New Jersey, recording four more songs.

With that session, they hit the jackpot. One of the songs recorded in Camden, "T For Texas (Blue Yodel)," was a national phenomenon, generating an excitement and record-buying frenzy that no one had predicted. The song, a Rodgers original composition, drew heavily on traditional blues while showcasing his unique guitar and vocal style and his characteristic yodel. The lyrics referred to Southern states ("T for Texas, T for Tennessee"), discussed trouble with women and work, and had a macho, slightly dangerous undertone ("Gonna shoot poor Thelma / Just to see her jump and fall"). Not only were these to be recurring themes in subsequent Rodgers songs (he re-worked these ideas for a total of thirteen designated "Blue Yodels"), they continue as popular themes in country music songwriting to this day.

By 1928, Jimmie Rodgers had experienced a meteoric rise from obscurity to stardom, foreshadowing the career trajectories of Hank Williams Sr. and Elvis Presley. Rodgers' years of hard living and grassroots entertaining served him well, as he scurried to meet the demands for live appearances and recording sessions. He continued to feature traditional songs like "Frankie and Johnny," such sentimental favorites as "Mother Was a Lady," railroad songs, and his calling-card Blue Yodels.

Rodgers also discovered a gold mine in the songwriting talents of his sister-in-law, Elsie McWilliams. Carrie's piano-playing sister had been in a three-piece dance band with Rodgers during his Meridian days, and McWilliams composed and collaborated extensively with him during the critical early phases of his recording career. Some of the well-known songs that bear her name are "My Rough and Rowdy Ways," "Daddy and Home," "My Old Pal," and "Mississippi Moon."

Setting a pattern for subsequent recording stars, Rodgers soon had songwriters and publishers pitching him material from every direction, augmenting his own prolific output. Reflecting the full array of current popular music, he and producer Peer recorded a staggering variety of songs and musical styles, from "Everybody Does It in Hawaii" backed with Hawaiian instrumentation, to "My Blue-Eyed Jane" with full Dixieland-style jazz band accompaniment, Rodgers embodied much of the music of his time. On his recordings, he was backed by a wide variety of instruments, including mandolin, jug, steel guitar, ukulele, banjo, tuba, musical saw, and harmony whistling. In addition to blues, lullabies, and novelty songs, he recorded Western material, train songs, comedy skits, sentimental parlor ballads, two duets, and one gospel song. He shared the studio with such musical icons as jazz great Louis Armstrong, pianists Earl "Fatha" Hines and Lillian Armstrong, fiddler Clayton McMichen (who wrote "Peach Pickin' Time Down in Georgia"), and guitarist Hoyt "Slim" Bryant (who wrote "Mother, the Queen of My Heart").

Through all of this, Rodgers somehow maintained an undeniable, very personable public identity. No matter how eclectic the setting, his distinctive voice, guitar playing, and yodel rendered each performance a reaffirmation of his own unique style and indomitable spirit. In addition, nearly half of his more than 100 recordings featured the sound with which he started in Bristol: simply his voice and his guitar.

The effects that his Bristol session and Ralph Peer had on Jimmie Rodgers, his life, and his career cannot be overestimated. While it is possible — even likely — that Rodgers would have, one way or another, found his way into a recording studio eventually, the unique circumstances of his Bristol session helped define him as an artist. Peer, as a producer and publisher, not only identified Rodgers' appeal as a rural entertainer but also recognized and encouraged Rodgers' more contemporary and adventurous side, urging him to write original songs and to record in a variety of musical settings. It is doubtful that another recording company executive at that time, searching the backwoods for indigenous folk talent, would have had Peer's perceptiveness.

Rodgers' Bristol session cemented his estrangement from the Tenneva Ramblers and started him confidently on his way to becoming a successful solo performer. The session also paid him $100, a substantial sum at the time. The recording contract he signed that day held no promises for the future, but it clearly gave Rodgers cause for optimism — so much so that he soon had "Victor Recording Artist" emblazoned on all of his publicity materials.

Rodgers' new career as a recording musician bought him a few more precious years of life, giving him incentive to fight his losing battle with tuberculosis. Given his pattern of behavior before moving to Asheville, Rodgers, had he not achieved success in music, would inevitably have gone back to railroading, a move that would have most certainly accelerated the progress of his disease. In the end, Rodgers lived out his railroading fantasies in song and in costume, through the persona of "the Singing Brakeman."

Rodgers' participation in the Bristol sessions forever linked him in the public imagination with the Carter Family, who also made their first recordings in Bristol and who, like Rodgers, saw great success under the guidance of Ralph Peer. However, Rodgers and the Carter Family never met in Bristol; musically and personally they could hardly have been farther apart. Yet, Rodgers and the Carter Family soon played their make-believe friendship for all it was worth, at Peer's request. In November 1929, Rodgers was teamed with Sara and Maybelle Carter for a short talking movie called *The Singing Brakeman*, in which the musician, who had adopted that nickname, sang a few songs and chatted awkwardly with the two women in a makeshift railroad station set. Neither of the Carter women sang in the film.

In June 1931, another effort was made to combine forces, this time in a Louisville, Kentucky, recording studio. In two rather awkward recordings, one entitled "Jimmie Rodgers Visits the Carter Family," the other "The Carter Family Visits Jimmie Rodgers," the famous recording stars exchanged some dialogue, first about "how pretty it is here in Virginia," then about "how big it is down here in Texas," followed by snippets of some of their best-known songs. Two charming duets sung by Rodgers and Sara Carter and featuring the fine guitar playing of Maybelle Carter make these sessions memorable. "Why There's a Tear in My Eye," a sentimental song written by A. P. Carter, displays a smooth vocal blend by Rodgers and Sara Carter along with some memorable harmony yodeling, while "The Wonderful City," co-written by Rodgers and his sister-in-law Elsie McWilliams, is notable as Rodgers' only gospel recording.

During his glory years of 1928 to 1933, Rodgers and his family lived a hectic yet exhilarating life of travel and wealth, which made them the envy of Depression-era America. Rodgers, his family, and audience knew all along that, as he wrote in a song, "Ain't no one ever whipped the T.B. blues," and his struggle made him an even more heroic figure. He finally succumbed to tuberculosis on May 26, 1933, while on a recording trip to New York City.

In death, as in life, the musician captured the imaginations and emotions of millions. Volumes of tribute songs were written, and a veritable yodeling army of Jimmie Rodgers imitators emerged. Some of these singers, including Gene Autry, Jimmie Davis, Hank Snow, and Ernest Tubb, went on to become marvelous talents in their own rights, once they developed their own personal styles.

Rodgers has influenced such musicians as Bill Monroe, Tommy Duncan, Bob Wills, Hank Williams Sr., Lefty Frizzell, and Merle Haggard, and he deeply affected the eventual formation of bluegrass, western swing, and honky-tonk music. Diverse modern interpreters — such as Bob Dylan, the Southern rock band Lynyrd Skynyrd, the British singer-songwriter Van Morrison, and Irish rock singer Bono — have recorded Rodgers' songs. In 1961, Rodgers became the first person inducted into the newly-inaugurated Country Music Hall of Fame in Nashville, earning him the sobriquet "The Father of Country Music." In 1970, he was voted into both the Songwriters Hall of Fame in New York City and the Nashville Songwriters Hall of Fame. In 1996, he was inducted into the Rock and Roll Hall of Fame, located in Cleveland, Ohio.

Norm Cohen, in his introduction to Johnny Bond's *The Recordings of Jimmie Rodgers: An Annotated Discography* (JEMF Special Series, No. 11), suggests the following as Rodgers' major contributions to country music:

a) Increased reliance on new compositions by contemporary writers and composers;

b) Increased reliance on studio musicians;

c) Popularization of yodeling;

d) Popularization of "white blues" — a hillbilly offshoot of the classic 12-bar blues popular with both white and black audiences in the mid-1920s;

e) Creation of a stable of lasting country music repertoire, still actively in use;

f) Creation of a singing and guitar style emulated by many major artists during his lifetime and afterward.

In his parting from the Tenneva Ramblers in Bristol, Rodgers symbolized country music's break from past traditions. Innovation, eclecticism, and professionalism — qualities that distinguished commercial country music from regional traditional styles — were Rodgers' significant contributions to a fledgling genre of popular music. He must also be viewed as representing the convergence of many disparate musical idioms, including blues, traditional folk, Western, Hawaiian, jug band, and early jazz. By combining these various elements in his strong personal style, Rodgers' recordings continue to inspire those who appreciate the roots of American music.

Portions of this chapter were previously published in the magazine *The Old-Time Herald*, Volume 3, Number 3; used by permission.

5. Something Old, Something New: The Carter Family's Bristol Sessions Recordings

Katie Doman

The Carter Family has become such an icon of country music that it is hard for twenty-first century fans to imagine a time before A. P., Sara, and Maybelle Carter were famous. However, when they arrived in Bristol in 1927 and appeared for their audition with Ralph Peer, the three musicians began on an equal footing with the other acts signed up for a chance at fame and fortune. Like virtually everyone else at the recording sessions in Bristol (other than Ernest Stoneman and the Johnson Brothers), the Carters were unknown. But two of the acts — The Carter Family and Jimmie Rodgers — emerged as country music stars. During his career, Rodgers sang about traveling, and travel he did, building a reputation for living the wild life. The Carters, on the other hand, always kept their focus on subjects suitable for family and home, singing songs that were morally and spiritually instructive or were derived from the old ballad tradition.

In the Carter Family's Bristol sessions recordings, one can easily identify the reasons for their success. They took old-fashioned, familiar songs and themes and turned them into new material — and though their harmonies and instrumentation were grounded firmly in Appalachian folk music, they took that tradition in new directions. It was their distinctive Carter sound — based firmly on Sara and Maybelle's lead vocals, A. P.'s bass harmony, and Maybelle's guitar work — that appealed to audiences and induced

66

them to buy records from the Victor Company. A. P. Carter's ability to rework songs gave the Carters a vast repertoire of fresh material to sing, but this modified material also appealed to Peer because it created opportunities for copyrighting and publishing. An examination of the Carter Family's Bristol sessions recordings, which managed to be simultaneously old-fashioned and innovative, reveals how the Carters served as a bridge between folk music and a newly developing commercial "hillbilly music" business. These recordings demonstrate the group's ability to retain the best of the old tradition, while reshaping it into such a fresh and appealing form that the Carter Family's material still proves relevant and even irresistible to present-day artists.

An investigation into the background of each of the members will help illuminate the origins of the Carter Family's music, due to the fact that their social and cultural background heavily influenced both their repertoire and their images as performers. As Michael Orgill observes in his 1975 biography of the Carters, *Anchored in Love: The Carter Family Story*, "The Carter Family participated in [the twentieth] century's initial expansion of the entertainment media, but ... their art was the product of an essentially self-contained and self-nurturing tradition. For them, the cradle of this tradition was their Clinch Mountain home."[1] All three of the Carters grew up in Scott County, Virginia, where the Appalachian musical tradition thrived. Undeniably the infrastructure of the Carter Family's music, the folk and gospel traditions of the mountains influenced each of the three musicians and infused their repertoire of songs, which according to Janette Carter, daughter of A. P. and Sara, eventually numbered around 300.[2]

The oldest of the three original Carter Family members, Alvin Pleasant Carter, was born in 1891 into a musical family. His father Bob Carter was a fiddler, and Mollie Bays Carter, A. P.'s mother, loved to sing both traditional and religious songs. Mollie was an especially strong influence on her son. In their 2002 biography of the Carter Family, *Will You Miss Me When I'm Gone: The Carter Family and Their Legacy in American Music*, Mark Zwonitzer and Charles Hirschberg write that "while she went about her daily chores, Mollie would sing the hymns she loved best" and that "she also sang traditional ballads, known [to her] as 'English' songs because the form — if not the songs themselves — had crossed the Atlantic with the English and Scotch-Irish who settled the southern mountains."[3] These traditional and religious songs, learned by A. P. early in his life and reworked later to suit the trio's voices and instruments, formed the basis of the Carter Family's repertoire of hits.

Both A. P. and his brother James could play the fiddle, though A. P. was the better musician. Zwonitzer and Hirschberg note that A. P. had a "supple feeling" for playing and that "if he heard a new song, he could generally chord it out on the fiddle by the end of the day."[4] But A. P. seldom chose to play in public, perhaps because "from the day he was born to the day he died, [A. P.] was possessed of a slight tremor, most noticeable in his hands," which meant that he could "barely keep his bow steady."[5] Interestingly, at the same time that his tremor detracted from his playing, it added something to his singing. It "gave him what the locals called a 'tear'" in his voice, and it "embroidered his singing with an almost otherworldly tenderness."[6] This "tear" is definitely audible in the Carters' Bristol sessions recordings of August 1st, 1927, especially on the songs on which A. P. sings harmony to Sara Carter's lead.

Fiddle tunes and the ballad tradition were not the only early influences on A. P. Carter. Mollie and her large brood were steadfast members of Mount Vernon Methodist Church. The church offered its members the opportunity to pray together, attend services each Sunday, and worship together through music. As musical director of the church, A. P.'s Uncle Flanders was in charge of putting together the church quartet. A. P. sang bass for the group. Flanders also taught shape note singing across the region, using material developed by James D. Vaughan, "a publisher whose close-harmonizing gospel quartets were the new musical sensation of southern choirs."[7] The gospel music that A. P. learned as part of the church choir and in shape note singing schools would later play a vital role in shaping the sound and repertoire of the Carter Family's music.

Marriage transformed A. P. Carter's music. He was traveling across the county selling fruit trees for a living when he stopped at the home of Melinda and Milburn Nickels on Copper Creek. The Nickels were raising their niece, Sara Dougherty, whose mother had died when Sara was a tiny child. Charles Wolfe, who has written extensively on the lives and music of the Carters, notes that Copper Creek offered no dearth of musical opportunities for the young girl; it was there that Sara developed an ability to play the banjo, the guitar, and the autoharp. As Wolfe explains, "She had learned to play [the autoharp] from a relative ... and ordered her first model from the pages of Sears Roebuck."[8]

The autoharp and Sara's lead singing would prove significant in the Bristol recordings that launched the Carters' musical career, but in 1914, Sarah was a teenager with a beautiful but untrained voice. That voice, which later garnered so much critical praise, caused A. P. Carter to fall in love with Sara Dougherty before he even saw her. Zwonitzer and Hirschberg offer Sara's own account of her first meeting with her future husband:

> I remember I was singing "Engine 143," an old song I learned as a little girl, and this fellow knocked on the door.... I remember that he stood

there while I sang ... and then he said something like, "Ma'am, that was mighty pretty playing and singing, and I sure would like you to play that again for me," and so I did.[9]

A. P. was spellbound, and for about a year he courted her relentlessly. She was reluctant to marry, but he persisted, and on June 18, 1915, Sara Dougherty became Sara Carter. "For the next ten years," Wolfe reports, "A. P. and Sara honed their skills at singing together."[10]

Although they became famous only after teaming up with Sara's cousin Maybelle (who was also A. P.'s sister-in-law through Maybelle's marriage to his brother, Ezra Carter), A. P. and Sara made a stab at recording commercially before they enjoyed success at the Bristol sessions. According to Wolfe, the couple sang for the Brunswick Record Company as a duo in 1926. They performed "Anchored in Love," accompanied by Sara on the autoharp. The representative from Brunswick, James O'Keefe, decided that the recording equipment did not pick up the sound of the autoharp well enough. After having them sing with a pianist instead, O'Keefe — who knew that A. P. could play the fiddle — decided against recording a vocal duet. He wanted instead "a good southern fiddler, somebody who could compete with Doc Roberts on the Gennett label."[11] Although A. P. had his first record deal at hand, he decided against trying to fiddle his way to fame. Wolfe notes that he may have decided against it because so many of his friends and family still considered the fiddle "the Devil's box," and A. P. was disinclined to make waves.[12] (Certainly, this fits with the Carters' personalities; even after achieving success, they kept their shows and their image clean, advertising their concerts with posters that made a clear announcement to fans: "This show is morally good.") Zwonitzer and Hirschberg offer two additional possibilities for A. P.'s hesitation to sign a record deal with Brunswick. They suggest that he may have been concerned about the tremble in his hands, which rendered him insecure about his fiddling. They also recount O'Keefe's comment that "women just didn't take the lead in combos, except maybe in race records,"[13] suggesting that the Brunswick representative was not progressive enough to sign a duo that featured a female lead singer. But A. P. seemed to think that his wife's voice was as important to their success as his own, so the couple went home to Maces Spring. The Brunswick experience disappointed them — especially A. P. — but the Carters kept playing music, and in the time between their first attempt at recording and their Bristol meeting with Ralph Peer, the couple added a key element in their eventual success: Maybelle Carter.

Maybelle Addington Carter was Sara's first cousin; their mothers were sisters. Maybelle was younger than Sara by more than a decade, but she had been born on Copper Creek while Sara still lived there, and the two girls knew each other. Maybelle was gregarious, sweet-natured and pretty, with startling blue eyes and a talent for music. Like Sara, Maybelle had opportunities in Copper Creek to learn to play instruments, and as a child she could play both banjo and autoharp. By the time she was 13, Maybelle was also playing the guitar. As Charles Wolfe tells it, she "had a little mail-order Stella and was trying to figure out how to play a little melody on it as she kept time"[14]

By Maybelle's own account, no one could have prevented her from learning how to play. "I have loved music all my life," she stated, "I guess I was just born that way."[15] She once outlined her early experiences:

> My sister used to play the banjo some; my mother would play banjo, and I would pull the autoharp down off the table to the floor and try to play it.... I played the banjo too when I was a kid, and me and my brothers used to play for squaredances ... and then when I was about twelve or thirteen one of my older brothers gave me a guitar and I started trying different ways to pick it, and came up with my own style, because there weren't many guitar pickers around.[16]

Like A. P. and Sara, Maybelle encountered ballads and religious music early in life. Her mother, Margaret Addington, taught her the traditional Appalachian ballads that had been passed down from generation to generation, and she also encouraged Maybelle to learn the gospel songs sung by the Women's Chorus at the Fair Oak Methodist Church.[17] Most certainly, Maybelle was influenced by Appalachian community gatherings, during which Copper Creek folks came together for fun, exchanging songs and playing fiddle music well into the night.

Old-time long-bow fiddler and 2002 National Heritage Award Fellow Ralph Blizard, a native of Kingsport, Tennessee, knew the Carters, and he often performed at the Carter Family Fold, a music venue at the site of A. P. Carter's store, near Hiltons, Virginia. Blizard confirmed that Maybelle's guitar style "just developed individually with her" and added that "she was an excellent guitar player" with a "soulful feeling."[18] He acknowledged her musical ancestry, saying that "her brother, Doc Addington, was a guitar player, but he played a different style from what Maybelle played. Completely different."[19] Maybelle learned the basics of instrument playing from her friends and family, but her innate talent gave her the ability to innovate — first on the guitar and later on the autoharp; her innovation on her chosen instruments was key to the success of the Carter Family.

At 16 years of age, Maybelle eloped with A. P.'s younger brother, Ezra Carter. The couple spent the first months of their married life in Mollie and Bob Carter's home.[20] Maybelle's new proximity to A. P. and Sara allowed ample opportunity for the three musicians to practice. Soon, the three were working diligently on their songs and musical arrangements.

Asked how her parents and Maybelle worked together during rehearsals, Janette Carter, daughter of Sara and A. P., remembers that "they'd sit and talk about it. Mommy and Maybelle would figure out the music leads — anyway, Maybelle would figure it out on the guitar."[21] According to Janette, her parents and aunt knew that the songs had to "follow a pattern."[22] Generally, songs were laid out in a "verse-chorus-instrumental-verse-chorus-instrumental-verse" order.[23] Ballads were reworked into shorter pieces containing fewer specific details; only the most essential themes were left intact. This was usually A. P.'s part of the process, and then the women took their turn: to make the song complete, "they'd work music leads in."[24]

The Carters cooperated on their music from the very beginning of their career together. Ralph Blizard credited the Carters' ability to make good music to their adherence to Appalachian tradition. He noted that the best old-time music groups have always recognized each member's strengths. "Within any group, you have individuals that come through as lead singers, and the others play and sing their parts. That's just a natural thing. When a group gets together, they work out their songs or tunes and ... they work out their parts, and they are professional enough to know who's coming over the best with [each] particular thing."[25] According to Blizard, the Carters were aware of each member's special talents, and they worked hard to use them to best advantage in each number they arranged.

Sara and A. P.'s granddaughter, Rita Forrester, agrees that the original Carter Family members had a knack for knowing how to take advantage of individual talents. Asked about what she sees as the individual strengths of each member, Forrester comments first on what initially caught A. P.'s attention — and during the Bristol sessions, Ralph Peer's:

> Well, of course, my grandmother's voice. I think that's what Mr. Peer would say convinced him to record them. She had that wonderful, clear, just hauntingly beautiful voice. My granddad's [strengths were] the composition, the organization of the material they sang, and that wonderful bass voice. You know, he rarely got in front of the mike or did anything but what he called "bass in," but if you listen to the songs that he did solo, his voice is every bit as beautiful as my grandmother's. He just let the ladies take the forefront, and he didn't mind that.... And then Maybelle, of course — her wonderful instrumentals. And her alto voice. And the harmony, the beautiful harmony.[26]

Forrester also notes that A. P. Carter was the driving force behind the band.[27] "The ladies just wanted to go home and take care of their babies," she explains, "They didn't want to [travel and sing]. Women didn't do that then."[28] Forrester remains convinced that it was her grandfather's belief in the talent of the women and his ability to talk them into performing that first gave the Carter Family a break in Bristol, and that kept them going afterwards.

Mary A. Bufwack and Robert Oermann, in their book *Finding Her Voice: The Saga of Women in Country Music*, suggest that A. P. "domineered" the women, choosing performance venues that brought in less money than the "wider show-business world of country radio barn dances or vaudeville bills."[29] The scholars claim that, "in retrospect, the two women could have probably done as well without him were it not for constraints against unchaperoned country women at that time."[30] "Domineering" may be too strong a word to characterize A. P.'s power over his two female musical partners. A number of sources credit the women with having plenty of input into the group's activities. Additionally, there were times when one of them simply chose not to appear for a performance, necessitating that A. P. ask his sister Sylvia or another family member to fill in. As for Bufwack and Oermann's supposition that the Carter women could have been performers without A. P., if not for him, Sara and Maybelle would not have been recording in the first place. As reluctant as they sometimes were to travel, the Carter women enjoyed singing — not to mention the fact that they usually needed the money that it brought in, especially in the early days of their singing career. As Janette Carter explains, "They were just trying to make a living, and [singing] was a lot easier than trying to farm. And they never did make but a very, very little amount of money. But they made more than they was a-making with [farming]."[31]

The Carter women had a voice in choosing the types of shows the Carter Family would perform. Sara and Maybelle, who were church-going, family-oriented women, surely balked at performing in the kinds of venues that Jimmie Rodgers favored. And A. P., also deeply religious and concerned with keeping the group's shows "morally good," probably had no desire to go that route himself. Musing on the Carter Family's performance schedule and her grandfather's "management" of the group, Forrester insists that family time "mattered most [to Maybelle and Sara].... They had their meals, their fellowship with their families — that was the important thing, and when that suffered, they let the other go."[32] Forrester admits that "they probably could have done more if they had gone out on the road like Jimmie Rodgers, just really hit the road, but they didn't want to do that. And my granddaddy wouldn't have wanted that, either. Family was always the most important thing to him."[33]

Forrester's opinions are supported by decisions that the Carter Family made later in their career. When the trio's success earned them a nationally broadcasted spot on XERA radio in Mexico during the late 1930s, they accepted the deal only because it allowed them time to attend to their families and farms. They traveled to Texas to do the show for six months, and then went back home to Maces Spring for the other six months to lead a relatively normal family life and manage their farms. When they did go to Texas, they often took their children with them. Their show, therefore, sometimes included other members of the family, adding to the show's appeal and keeping it within the Carters' "morally good" comfort zone.

Anyone listening to their recordings can hear that the Carters genuinely enjoyed singing together during those early years. In the summer of 1927, though, only A. P. had a real yearning to try recording again. Distinguished by three fine voices (Sara's impressive contralto, A. P.'s trembling bass, and Maybelle's alto) as well as Maybelle's guitar leads, the Carter Family packed their borrowed car with instruments and children and headed for Bristol to meet Ralph Peer. A. P. had seen an advertisement in the Bristol paper stating that: "The Victor Co. will have a recording machine in Bristol for 10 days beginning Monday to record records — Inquire at our Store."[34] Inquire A. P. did, and he learned from Cecil McLister, a local furniture store owner, that Peer had "asked [McLister] to put the word out and line up some music acts Peer could audition in Bristol."[35] A. P., trying to talk his wife into making the trip to the nearby city, told Sara that they would earn fifty dollars for each side they recorded — no small sum in those days. The immenently practical Sara was unconvinced. "Ain't nobody gonna pay that much money to hear us sing," she told him.[36] But A. P. was resolute, and even convinced Maybelle, who was about a month from delivering her first child, to travel with them to participate in the Victor sessions.

The Carters arrived in Bristol on the last day of July 1927, tired after their grueling trip. The roads had been hot and bumpy, and A. P. had had to fix several flat tires along the way. They were staying with Virgie and Roy Hobbs — A. P.'s sister and her husband — who lived in Bristol. Though "A. P. had hoped to rehearse that night ... the two women simply said no; they were off to bed."[37] In the morning, the three of them made their way to where Peer had set up his portable recording studio and began singing the songs that would make them famous. During their first Victor session, the Carter Family recorded six songs: "Bury Me Under the Weeping Willow," "Little Log Cabin By the Sea," "The Poor Orphan Child," "The Storms Are on the Ocean," "Single Girl, Married Girl," and "The Wandering Boy."

Interestingly, the very aspect of the Carters' singing that the Brunswick representative had earlier noticed and then rejected was the first aspect of the Carter Family's sound to pique Ralph Peer's interest. The same voice that had enchanted A. P. back on Copper Creek immediately caught the talent scout's ear. Peer later claimed that "as soon as I heard Sara's voice, that was it. I knew it was going to be wonderful."[38] It didn't altogether bother Peer that Sara and Maybelle were the featured singers in the group — in fact, it made them different. Bufwack and Oermann note that "Sara and Maybelle's musical sisters were few. Only about five percent of country's earliest recordings feature female performers,"[39] and that their unusually feminine sound led them to become "the foundation female act of country music history."[40] Peer intuited that the Carters' predominantly female vocals were not necessarily a bad thing — especially considering the themes of the songs they chose to sing. The songs tended to deal with the domestic sphere, stressing themes of home and hearth. There might be women fronting the group in these recordings, yet they were singing about subjects that offered no challenge to the cultural expectations or social order of their era — and they sounded great.

Jack Tottle — a bluegrass musician who directs the Bluegrass, Old-Time, and Country Music program at East Tennessee State University in Johnson City, Tennessee — suggests that the Carters' choices of subject matter were based not just on what would please their audience, but also on their own personal experiences and convictions. Tottle notes that many of the musicians who became commercially successful during the same era as the Carters sang songs about "mother" and "home." He attributes this to the fact that often "it was [the musician's] mother who was the one in the family who sang or played the banjo. There are a lot of songs [from that era] about mother, and there are few about 'daddy.'"[41] Sara had not known her mother for long, but Tottle's comments fit for both A. P. and Maybelle, who learned a great deal from their mothers.

However, the Carters' songs, while they were nostalgic and sentimental, were also innovative and a little edgy — and not just because the women's voices were featured over A. P.'s. Maybelle's guitar style certainly offered something new to listeners. Most accompanists in old-time music simply backed the singers by playing chords to support the vocals. If anyone in an old-time string band took an instrumental break, it was the fiddler. But Maybelle defied tradition and picked out the melody in her guitar breaks between the vocals, inventing what would later come to be called the "Carter scratch" or the "Carter lick." It's been noted that "by the end of the twenties, Maybelle's Carter scratch ... was the most widely imitated guitar style in music. Nobody did as much to popularize the guitar, because from the beginning, her playing was as distinctive as any voice."[42]

A number of musicians have acknowledged Maybelle's influence on them, including Chet Atkins, Elvis Presley, Bob Dylan, Marty Stuart,

Emmylou Harris, and, of course, Johnny Cash, who married June Carter and became Maybelle's son-in-law. Rita Forrester admits that "there are so many [musicians who credit Maybelle's influence] that it's hard to remember who all they are. I'm sure that anybody who has ever played a guitar has used something of Aunt Maybelle's — they've had to. There's no question in my mind."[43] Forrester also suggests that Maybelle's influence has so infused popular music that people may not even realize its origin: "Maybe [a guitar player] is influenced by one person, and [Maybelle] influenced that person and laid the groundwork — it would be hard for [anyone] not to be touched by the way she played."[44]

Jack Tottle agrees. He cites several reasons why Maybelle's guitar licks revolutionized guitar playing: "[Her playing] gives you the melody of the song. It's very satisfying, and it is incredibly even, polished, and smooth in a way that was not all that common at that time."[45] He adds that "people who were listening to mountain-type singing weren't used to hearing a guitar pick out a melody. When Maybelle [played lead], a person who played the guitar a little bit thought, 'I'll bet I can do that.' So she was connecting with her audience on more than one level, and encouraging participation."[46]

Of course, on first hearing the Carter Family's 1927 Bristol sessions recordings, a twenty-first-century listener might consider them primitive and rough — especially if that listener is accustomed to the slick, elaborately produced country music coming out of Nashville today. To such a listener, the Bristol sessions recordings — made when the recording industry was new and equipment was less sophisticated — might initially sound a bit tinny and coarse. But on subsequent listenings, the Carter Family's earliest recorded music transcends the limitations of early-twentieth-century technology. The elemental and earthy quality of the Carters' music — drawing on deep, sturdy roots in the Appalachian ballad and gospel traditions — ultimately commands the attention of modern listeners because, as Ralph Blizard put it, their music is so "sincere" and "soul-felt."[47]

That sincerity and soulfulness caught Peer's ear during the Carter Family's morning audition on August 1, 1927, and prompted him to invite them back for an actual recording session. On that first afternoon, the Carters recorded four songs. The first number they sang was "Bury Me Under the Weeping Willow." Both Sara and Maybelle had sung this song as children.[48] Descending from the sentimental Victorian-era tradition of "corpse poems," in which the speaker, generally female, is either dead or dying because her heart has been broken by a deserting male lover, "Bury Me Under the Weeping Willow" chronicles an idealized case of unrequited love. In such songs, sleep is often used as a euphemism for death, and in this particular song, a willow is clearly a symbol of mourning.

In the Carters' version of "Bury Me Under the Weeping Willow," the speaker hopes to hold power over the absent lover in death that she had been unable to wield in life. The themes in this genre of nineteenth-century popular song — women dying of broken hearts, men proving false, ruined weddings — connect closely with the older and more violent Appalachian ballads that were so familiar to the Carters. Here, the female speaker wonders if her false male lover, who has deserted her just before their wedding day, will at least be sorry to learn that she has died. Her attitude is submissive rather than vengeful or angry. Her request to be buried under the willow so that her lover will know where she lies is rendered more poignant by the acknowledgement that he may not care at all about her death; the last line of the chorus says, "*perhaps* he will weep for me," suggesting that even as she hopes to garner his attention by dying, she recognizes the extent of his desertion and also understands that he may never mourn for her as she does for him.

In the wrong hands, the song could be cloyingly sentimental, but the Carters' arrangement saves it. The driving rhythm of the autoharp offers a counterpoint to the subject matter, and Maybelle plays her part so energetically that, as Charles Wolfe notes, "some of her strings [slap] against the guitar."[49] The three-part harmony of the Carters does not whisper; it lends a powerful exigency to the woman's request for her false lover's attention. Perhaps the Carters were singing "Bury Me Under the Weeping Willow" so vigorously because of the recording equipment. A. P. and Sara might have remembered their previous recording experience, in which the autoharp did not make enough sound for the machine to record it appropriately. Whatever the reason, their version of this song has an undeniable and powerful urgency.

In "Little Log Cabin by the Sea," the second song they recorded during the Bristol sessions, the Carters offered Peer their first gospel song. Many of the religious numbers that A. P. arranged for the group came from his experience with church-sponsored singing schools and shape note songbooks. Wolfe points out that "Little Log Cabin by the Sea" originates from such a source. The original version of the song, named "The Bible In The Cabin by the Sea," was written in the nineteenth century by W. C. Hafley, and was published by A. J. Showalter in 1903.[50] Since the Carters' version departs somewhat from the originally published lyrics, A. P. probably rearranged and rewrote the original to suit the Carters' purposes.

The content of "Little Log Cabin by the Sea" reflects the Carter Family's usual themes and concerns — it is a celebration of mother, home, and the christian faith. Again, in their rendering of the song, the Carters restrain the sentimentality of the material by maintaining a driving instrumental rhythm under their vocals. They keep tight time, and play with gusto — the listener can almost see Sara's arm flying over the strings of the autoharp and Maybelle's look of concentration as she bends over her guitar. Maybelle's voice is absent in this number, but her guitar is an undeniable presence when she takes her two instrumental breaks. Sara sings a strong, sure lead. A. P.'s repetition or "echo"[51] of the phrase "by the sea" in the chorus offers just the right amount of artistic interest to the song without making the arrangement too busy. On this recording, the Carters sound vigorous and committed.

"The Poor Orphan Child," the third number recorded by the Carters on that first day, combines the sentimentalism of "Bury Me Under the Weeping Willow" and the religious feeling of "Little Log Cabin by the Sea." The song "[appeared] in at least five gospel songbooks between 1899 and 1907," and was probably written by H. W. Elliot in 1899.[52] In his book *Don't Get Above Your Raisin': Country Music and the Southern Working Class*, Bill C. Malone wrote that the song was "originally titled 'Saviour, Lead Them,'" and was written as a tribute to the "Orphans Homes of Texas" as a "compassionate and sentimentalized plea for orphan children, and only incidentally an endorsement of the benevolent and fatherly role of God."[53] Malone theorizes that in choosing such material, "the Carters ... had no evangelistic intent, but instead were falling back on the cherished souvenirs of a past shared with their listeners."[54] Although the Carters probably had no direct evangelistic purpose, the depth of their religious convictions suggests that they chose the song partly because it *was* religious, and in its indirect way, it reflected a Christian ethos that was important to them. However, the Carters probably chose the song primarily because they liked it, they knew it well, and they thought that it would sound good on a recording.

The arrangement of "The Poor Orphan Child" is similar in many ways to that of "Little Log Cabin by the Sea." Once again, the Carters sing a duet in which Sara's strong lead vocal is supported by a driving rhythm underneath. On this recording, Sara plays autoharp, while Maybelle plays guitar without taking a break — perhaps the Carters felt that none of the verses of this song could be omitted and still have the story make sense. A. P. again sings church music–style harmony with an echo on the chorus, this time offering a slight variation on the lines rather than a straight repetition of the words as in "Little Log Cabin by the Sea." The theme of this song — the separation of children and parents — not only resembles the Carters' previous number, but also anticipates the same theme in the sixth song that the trio recorded during the Bristol sessions, "The Wandering Boy."

The last song recorded by the Carters on August 1, 1927, was "The Storms Are on the Ocean." Like "Bury Me Under the Weeping Willow," this song depicts the parting of lovers, but this time it seems to be necessity, rather than lost love, that parts them. The young man is going to sea, probably to make money so that he can come back and marry his true love. Although it is rearranged into more modern form with verses and a chorus, the song exhibits several traits inherited from the ballad tradition. First, as in a number of traditional ballads from the British Isles, two speakers within the song are engaged in a dialogue. Also, the song contains what ballad scholars call "commonplace" or "floating" verses — that is, verses incorporated into numerous ballads; for instance, the verse beginning with "Who will dress your pretty little feet" appears with slight variations in several different traditional ballads, as does the verse about the "mourning doves flying from pine to pine." According to Wolfe, the song is descended from a Scottish ballad with a "great long story" called 'The Lass of Loch Royal,' but when it got to the mountains, only the lyric parts survived."[55]

For "The Storms Are on the Ocean," the Carters slowed the tempo to a lilting waltz time. All three Carters sing on this song, with Sara providing the lead. Maybelle and A. P. harmonize, and Maybelle plays two instrumental breaks on her guitar. In some places, Sara and A. P. sing different words: at one point during the female speaker's verse, she sings "you," while A. P. sings "I," the logical word for the male speaker. In another line, Sara sings "you *can* kiss my rosy red cheeks," and A. P. sings "you *may* kiss." Far from marring the performance, these slight incongruities simply make the recording seem more like a live performance. The Carter Family's version of the song swings back and forth in an easy rhythm, but at a faster pace than more recent interpretations, which tend to be slower and sweeter and to play on the pain of separation between lovers. The Carters' earnest approach to the song instead seems to emphasize the seriousness with which the lovers make their promise to remain true.

The two Carter women returned to the Bristol studio for another recording session the next day, August 2, 1927, but A. P. was not with them. Much to Sara's chagrin, Peer wanted her to record a song called "Single Girl, Married Girl." Perhaps Sara's reluctance to sing the song, as a number of biographers have speculated, stemmed from the fact that it too closely resembled her real life. Such writers point out that since her wedding, Sara had certainly taken on more than her share of domestic responsibility. She knew what it was like to care for a home and babies when money was scarce. Because her husband was regularly gone while working or collecting songs, Sara often took on the task of running the farm as well as their home. But there may be another element to the song. Based on descriptions of Sara offered by family and friends, it is also likely that the rather stoic Sara was simply unwilling to sing something that sounded like a complaint. In any case, Peer prevailed, and Sara recorded the song.

According to Wolfe, a friend had taught Sara "Single Girl, Married Girl" in 1905.[56] Variants of the song existed all over Appalachia in 1927. Even today, versions of the song are in circulation; for example, Sheila Kay Adams, a seventh-generation ballad singer from Sodom, North Carolina, sings a version called "Single Girl."[57]

In the Bristol sessions recording of "Single Girl, Married Girl," Sara sings lead and plays autoharp, as usual. But there is something different about this cut. Part of it is the complete lack of sentimentality in the lyrics, marking a departure from the Carters' other Bristol sessions selections. There is no pain of separation here, though the song's protagonist reflects upon her "single" days. But much of the difference in this recording results from the way that Maybelle plays her guitar: she picks out the melody rather then simply chording under Sara's singing, and Maybelle matches Sara's voice almost note for note. An additional point of interest in "Single Girl, Married Girl" is that it is structured more like the old Appalachian ballads than the previous four cuts, in that the song does not have a chorus. The women play the same melody with every verse — even the guitar breaks stick to the same tune. The interest in this song derives not from the harmony singing, as in the first four selections, but from Maybelle's playing the melody line on guitar under the singing and from the unusual positioning of the guitar breaks. "Single Girl, Married Girl" actually begins and ends with instrumentals rather than with vocals, and there is also an instrumental break in the middle. This particular recording underscores the Carter Family's innovation, versatility, and the breadth of their repertoire.

The Carter women ended their Bristol sessions recordings with "The Wandering Boy." As Wolfe put it, "this song [seems] to have roots in the gospel songbook tradition, though its exact provenance is cloudy."[58] The song, with its emphasis on a heavenly reunion, connects with the gospel tradition of "Little Log Cabin by the Sea" and "The Poor Orphan Child." But because it bears the point of view of a woman who misses a loved one, "The Wandering Boy" resembles the sentimentality of "Bury Me Under the Weeping Willow" and "The Storms Are on the Ocean."

The phrasing and rhythm of "The Wandering Boy" seem a bit odd at first to the modern listener, because the song's autoharp and guitar accompaniment is quite urgent — such sentimental lyrics would be treated today with a sweeter, slower instrumental arrangement. But again, the Carters place their song's emphasis on the earnestness of the protagonist's emotional perspective and thus prevent the song from becoming maudlin. The pulsing rhythm seems to underscore the emotions of the mother whose son is far from her, and Sara's voice carries the poignancy of the words without the assistance of a self-conscious arrangement. She imbues the first two lines of the chorus with particularly intense longing. When Sara sings, "Bring back my boy, my wandering boy / Far, far away wherever he may be," her voice becomes stronger and louder, taking on a keening edge as if she is actually calling out to an absent son. Maybelle takes no breaks on this recording; she simply keeps time with Sara's autoharp and vocals. The listener can imagine Maybelle concentrating on Sara's face, watching for the subtle changes that signal a change in chords.

The Carter women finished recording before lunchtime on August 2. The family then piled into the car with their instruments and went back home to spend a few quiet months waiting to see what would come of their Bristol recording sessions, if anything. About four months after they sang for Ralph Peer, the lives of the Carters began to change.

During the late 1920s, commercial records were released with one song on each side. The first release of music by the Carter Family featured "The Poor Orphan Child" on one side, with "The Wandering Boy" on the other. The record sold rather well, and the Carters earned some royalties. But to Sara's amazement, a subsequent release, "Single Girl, Married Girl," eventually became the biggest seller of all the sides they recorded that day, as a growing number of listeners related to the song that Sara had been so hesitant to record. In fact, it was the success of this release, with "The Storms Are on the Ocean" on the other side of the record, that prompted Victor to invite the Carters to a later recording session — this time in Camden, New Jersey.[59]

The Carter Family's Bristol recordings proved what Peer had already guessed about the Carters as soon as he heard them audition — that their sound was good enough to prompt record sales. Ralph Blizard comments that "Peer had the talent to recognize ... what people wanted to hear, what they liked.... He had a pretty good idea of what would go over. All that sincere, soul-felt music he was hearing [from the Carter Family] was coming across."[60] But Peer saw something else of value in the Carters' songs. He could publish them and profit from the royalties. Recording technology was very new in 1927, and so were the laws that pertained to intellectual property. Peer paid the Carters for each recording that he could sell as a commercial record, but he also offered royalties to A. P. for songs he could write, collect, or rework for copyright — and as the publisher of A. P.'s songs, Peer was entitled to part of the royalties for each one.

A. P. Carter has sometimes garnered criticism for his copyright applications on songs that were in the public domain — or, more controversial even, on songs that were derived from earlier material with clear provenance. As previously suggested, the songs that the Carters sang during the Bristol sessions were often reworkings of older songs, whether traditional or com-

Carter Family Songbook: The Carter Family, featuring husband and wife A. P. and Sara Carter and Sara's younger cousin Maybelle Carter (who was married to A. P.'s brother Ezra), became major country music stars in the months after making their first records at the 1927 Bristol sessions. One of the trio's great strengths was A. P. Carter's ability to craft memorable new songs that sounded like they had always been around. Songbooks containing the words and tunes of A. P.'s songs soon became widely popular. Collection of Charles K. Wolfe.

mercial. Critics sometimes have taken A. P. to task for copyrighting songs that someone else originated. Much of the controversy over A. P.'s copyright practice is unwarranted in light of his cultural background and the newness of copyright law in the late 1920s. Unlike ballad collectors like Cecil Sharp and other academics, A. P. Carter came from within the Appalachian folk tradition, in which people had been swapping tunes and songs for generations. When scholarly collectors began to travel through Appalachia around the turn of the century, they carefully collected the region's ballads and songs and wrote them down note for note because they wanted to preserve them in their "pure" forms.[61] In contrast, Appalachian musicians historically traded tunes and songs with the expectation that each player or singer would put his or her "mark" on a piece. Ralph Blizard commented that it was still common practice for him, as an old-time musician, to learn a tune from someone else, "[but] play it the way that *I* do it."[62] This practice includes making changes — sometimes substantial ones — to both melodies and lyrics. Blizard called this "putting your own complexion on a song."[63] In his song collecting and his songwriting, A. P. followed these traditional methods of changing the tune or lyrics to suit his group's needs.

Although he defended A. P. Carter's song collecting methods, Blizard acknowledged the reasons for today's much tighter copyright laws, admitting that "copyright law ... was necessary, of course, in order to protect people's rights"; but Blizard also maintained that in the earliest days of the recording industry, "a lot of people got copyright on songs they did not really write themselves. Back when I was coming up, songwriters were selling their songs very cheap — they'd sell them, and whoever they sold them to 'wrote' them."[64]

Rita Forrester thinks that people "misunderstand" her grandfather's methods and intent.[65] "There were no rules," she says, "Mr. Peer and the Carter Family were in new territory" when it came to copyright law.[66] She offers insight into the Appalachian tradition, saying that "a lot of times, people would give them things that they knew simply so that they would be preserved. It [might have been] a verse or a poem — just something that they had learned. It was common practice for people to give [them] material."[67] She acknowledges that ballads were source material for her grandfather's songs, but so were other songs "that [the Carters] had heard all their lives ... [though] maybe they changed them around, rearranged then and worked them to where they felt comfortable with them."[68] She points out that several of the songs on which A. P. claimed copyright were in fact fully his own. About "The Cyclone of Rye Cove," she says, "I know that ... my granddad wrote it after he had actually been to Rye Cove and seen what happened.... That was just straight out because he had lived that, and it moved him so."[69]

She also recounts a story about the song "Sweet Fern": "I've heard Mom talk about him walking in the woods and [seeing] a bird up on a limb, and that brought 'Sweet Fern' about.... [He] was very outdoorsy. He loved the outdoors and nature and animals ... so a lot of his songs came from that."[70]

Forrester agrees that the Carter Family served as a bridge between the folk process and the new commercial music. "It was a new experience for all of them," she says, "The recording industry was in its infancy.... Just a few years of recording had taken place when they started, so it was brand new to all of them."[71]

Those who focus on the controversy over A. P. Carter's copyright practices tend to base their judgment of the situation too heavily on today's norms, and they tend to miss the real point of his genius, which was his ability to identify interesting material and to craft memorable arrangements. He was extremely skilled in both these areas, despite the many limitations he faced in compiling a repertoire for the Carter Family — that is, he had to choose material that was "morally good"; it had to have the old-fashioned qualities that fans loved, but with a new twist; and it had to be three minutes or less in length in order to fit on the wax master discs used for recording. The last of these limitations is one that no longer exists for recording musicians. They can record much longer songs, and they can certainly include more than two sides on one release. But in working up songs for the Carter Family to record, A. P. Carter had to keep in mind that the equipment simply could not accommodate anything over three minutes long. Traditional ballads had to be changed in format. As Rita Forrester conveys, "It was common for songs to have thirteen, fourteen verses — even fifteen. 'Course, they couldn't use all that, so they had to shorten things"[72]

The Bristol sessions recording of "The Storms Are on the Ocean" serves as a good example of how masterfully A. P. Carter could rework a song to suit his audience's tastes and stay within a three-minute format. The oldest elements of the song — the verses that derive from the ballad tradition — set up the theme of parting, and outline the journey of the young man over the sea. But A. P.'s rendering departs from the ballad tradition, which often mentions characters' names and the names of locations referred to in a given ballad. A. P. Carter would borrow parts of a ballad but would leave out names and locations, which would render a song more universal. Such a song by A. P. would also depart from the ballad tradition by adding a chorus; ballads traditionally featured the same melody all the way through. The chorus of "The Storms Are on the Ocean" reinforces the lovers' earnest love for one another, and it reminds listeners of the theme of the song despite the absence of the original details. And, most important of all, the song was short enough to be captured by Peer's recording equipment.

A large component of the Carter Family's initial fanbase — that is, the people who bought those first releases — consisted of people who were born and raised in Appalachia but who were living in other parts of the country for economic reasons. As Ralph Blizard pointed out, "what people don't realize mostly is that our traditional music had a footing in [the North] even before World War II."[73] Blizard also recalled that "a lot of the people moved from the South to the North to get jobs, because we didn't have much in the south — not as much as there was up there."[74] The traditional elements of "The Storms Are on the Ocean," coupled with the Carters' accents, would certainly appeal to misplaced Appalachians, many of whom longed to return home. Many of these fans would identify with the plight of the lovers depicted in the song, who had parted for economic necessity and not by choice. After all, they had left friends and family behind to find employment in the factories up north, and many of them did not know when they would be able to return. A. P. Carter himself had left to work up north for a time, so he knew how it felt to be far from home and loved ones. In addition, Jack Tottle points out that the Carter Family pronounced their words in a distinctively Appalachian manner, which would have given the songs a special appeal to transplanted Appalachian people who had migrated and were now surrounded by unfamiliar cultures and speech patterns.[75]

The Bristol sessions recordings would change everything for the Carters — and for American music in general. As Bufwack and Oermann put it:

> It would be hard to overstate The Carter Family's importance to popular music history. Country's first star group is unmatched as a preserver and popularizer of folk and parlor songs. Maybelle's then-revolutionary guitar style helped transform the instrument from background rhythm to the dominant lead sound in pop culture. [55]

Seventy-five odd years after they were made, the Carter Family's recordings from the Bristol sessions still attract the attention of fans as well as of other musicians. They operated in the gray area between folk and commercial music, giving a nod to the old days, but at the same time, updating the music. The Carters' music, today, sounds careful and professional, not at all amateurish. And even though some of their material could be faulted for over-the-top sentimentalism, many of the trio's songs are regularly included in the repertoires of folk, old-time, and bluegrass musicians. The Carter Family's songs may be old-fashioned, but they continue to please audiences because they concern the universal things that people still care about in the twenty-first century.

Notes

1. Michael Orgill, *Anchored in Love: The Carter Family Story* (Old Tappan, New Jersey: Fleming H. Revell Company, 1975): 31.

2. Janette Carter, interview by author, February 1, 2003, near Hiltons, Virginia. Cassette recording. Interview on file in the Archives of Appalachia at East Tennessee State University, Johnson City, Tennessee.

3. Michael Zwonitzer with Charles Hirschberg, *Will You Miss Me When I'm Gone: The Carter Family and Their Legacy in Country Music* (New York: Simon and Schuster, 2002): 24–25.

4. Ibid., 29.

5. Ibid., 29–30.

6. Ibid.

7. Ibid., 32.

8. Charles Wolfe, liner notes to boxed CD set, *The Carter Family: In the Shadow of Clinch Mountain*. Boxed CD set. BCD 15865 LK. Bear Family, 2000.

9. Zwonitzer and Hirschberg, 35.

10. Charles Wolfe, liner notes, 8.

11. Ibid., 9.

12. Ibid.

13. Zwonitzer and Hirschberg, 77.

14. Charles Wolfe, liner notes, 10.

15. Mary A. Bufwack and Robert K. Oermann, *Finding Her Voice: The Saga of Women in Country Music* (New York: Crown Publishers, Inc., 1993) 53.

16. Ibid., 53.

17. Ibid.

18. Ralph Blizard, interview by author, January 13, 2003, Blountville, Tennessee. Cassette recording.

19. Ibid.

20. Zwonitzer and Hirschberg, 60–61.

21. Janette Carter, interview by author.

22. Ibid.

23. Zwonitzer and Hirschberg, 108.

24. Janette Carter, interview by author.

25. Ralph Blizard, interview by author.

26. Rita Forrester, interview by the author, February 1, 2003, near Hiltons, Virginia. Cassette recording on file in the Archives of Appalachia, East Tennessee State University, Johnson City, Tennessee.

27. Ibid.

28. Ibid.

29. Bufwack and Oermann, 57.

30. Ibid.

31. Janette Carter, interview by author.

32. Rita Forrester, interview by author.

33. Ibid.

34. Zwonitzer and Hirschberg, 77.

35. Ibid.

36. Charles Wolfe, liner notes, 12.

37. Ibid., 16.

38. Ibid., 17.

39. Bufwack and Oermann, 59.

40. Ibid., 55.

41. Jack Tottle, interview by author, January 15, 2003, Johnson City, Tennessee. Cassette recording.

42. Zwonitzer and Hirschberg, 109.

43. Rita Forrester, interview by author.

44. Ibid.

45. Jack Tottle, interview by author.

46. Ibid.

47. Ralph Blizard, interview by author.

48. Charles Wolfe, liner notes, 46.

49. Ibid., 17.

50. Ibid., 46.

51. Ibid., 17.

52. Ibid., 46.

53. Bill C. Malone, *Don't Get Above Your Raisin': Country Music and the Southern Working Class* (Urbana: University of Illinois Press, 2000): 93.

54. Ibid.

55. Charles Wolfe, liner notes, 17.

56. Ibid., 46.

57. Adams' version can be heard on her 2000 release *My Dearest Dear*, a self-published CD with 15 cuts, including traditional ballads learned from her family and one original. The CD is of interest to Carter Family fans because it contains variants of other traditional songs sung by the trio, such as "I Never Will Marry" and "Black Jack Davy."

58. Charles Wolfe, liner notes, 46.

59. Ibid., 19.

60. Ralph Blizard, interview by author.

61. This concern for exact transcripts of words and songs for ballads sometimes

puzzles and amuses folk musicians and
scholars, who point out that by the time
the academics were collecting them, the
songs had already been through generations of changes, so they could hardly be
deemed "pure" in form.

62. Ralph Blizard, interview by author.
63. Ibid.
64. Ibid.
65. Rita Forrester, interview by author.

66. Ibid.
67. Ibid.
68. Ibid
69. Ibid.
70. Ibid.
71. Ibid.
72. Ibid.
73. Ralph Blizard, interview by author.
74. Ibid.
75. Jack Tottle, interview by author.

Works Cited

Blizard, Ralph. Personal interview. January 13, 2003.

Bufwack, Mary A. and Robert K. Oermann. *Finding Her Voice: The Saga of Women in Country Music*. New York: Crown Publishers, Inc., 1993.

Carter, Janette. Personal interview. February 1, 2003.

Forrester, Rita. Personal Interview. February 1, 2003.

Malone, Bill C. *Don't Get Above Your Raisin': Country Music and the Southern Working Class*. Urbana: University of Illinois Press, 2000.

Orgill, Michael. *Anchored in Love: The Carter Family Story*. Old Tappan, N.J.: Fleming H. Revell Company, 1975.

Tottle, Jack. Personal interview. January 15, 2003.

Wolfe, Charles. Liner notes to boxed CD set, *The Carter Family: In the Shadow of Clinch Mountain*. Boxed CD set. BCD 15865 LK. Bear Family, 2000.

Zwonitzer, Michael, with Charles Hirschberg. *Will You Miss Me When I'm Gone: The Carter Family and Their Legacy in Country Music*. New York: Simon and Schuster, 2002.

6. The Blackard-Shelor Story: Biography of a Hillbilly String Band

Tom Carter

Dad Blackard's Moonshiners, alternatively billed as the Shelor Family, recorded four sides for Victor in 1927.[1] On these recordings Joe Blackard sang the lead and picked the banjo; his daughter Clarice Blackard Shelor sang harmony and provided piano accompaniment. The fiddlers were Jesse Shelor (Clarice's husband) and his brother Pyrhus. This band, for convenience referred to here as the Shelor Family, hailed from Meadows of Dan, Patrick County, Virginia. Both the Blackards and the Shelors play an important role in the musical history of this region and are particularly noteworthy because their lives span three distinct eras of outside involvement in the folk music of the Southern Appalachians. Cecil Sharp, the English folksong collector, visited and notated Joe Blackard's singing in 1918[2]; the two families combined in 1927 to make commercial discs for the early recording industry; and, finally, the urban folk revival of the 1960s led to their "rediscovery" and subsequent re-recording. The history of this band and its music perhaps can best be illustrated by tracing the development of its individual members.

Joe Blackard was born "down the mountain"[3] near the town of Stuart, one of the children of Willoughby Blackard, in 1859. The Blackards moved up to the top of the Blue Ridge in the early 1860s and lived at Connors View, not far from the present Meadows of Dan post office. Shortly thereafter, Willoughby was killed during the battle for the defense of Richmond — one

Reprinted from *Old Time Music* 24 (Spring 1977): 4–7. Used by permission of the author and that periodical's editor Tony Russell.

of the closing battles of the Civil War. In 1867, young Joe started to attend the first public school in Patrick County. Apparently he immediately began to pick up and digest the songs then popular in the community. The origins of his banjo style are obscure; some evidence indicates that Joe's was the first generation to incorporate the banjo into the rural repertoire. Whatever the case, he played his breakdown tunes in a basic clawhammer style and seconded his singing in what sounds like a single-note, melodic technique. (Fortunately, Joe Blackard's large and varied repertoire was preserved by his daughter Clarice.) Joe married in 1892 and settled down to the life of a farmer and rural mail carrier. He was in constant demand as a dance musician and regularly taught shape note–singing school in the community.

Clarice Blackard, the younger of Joe's two children, was born on March 24, 1900. She quickly demonstrated a love for her father's style of music — an interest that Joe undoubtedly recognized and nurtured. Her father bought a piano around 1910, and Clarice joined in as his accompanist. In 1919 she married Jesse Shelor. Jesse often worked on Joe Blackard's farm and had known Clarice since childhood.

The Shelors, of German ancestry, undoubtedly were part of the stream of immigration that flowed down the Valley of Virginia during the late 1700s. Jesse Shelor was born in 1894, one of 14 children of Billy Shelor and Sarah Brammer. The Shelors lived on the mountain, close to Meadows of Dan, but Sarah Brammer came from below the mountain near Stuart. Then, as now, Meadows of Dan was tied closely to the "down the mountain" communities — a relationship manifested in the many marriages between people from the two areas. Billy Shelor was a Baptist minister. Jesse recalled his father playing the fiddle only once: "He come in one night, picked up the fiddle, played the most beautiful 'Sandy River Belles' you ever heard, put it down and never did it again. That's when I knew he once had been a fiddler." Despite Billy's denial of his own musical abilities, 12 of the 14 children could play either the banjo or the fiddle. Jesse's main musical training came from an old fiddler living in Meadows of Dan named Wallace Spangler. (Pyrhus, six years older than Jesse, died in the 1930s. We may assume that the situation of learning was quite similar for the two brothers.)

Wallace Spangler (1851–1926) is generally regarded as the premier old-time fiddler from Patrick County. His name is almost synonymous with fiddling in this section of Virginia, and his influence on younger fiddlers was incredible. As a young boy Jesse followed Spangler closely and tried to learn the older man's tunes and styles, duplicating them as well as he could. According to Jesse, "anybody that ever heard him [Spangler] play would have been ashamed to sit down and play, he was that good. But we used to play together a whole lot." Clarice remembered that "he used to come down to

Pa's a lot, they was kind of buddies, you know. Pa played the banjo and him the fiddle. Pa thought a lot of the old man Wallace." Taylor Kimble, a fiddler from nearby Laurel Fork, remembered Joe Blackard, Wallace Spangler, and Clarice coming to a Fourth of July celebration once held near his home. The trio arrived in a flat-bed truck that carried Clarice's piano. The truck was backed up on the festival ground and the musicians performed on the bed of the truck, which served as a stage. By 1906, Jesse had assimilated much of Spangler's music, but his relationship with the old fiddler was broken for a time when the Shelor family moved to Spray, N.C., a move that offered employment opportunities for the family and new musical influences for Jesse and Pyrhus.

Between 1906 and the beginning of World War I, Billy Shelor moved his family several times between the area near Danville and Spray, where the factories were located, and Meadows of Dan. For a number of years, he operated a rooming house in Danville. Jesse remembered his father reading Western novels and other stories nightly to the mill workers who boarded with him. The Shelor children were also soon employed in the cotton mills, Jesse for the first time when he was 12 years old. It was while living and working in Danville that he and Pyrhus first met Charlie LaPrade, of Blue Ridge Highballers fame.[4] For a period of years, LaPrade lived directly across the street from the Shelors. Jesse and Pyrhus would get together with him two or three nights a week for music. Jesse recalled that LaPrade's fiddling was somewhat different than he was accustomed to hearing Wallace Spangler play:

> He played, well, more high-class music than we did. He knew a lot of tunes. He'd hear people play them on pianos and pick up new pieces like that, I guess. He was good, there's no question about that. He played tunes like "Under the Double Eagle" and "Over the Waves" and, well, he could play anything he wanted to. Now I never heard him play anything like "Mississippi Sawyers" or these old-time tunes, like we played, but we still played a lot together. Pyrhus and I played the fiddle, my brother Charlie the banjo, and Charlie would come over and play for half a night's time.

We know from LaPrade's recordings that he *did* play some of the old dance tunes of the region, pieces like "Darneo" and "Sandy River Belles." What undoubtedly struck Jesse was the appearance of newer pieces like "Under the Double Eagle," "Lynchburg Town," etc.— tunes that didn't fit the old fiddle pattern. Jesse pointed out that it was from LaPrade that he picked up "new" tunes. Wallace Spangler, according to Jesse, was quite intrigued with the music that his young protégé was bringing back from Danville:

I never hated to play before anybody as bad in my life as I did [before] Wallace. And one day he said, "Jesse," said, "Come over here." He handed me his fiddle and said he'd been hearin' about me playin' "Over the Waves" and "Under the Double Eagle," and he made me play both tunes. I never was so embarrassed because I couldn't hold a light to him on the fiddle, but he enjoyed it. But he said, "I never could learn to play a piece like that."

Clearly, the Danville/Spray area, with its cotton mills and heterogeneous population, was attractive to Patrick County people not only as a source of paying jobs but also because of its intrigue as a center of city life. The mill towns served to introduce many modern and popular forms into this vicinity. The mill owners brought trained musicians into the Danville area to "enlighten" their employees (and keep them peacefully occupied in their spare time). Jesse's brother Frank learned guitar and wind instruments from some of those musicians. Judging from Kinney Rorrer's material on LaPrade (in the notes to County Records 407), this progressive fiddler might also have profited from such exposure. As a source area for new and popular musical styles, the Danville area is vitally important and deserves a detailed study.[5]

When America entered World War I, both Jesse and Pyrhus were drafted into the army. Pyrhus went overseas, and Jesse, while in basic training near Washington, D.C., came very close to being a victim of the influenza epidemic that swept the country during the war years. His unit was nearly wiped out by the disease; he remembered that men died so rapidly that burial details could not keep up. Discharged, he returned to Meadows of Dan to recover and to renew his relationship with Clarice Blackard. When they married in 1919, they took over a part of Joe Blackard's farm.

Joe, Clarice, and Jesse now began playing together regularly. Pyrhus returned from Europe in 1920 and joined the musical get-togethers. It should be noted that they were not a band in the performance sense. They merely played music with each other and provided entertainment at such community events as dances, school breakings (the last day at school was always an occasion for a program), and other celebrations. Music was an informal situation for them; Pyrhus was farming, Jesse had recently initiated his 40-odd-year tenure with the state road department, Clarice was keeping house and raising a family, and Joe — though he had ceased carrying the mail — continued to operate his farm. The group did not have a band-name; they had no need of one until they recorded for Victor. The records they made together, probably like a lot of others that were waxed in the first years of recorded country music, were of an accidental nature and in no way reflected a desire to become professional musicians.

The Shelors (from left-to-right: Pryhus Shelor, Joe Blackard, Clarice Shelor, Jesse Shelor): According to group member Clarice Shelor, the Shelor Family — a string band from Meadows of Dan, Virginia — was primarily interested in instrumental arrangements before arriving in Bristol, yet Ralph Peer requested that they accentuate vocals on their Bristol recordings, revealing the producer's notion that people were more likely to purchase records featuring songs than those containing instrumentals. Courtesy Birthplace of Country Music Alliance.

The record industry was making inroads into the Southern market in the late 1920s, in many cases encouraged by local entrepreneurs who operated phonograph machine outlets. These local businessmen were eager to push the recordings of local talent in an effort to promote record sales, which in turn would increase the purchase of phonographs. The records made by the Shelors seem to have evolved from such a situation. The arrangement was made, as Clarice told it:

> There's a man named Howlette, in Hillsville, who sold records and record players. That was about all he handled. Walter Howlette was his name, but he has been dead a long time. Well, Pa had friends up there in Hillsville, and they told him about Pa, and he sent down here for Pa to come up there, and we all went up there and played some for him. In a few months, we got a call to go to Bristol to play. We drove in Pa's truck.

On August 2, 1927, the band drove to Pulaski and spent the night with friends. On the morning of the next day, they drove to Bristol, crossing the New River by ferry at Hillsville. Arriving at Bristol, they reported to the Victor recording studio. Neither Clarice nor Jesse recalled meeting any specific individuals, and whether they encountered Ralph Peer is uncertain. The Victor men immediately began the process of screening pieces for recording. Clarice described this:

> They had Pa name some old pieces and they'd say, "We got that, we've got that, we've got that," and Pa said, "Well, I'm about named out." And he knew a lot of old pieces. But he finally mentioned some pieces they didn't have. They had all the tunes they already had in a big book. And they said they had more instrumental than singing records and said that singing helped sell the records.

The material chosen by Victor placed them in some difficulty — they had not practiced specifically for recording, and the singing numbers had to be worked out on the spot, as revealed in the author's conversation with Clarice Shelor:

> TC: "So you didn't really practice anything to go over there?"
> CS: "No, we didn't have any idea. I had to sit down over there and write out the words to that 'Big Bend Gal.' Lots of times, I would sing just a verse here and there but I never had tried to sing it all. They wanted it all sung and I didn't know it, and Pa says, 'You sing it with me,' and I said, 'Pa, you'll have to give me the words.' So he had to write that out and then after they wanted that 'Billy Grimes, the Rover,' we had to sit and write the words out to that too. Had the words sitting on the piano."

Once the numbers to be recorded were selected and arranged, the recording session began, though not without some difficulty.

> CS: "The recording man was just as nice and friendly as he could be. We were making the record and Pyrhus patted his foot the loudest of anybody I ever saw playin', it would just drown the music out sometimes, and we played in an old milliner's shop, this great big old piano they had sittin' in there."
> TC: "A milliner's shop?"
> CS: "Where they made the hats, you know. And they had great big benches of hats and things to sell up in there. I reckon it's 'cause it was so large they put that piano in there. And Pyrhus just pat that foot, you know, just so loud. And they put a pillow under it and they told him not to pat his foot so loud. Well, he went on pattin' his foot, just couldn't play, it didn't seem like, without gettin' time...."

JS: "Well, I can't play without pattin' my foot."
CS: "And he [Pyrhus] said, 'I'll be damned if I can remember that.' And that went on the record too, they was cuttin' a record."
JS: "When Pyrhus said that and it went on the record, that tickled the man that was trying to work and fix it, so he said, 'We'll have to try that over, we won't send that out.'"

Neither Clarice nor Jesse remembered seeing other bands there for the recording session. They arrived, cut their allotted number of tunes, and departed, driving all the way back to Meadows of Dan that night.

CS: "We were the only ones that day, but they had been doin' that several weeks up there, I think. But we had our time and they told us what time to come. Be there in the afternoon. We had our dinner and all before we went in. We left directly after."

Several months later, Victor contacted the band to return to the recording studio, but Joe Blackard's failing health (due to cancer) prevented the trip. In the years following, music became less and less a part of the lives of Jesse and Clarice. They left it to their children, all of whom learned to play instruments. The three boys, Paul, Joe, and Jimmy, are especially excellent musicians, particularly in their performances of Delmore Brothers–style tunes.

Notes

1. Details of the recordings are as follows:
Vocal group with two fiddles, piano, banjo.
Bristol, Tennessee, Wednesday, August 3, 1927

39761–3	Big Bend Gal	Vi 20865; RCA LPV-552*
39762–2	Suzanna Gal	Vi 21130
39763–2	Sandy River Belle [*sic*]	Vi 21130; Cy 504
39764–2	Billy Grimes, the Rover	VI 20865

The tunes that the Shelors recorded represent the two distinct groupings of their repertoire: fiddle tunes and songs. "Suzanna Gal" is popular throughout the Blue Ridge region in Virginia and North Carolina. The Shelors' second or high part, similar to "Sally Ann," is indicative of Patrick County versions of the tune. "Sandy River Belles" is particularly associated with the Patrick County area but found also towards Martinsville to the east and northward towards the West Virginia line. Clarice maintains that Joe Blackard's banjo was tuned standard, gDGBD, for this tune. There is, however, locally a specific

*Vi 20865 is labeled as the Shelor Family, Vi 21130 as Dad Blackard's Moonshiners.

"Sandy River Belles" banjo tuning, gDGDE. (Older Patrick County musicians are normally tuned one whole tone lower than standard; thus, on the discs, this piece turns out to be in the key of F.)

2. Cecil Sharp, *English Folk Songs from the Southern Appalachians* (London: Oxford University Press, 1932). Sharp prints five songs from Joe Blackett [*sic*] and mentions recording some sixteen songs from Meadows of Dan performers August 27–29, 1918.

3. Meadows of Dan is located at the top of the Blue Ridge, which runs through the western part of Patrick County. Stuart is situated in the Piedmont section of the county, about 16 miles distant and 1000 feet below.

4. C. Kinney Rorrer, notes accompanying *The Blue Ridge Highballers* (County Records 407).

5. Although much material has been published concerning commercial recording groups from the Danville/Spray area, little research has dealt with the older folk music traditions of the area, or with the specific effects of urbanization on this older music. Take for example Tony Russell's article on Walter "Kid" Smith (*Old Time Music* 17). In expertly relating details of Smith's life and recording experiences, Russell mentions two locally prominent fiddlers, Dan Carter and Will Heffinger. Ironically, we know nothing of Carter's playing except for the fact that two of his pieces, "Dan Carter's Waltz" and "Rustic Dance," appeared on the out-of-print compilation *Back Home in the Blue Ridge* (County Records 723).

7. Gospel According to Bristol: The Life, Music, and Ministry of Ernest Phipps

Brandon Story

Reconstructing the life of an Appalachian preacher who died in 1963 is not an exact science, but reconstruction may be the only means of discovering the story of Ernest Phipps (1900–1963), one of the more legendary musicians who recorded at the Bristol sessions. Names, places, and dates supply a skeleton, but a life is more than just data. Records of a birth, marriage dates, military service, and a death date for Phipps fortunately still exist, but, more importantly, some people who knew Phipps are still living.[1] There is a gap in Phipps's story, though, from about 1923 until 1940. Fortunately, the six sides he recorded in Bristol, Tennessee, in 1927, and the six sides he came back to record there in 1928 help fill in the picture. Unfortunately, analyzing those sides raises as many new questions as it answers old ones. Best known for the celebrated company they keep alongside the other recordings of the Bristol sessions, Phipps's recordings are remarkable themselves for being the "first (and only)" Holiness music to be recorded in that era.[2] The Bristol sessions are sometimes referred to as the "Big Bang of country music"; however, the Phipps recordings are pioneering examples of a separate but related genre: Southern gospel. The story of Phipps's life and ministry reveals a remarkable man with an unfulfilled vision for evangelism and media. His story is pieced together in this essay from interviews with his sister, his two stepsons, and his granddaughter; from court records and legal documents; and most importantly, from the music he recorded from 1927 until 1930.

Ernest Phipps was born May 4, 1900, in Knox County, Kentucky. He was the second-born, and the second son, of James and Bessie (Owens) Phipps's six children. The family lived between Gray and Rossland, Kentucky, southeast of Corbin, in a coal camp at Bertha's Switch. Coal trains coming from Corbin would back into a sidetrack called Bertha's Switch to be loaded with coal. James Phipps worked on the railroad at the coal tipple (a mound of coal and dirt where trucks dumped their loads into train cars). Named for its proximity to Bertha's Holler, Bertha's Switch no longer boasts a coal camp or tipple, and the entrance to Bertha's Holler is now guarded on either side by a giant lumber mill. A few families still live in Bertha's Holler, but the locality now is a lumber camp for timber workers who supply the mill.

The Phipps children went to school in Gray, and Ernest studied up to the third grade.[3] Once the oldest boys, Howard, Ernest, and Elmer, were old enough, they went to work in the mines. Howard and Ernest probably worked around Gray, but Elmer worked for the Black Star coal company in Harlan. The younger children — Hazel, Robert, and Lillian — attended school longer than their siblings did, through the eighth grade.

Lillian McDaniel, Phipps's youngest sister, does not remember her parents playing any instruments, but several of the Phipps children were musical and played in church from their early years.[4] Music and religion were clearly connected in the Phipps family and in the heart of Ernest Phipps. Elmer played the French harp, and both Lillian and Hazel were church pianists. No one recalls Ernest playing an instrument, but Lillian reports that he sang in church "all the time."[5] The Phippses were Baptists when Ernest was growing up, but during his teen years, the family attended the Gray and Rossland Holiness churches. During those years, Ernest was already settling into a pattern he would follow for the rest of his life: working coal, singing in church, and fishing and hunting for fun.

On May 9, 1918, five days after his eighteenth birthday, Ernest was married to Mary Hammons, a 17-year-old Knox County–born girl.[6] The wedding took place in Gray, and Ernest's father, James, signed the marriage certificate, but Mary's parents, John and Anne Hammons, did not; this is significant because the marriage was not to last long. According to W. R. Mays, Ernest's older stepson, the marriage was annulled shortly after the wedding because of the age of the bride.[7] In the Knox County book of marriage records, notes from the parents of brides under the age of eighteen accompany many marriage certificates. These notes say something along the lines of "I give my daughter, Sally Brown, permission to marry Bill Jones.

Signed, John and Sarah Brown." No letter of release is recorded with Ernest and Mary's marriage certificate, which supports W. R. Mays's theory of the annulment. Randall Mays, Ernest's younger step-son, remembers differently, recalling that Ernest's first wife died very young, possibly in a flu epidemic, in 1919. No articles appeared in the *Corbin Daily Tribune* about a flu epidemic in that year, but a local outbreak in a small community like Gray may not have made the newspaper.

Supporting Randall's theory is the marriage certificate of Ernest and his second wife, Minnie Douglass. Ernest and Minnie were married January 10, 1920, just twenty months after his marriage to Mary.[8] Ernest was now nineteen and his new bride was only sixteen. His marital condition is listed as "widowed," and his occupation is listed as "miner." Minnie was also from Knox County, Kentucky, and along with the marriage certificate is a handwritten letter:

> Mr. County Court Clerk,
> Dear Sir,
>
> I am willing to give my daughter, Minnie Douglas to Mr. Ernest Phipps. Minnie Douglas age 16.
>
> Mrs. Bessie Evoy,
> Ernest Evoy[9]

A witness to the wedding was J. E. Champlin, better known as Johnny Champlin, one of Ernest's lifelong friends and a fellow Holiness preacher, who eventually became Ernest's brother-in-law when Johnny married the older of Ernest's two younger sisters, Hazel.

Ernest and Minnie lived in the coal camp at Bertha's Switch, and in February 1921 their first child, Charles, was born. No records or recollections verify that Ernest was preaching at this time, but it is probable that he was already involved in ministry, singing, and preaching. Helen Eulene, Ernest and Minnie's second child, was born in January 1923; the 22-year-old Ernest was now a husband, father, miner, preacher, and singer. The first record of the family during the 1920s is from the July 1, 1927, issue of the *Corbin Times Tribune*— interestingly, just weeks before he traveled to Bristol. In a small column of news from Gray, "Mr. and Mrs. Ernest Phipps and their children" were noted to have been among the many families who attended a party in Gray.[10]

The *Corbin Times Tribune* did not print articles about Phipps's journey to Bristol or his recordings; however, around July 25, 1927, Ernest Phipps and His Holiness Quartet (Roland Johnson on fiddle, Ancil McVay on guitar, and an unknown backup singer) made the trip from Knox County, Kentucky, to Bristol, Tennessee. It is possible that Alfred G. Karnes, a Baptist preacher likewise from the Corbin area, traveled with them down U.S. 411, a new road built in 1925 from Corbin, through the Cumberland Gap, to Bristol, Virginia.[11]

In the years immediately preceding the Bristol sessions, Southern gospel music was emerging as a distinct genre. The Lawrenceburg, Tennessee–based James D. Vaughn Music Publishing Company and the Dallas-based Stamps-Baxter Publishing Company organized singing quartets as marketing tools to sell shape note hymn books; to accomplish this, the quartets would travel to churches and singing schools to demonstrate arrangements from the newest shape note books.[12] The most popular of these hymns would make it into the hardcover shape-note hymnals.[13] As early as 1910, these quartets, made up of the best singers at singing schools and conventions, sang on tours underwritten by the publishing companies that supplied the groups with their names (such as the Vaughn Radio Quartet).[14] These singing groups consisted of four men who sang four-part harmony a cappella, or sometimes they were accompanied by one of the members playing piano.[15] By the late 1920s, a pianist was often a group's fifth member.[16] Recordings of such groups appeared on Vaughn's own record label as early as 1921.[17] In October 1927, Ralph Peer, a producer and talent scout for the New York–based Victor Talking Machine Company, recorded in Atlanta an "all-star" group of quartet singers, including Frank Stamps.[18] The group, known as the Stamps Quartet, would go on to record 25 sides between 1927 and 1932.[19] By the 1930s, the Vaughn company sponsored several groups, based in different southern states, that traveled and promoted their hymn books.

Three months before recording the shape-note singers in Atlanta, Peer was in Bristol, Tennessee, making records of, among others, Ernest Phipps. The music of Ernest Phipps came not from a publishing company's marketing department, but from the Holiness churches of eastern Kentucky. The rough-hewn playing and singing on Phipps's Bristol recordings contrast dramatically with the clean four-part harmony of the shape-note quartets and thus offered a different template for subsequent Southern gospel recordings.

Peer came to Bristol to record hillbilly records, a growing genre in the fledgling record industry, and comprised of "pre-war melodies and old mountaineer songs."[20] Gospel songs were a part of many Appalachian musicians' repertoires, but very few musicians from Appalachia were strictly gospel acts, and Peer was not specifically seeking to record gospel music. Peer identified Bristol as an ideal place to make hillbilly records through his association with Ernest "Pop" Stoneman, a Galax, Virginia, native who had recorded with Peer since 1924 on the OKeh label, and who had moved, with Peer, to

Victor by 1927.[21] Bristol, though a relatively small city, was centrally located between, and accessible from, the mountains of eastern Tennessee, southwest Virginia, and western North Carolina. The 1927 Bristol sessions, which took place over the last week of July and the first week of August 1927, were not so remarkable at the time, as recording sessions were held in other Southern towns during the 1920s, but over the next decade and beyond, two of the acts "discovered" in Bristol, the Carter Family and Jimmie Rodgers, would become the first country music superstars. The Bristol sessions, in turn, became a point of fascination for fans of country music, much as the various sessions at Sun Studios in Memphis, Tennessee, have fascinated aficionados of rock and roll.

The article about Ralph Peer and his recording sessions that ran in the *Bristol Herald Courier* on Sunday, July 24, 1927, reported that "Several well-known native record makers will come to Bristol this week to record. Mr. Peer has spent some time selecting the best native talent."[22] As Charles Wolfe has suggested, the implication of the article was that Peer had in mind exactly who would record the first week and that he hoped new talent would appear to record the second week.[23] The fact that Phipps recorded on Tuesday, July 26, 1927 — the second day of the sessions and the day after the appearance of the Stonemans, an already-signed Peer act — raises questions about how Phipps learned about the sessions and why he felt confident enough to go to Bristol. It is unlikely that Pop Stoneman, who was deputized by Peer to find acts for the Bristol sessions, discovered Phipps.[24] Somehow, either Phipps found out about the sessions or Peer found out about Phipps. Whether Phipps was the leader of a popular, traveling gospel act, or a young country preacher who caught the attention of a New York record man, the timing of Phipps's session implies that Peer came to Bristol knowing he was going to record Phipps, and that Phipps came to Bristol to record, not audition, for Peer.

While the activities of Peer in Bristol have been well documented by Charles Wolfe, little is known about what Phipps and the other members of his quartet did in Bristol other than recording six songs on July 26: "I Want to Go Where Jesus Is," "Do, Lord, Remember Me," "Old Ship of Zion," "Jesus Getting Us Ready for That Great Day," "Happy in Prison," and "Don't Grieve After Me."[25] McVay and Johnson — who would be back in Bristol with Phipps on October 29 and 30, 1928, to make additional recordings for Peer, and who would record two sides of their own for Columbia on October 17, 1929, in Johnson City, Tennessee — were the guitarist and fiddler.[26] The back-up vocalist remains unidentified, but could be McVay or Johnson. Guitarist Alfred Karnes's distinctive bass runs are audible in Phipps's 1927 recordings, and Karnes may have been a de facto member of the Holiness

Quartet for these sessions. He recorded his own solo sides on Friday, July 29. No one knows how Karnes caught Peer's attention; playing in the Holiness Quartet may have given Karnes his opportunity to audition for Peer.[27] A Baptist preacher from the Corbin, Kentucky, area, Karnes later pastored and held revivals in other parts of Kentucky, in Ohio, and Florida. By all accounts, he was a talented man who, later in life, painted and led a family band in which he played fiddle. His 1927 sides feature his stark, powerful baritone, accompanied only by his harp guitar, and those sides are a sharp contrast to the rolling rhythms, mountain harmonies, and string band instrumentation on the Phipps sides. Although Phipps and Karnes came from the same time and place and both played gospel music, their approaches were worlds apart. That Ralph Peer recorded both of them illustrates the variety of music at the Bristol sessions.

Phipps's recordings feature his own strong baritone voice, a higher vocal harmony part, strummed guitar rhythm, a simple fiddle melody line, and guitar bass string runs that connect vocal phrases. All six of Phipps's 1927 sides are upbeat, are fast or mid-tempo, and are in 4/4 time. Most of the sides have eight-bar repeating verses, for example on "I Want to Go Where Jesus Is": "I want to go, Lord, I want to go, I want to go there, too, / I want to go where Jesus is, Lord, I want to go there, too." In that particular song, these lines act as a refrain, while the melody remains the same for verse, chorus, and fiddle solo. The verses partially change the repeating lyrical pattern: "If you get there before I do, Lord, I want to go there, too, / Just look for me, I'm coming, too, Lord, I want to go there, too." Two other verses are the same, except for the substitution of Father for Mother in the line: "My loving Mother, gone so long." Of the six 1927 Phipps sides, "I Want to Go Where Jesus Is" is of average lyrical complexity. All the sides feature repeating lines, and some songs, like "Old Ship of Zion," sung to the tune popularly known as "She'll Be Coming Around the Mountain," offer only one line per verse:

> It's the old ship of Zion when she comes (when she comes),
> It's the old ship of Zion when she comes,
> It's the old ship of Zion, the old ship of Zion,
> The old ship of Zion when she comes.

Only one Phipps song, "Happy in Prison," contains verses with non-repeating lines and melodic variation in the chorus. In her book *Appalachian Mountain Religion: A History* (1995), Deborah Vansau McCauley relates that the lyrics of Holiness songs, even today, are printed in "unlined hymnals or hymnals without musical notation ... [while] the hymn tunes are part of the oral tradition."[28] This would seem true for Phipps's Bristol sides. The tunes, simple and familiar, do not account for the appeal of this music, and the music generally lacks lyrical or instrumental complexity. Phipps's recordings are instead memorable for their energy and spirit. These qualities, fundamental to Holiness theology, give the recordings their power.

In her discussion of Holiness worship, McCauley cites an early account of Holiness music by Capwell Wyckoff, a missionary for the Presbyterian Church in the U.S.A. who worked in the Ozarks and Appalachians and who in his book *The Challenge of the Hills* (1931) devotes a chapter to the religious music of "mountain people." Wyckoff's account suggests that he might have been listening to Ernest Phipps:

> The people of the mountains enjoy singing ... and in many of the homes a banjo or guitar, suspended from the wall or dusty on a shelf, testifies to this fact. Many of the roving religious sects of the mountains hold their services out of doors and the hymns are vigorously played on the banjo, imparting to the sacred music a swing not in keeping with the general tenor of holy things.[29]

The "galloping melodies" and "rollicking swing" Wyckoff goes on to discuss are a fitting description of Phipps's 1927 sides. Wyckoff, writing in 1931, was contemporary to the Bristol sessions, and one may infer from his descriptions that Phipps's music, the earliest recorded Holiness music, represents a rather common strain of Appalachian sacred music from that era.

The spirit behind Phipps's recordings deserves some discussion. The Holiness (later, the Holiness-Pentecostal) church placed great emphasis on the churchgoer being moved by the spirit, or Holy Spirit, in the worship service. This emphasis has generated curiosity among non–Holiness people, who become fascinated by the more sensationalistic aspects of Appalachian religion, such as glossolalia, or speaking in tongues, and the rare if notorious practice of handling snakes and drinking poison. Phipps spoke in tongues, but he never handled snakes or took strychnine. Anthropologist Troy D. Abell's book *Better Felt Than Said* (1982)— primarily an oral history of Holiness-Pentecostal beliefs and practices collected during Abell's visits with Holiness-Pentecostal people in Coal Creek, Kentucky, in the mid-1970s — also features Abell's own observations and analyses of those traditions. He writes that an "important assumption among Holiness-Pentecostals is that outward action (saying 'amen,' clapping hands, stomping feet, running the aisles, dancing in the spirit, shouting, jerking, speaking in tongues) is a manifestation of God's presence in a person's life."[30] Clearly, Ernest Phipps's 1927 and especially 1928 Bristol recordings were intended to help audiences "feel the spirit." As Charles Wolfe has noted, Phipps's 1928 sides in particular "give us some sense of the power and drive of a real Holiness service." [31]

Although the commercial Southern gospel boom occurred after the Bristol sessions, one might well wonder if Phipps changed the way he played his music when he first recorded commercial sides in Bristol in 1927. That seems unlikely, because Peer probably at some point auditioned Phipps for the recordings, and Peer obviously liked what he heard at the audition. However, when Phipps returned to Bristol in 1928 to record more sides for Peer, his music had definitely evolved. In October 1928, Peer explained to the *Bristol Herald Courier* that "only 75 records would be made this year, and that these had already been booked."[32] Peer and his engineer planned to spend ten days in Bristol that year, recording in the Peters building behind the City Bank.[33] The alley Phipps would have walked along to get to the Peter's building is now known as Bank Street, and it runs between the Paramount Theatre and the Gold Man building. Ernest Phipps and his Holiness Singers, as the 1928 group was called, made four recordings for Peer on October 29: "If the Light Has Gone Out in Your Soul," "Went Up in the Clouds of Heaven," "I Know That Jesus Set Me Free," and "Shine on Me." The group cut two more sides on October 30: "Bright Tomorrow" and "A Little Talk with Jesus."

Phipps's 1928 Bristol recordings were, in Wolfe's words, "much wilder," containing a great deal more of the outward actions of Holiness worship, such as clapping, stomping, and shouting; Phipps's music, by then, was in many ways more sophisticated.[34] The 1928 sides featured a larger group of singers, including Minnie Phipps, Nora Byrley, and A. G. Baker; the quartet included Ernest singing lead, A. G. singing bass, and the women taking high tenor and alto parts. On the song "A Little Talk with Jesus," the high female voice takes the lead, and Ernest sings the tenor below her. These later sides also incorporate more instruments than Phipps used in 1927: McVay and Johnson returned to play mandolin and fiddle, respectively, and were joined by Ethel (Hicks) Baker on piano, Eula Johnson on banjo, and Shirley Jones on guitar.[35]

The fuller sound achieved by the addition of female voices and additional instrumentalists gives Phipps's 1928 recordings the feel of actual Holiness congregational music making, whereas the 1927 recordings had featured only two male voices accompanied by a smaller string band. The material from the 1928 sessions is also more complex. Unlike the 1927 material, the 1928 songs have non-repeating verses and repeated choruses or refrains. The most interesting 1928 side, "Shine on Me," incorporates a verse from the Protestant hymn "Must Jesus Bear the Cross Alone?":

Must Jesus bear the cross alone
And all the world go free?
No, there's a cross for everyone
And there's a cross for me.

"Shine on Me" begins with this verse, sung slowly and accompanied by fiddle and piano, followed by a likewise slow refrain: "Shine on me, Lord, shine on me / Let the light from the lighthouse shine on me." Next are another slow verse and refrain, after which the whole group kicks in with a quick, stomp-and-clap-accompanied refrain that leads into the high-spirited second half of the song.

This recording is distinct among the 1928 sides not only because of its slow introduction and its tempo shift, but also because it offers an *arrangement*. Phipps's 1927 sides are, to a degree, arranged, in that they follow a repeated pattern: chorus, verse, chorus, and a fiddle break playing the verse melody. But "Shine on Me" reveals that the 1928 sides are both practiced and polished. Anyone familiar with Holiness services could jump in and sing "I Want to Go Where Jesus Is" from the 1927 sessions, but few could follow "Shine on Me" without having heard the song and without having paid attention to its arrangement. If Phipps's 1927 sides sound like Holiness congregational songs, with their simple lyrics and improvised melodies, his 1928 recordings at Bristol represent a more self-consciously constructed music. At the 1928 Bristol sessions, Phipps and his fellow musicians were not merely following the style of the singing school quartets: they were defining their own path, utilizing more sophisticated instrumentation and harmony singing. "A Little Talk with Jesus," with its female lead voice, was not preacher Phipps leading the congregation before he preached: it was white Southern gospel music — arranged, practiced, and recorded to appeal to the commercial recording market.[36] And ironically, though the 1928 sides have a more commercial sound, they are even closer than the 1927 sides to projecting the feel and drive of a Holiness service.

According to a few sources, Phipps, as a Holiness singer, would likely have been looking for new, recently published songs, something he and Peer had in common. Randall Mays remembers Phipps singing the hymn "I Want to Know More About My Lord" — a song copyrighted in 1949 — in the 1950s, when it would have been brand new.[37] Wyckoff, writing in 1931, laments the tendency of some Appalachian denominations to ignore old standard hymns in favor of new ones:

My experience was to go into a service, hurt my throat by singing hymns picked by the local song leader, and then wonder who had ever written such high-pitched, galloping melodies. A glance at the tops of the pages showed that they had been written within the last five or six years. Indeed, a careful check through a mountain hymn book showed the astonishing fact that not one hymn had been written before 1926! Much as he loves old customs, the mountaineer likes his hymns up to date.[38]

Although they sound dated now, Phipps's records were, for that era, thoroughly modern, boasting what then was new Holiness and Southern gospel music. Perhaps after Phipps's 1927 Bristol sides achieved some popularity, Peer realized the broad audience to which this music could be marketed, and this likely prompted Phipps to change the music to make it more accessible to a wider audience. Or, perhaps after Phipps had proven himself as a recording act, he felt the freedom to expand his group, to evolve as a musician by adding more singers and players to the lineup and by finding new, exciting songs with stronger lyrical content and musical texture. It is possible that, between the 1927 and 1928 Bristol sessions, Phipps — exploiting his modest fame to expand his ministry — began preaching and singing at more churches in the Corbin, Kentucky, area, bringing his "Holiness Singers" with him when he preached.

Ernest Phipps's ministry was that of a local, traveling, singing evangelist. The Holiness churches in Knox County, Kentucky, in the 1920s were not formally allied in an association, but it was common for those who attended one church to attend revival meetings and special services at the other churches, so the congregations knew each other.[39] W. R. Mays describes Phipps's ministry this way: "Well, it would be kind of hard to describe, I guess, by today's standards. He went to church different places. They didn't just get in a church and stay as such, they just traveled from place to place. He almost always preached wherever he went. They invited him to preach, so if he was there he almost surely would preach."[40]

Randall Mays adds that wherever Phipps preached he also sang, but that he never went to a church strictly to sing.[41] He probably never traveled far from Corbin to preach. Although by 1927 Phipps was a preacher, singer, and recording act, he was still employed full time in the mines. He was undoubtedly paid Peer's 1927–1928 rate of fifty dollars per side for the twelve sides he recorded during these sessions, and even with the expenses of traveling with a large band, he probably pocketed a little money. Nevertheless, he returned to work in the coal mines shortly after recording. Acts like the Carter Family and Jimmie Rodgers, who were able to make a career in the music business, were an exclusive minority. Wolfe reports that "If the Light Has Gone Out in Your Soul" sold almost 12,000 copies, a respectable number for most recordings from that time, but not enough to make Phipps a recording star.[42]

The Big Bang of Country Music - Bristol, TN/VA

April 23, 2006   Mon. 7/25 – Friday 8/5
Ralph Peer

Presented by Jim Murphy

Sequence	Media	Time	Running Time	Subject
1	Jim Murphy	1:00pm	20	Introduction
2	DVD-1	1:20pm	24	Carters/Bristol/Charles Wolf/ Ted Olson/Jim & Jesse McReynolds/ John Lilly
3	Jim Murphy	1:45pm	15	5 Jimmy Rodgers Songs
4	DVD-2	2:00pm	8	Katie Doman
5	Jim Murphy	2:08pm	2	Intro Carters
6	DVD-3	2:10pm	2	Carter Family Reenactment
7	Jim Murphy	2:12pm	15	5 Carter Songs
8	DVD-4	2:30pm	6	Carter Family Videos
9	Jim Murphy	2:36pm	10	Conclusion of A/V portion
10	Intermission	2:45pm	30	Intermission

11/27 (Camden)

5/28

– Intro Ron McConnell

000 ——→ 80#   "Fiddlin' John (Atlanta)

#1 - Play 4 songs (1923, 24, 25, 26)   Samantha Bumgarner + Eva Davis
Talk - ~~recatergory of Stonoroup + the Cost Heston~~   Charlie Poole + NC Ramblers
                                        Al Hopkins + B.B.'s "Hill Billies"

#2   Jimmie Rodgers ("1927 Camden, NJ)
     807 ——→ By#1, In the Jailhouse (Memphis Blues, By#4

#3   Original Carter Family (8/1,2 /1927 + Bristol)
     Little Log Cabin by the Sea,) Poor Orphan Child, Storms are on the Ocean
     (8/2) Single Girl, Married Girl, Wandering Boy

The topics of the songs recorded by Phipps in Bristol reflect the spiritual issues affecting him and his denomination. Of the twelve songs he recorded in 1927 and 1928, seven concern either the second coming of Christ or life with Christ after death: "Jesus Getting Us Ready for That Great Day," "Do, Lord, Remember Me," "Old Ship of Zion," "I Want to Go Where Jesus Is," "Don't Grieve After Me," "Went Up in the Clouds of Heaven," and "Bright Tomorrow." Of these, "Jesus Getting Us Ready for That Great Day" projects the vivid images of the apocalypse one might expect in a fiery Holiness sermon: "The earth will be a rocket on that great day, / the sun will turn to darkness on the great day, / the moon will be a-bleeding on that great day, / the stars will be a-falling on that great day."

Phipps's other songs concern the Christian life. Three songs, "If the Light Has Gone Out in Your Soul," "Bright Tomorrow," and "Shine on Me," speak of the illuminating qualities of God and His Spirit. "If the Light Has Gone Out in Your Soul" reminds the listener, in rich imagistic phrasing, that "When the sun of your life has gone dim, / And the clouds in the west turn to gold, / When you come to the end of the way, / When life's story for you has been told, / The spirit of God will attend / If the light has gone out on your soul." Two other songs — "I Know That Jesus Set Me Free" and "Happy in Prison" — characterize the weary life of humankind on Earth as a bondage from which God saves us. In the latter song, Phipps sings, "I'm happy in this prison, yes I'm happy everywhere, / Oh glory glory, hallelujah, sinner lay those burdens down." He also speaks of receiving a crown, signifying a deliverance from the prison of sin, as well as from the prison of poverty. "A Little Talk with Jesus" celebrates prayer as a means for getting the Christian through hard times. Phipps is remembered as a prophetic preacher, and we can surmise that this range of topics, illustrating the priorities of his singing ministry, also approximate the priorities of his preaching: the apocalypse, the redeeming light of God, the bondage of the sinful life, and prayer.

One complication of the Ernest Phipps story is a 1930 record on the Vocalion label by the "Kentucky Holiness Singers." The sides, "I'm on My Way" and "I Will Not Be Removed," were recorded in Knoxville, Tennessee, on Saturday, March 29, 1930.[43] The session was the second of two Knoxville sessions for the Brunswick recording company, the first taking place in late August 1929.[44] According to Wolfe, these were among the "last great sessions of the stringband era," and some of the last old-time sessions before the onset of the Great Depression.[45] In addition to such famous acts as Uncle Dave Macon, the Tennessee Ramblers, and McFarland and Gardner, these sessions also yielded "some of the rarest and most obscure music" with "many of the bands and music still unknown."[46] The sessions were most likely produced by a Chicago-based jazz musician named Richard Voynow, one of only a few producers during that era (one of the others being Ralph Peer) who produced jazz and blues records as well as recordings of old-time music.[47]

The two Brunswick sides by the Kentucky Holiness Singers complicate the story of Ernest Phipps. After listening to those recordings, one would not surmise that Phipps was part of the group. Wolfe writes that the Kentucky Holiness Singers seem "to be a stringband doing gospel numbers. The style is definitely not that of Ernest Phipps, and no one seems to know much about them."[48] He is right that the style is not that of Ernest Phipps in 1927 or especially in 1928. The 1930 recordings, "I Will Not Be Removed" and "I'm on My Way," are from a smaller group of musicians than Phipps used on the 1928 sides. The 1930 sides feature a trio of male singers backed by a guitarist playing chords and some bass runs, a banjoist playing chords, and a mandolin restating the melody along with the singers and through the instrumental breaks.

The music by the Kentucky Holiness Singers resembles in some respects (but not in others) the musical approach employed in Phipps's 1927 sessions. They have in common a lead baritone male singer, but where the 1927 sides feature a high tenor male harmony, the 1930 recordings possess an alto male harmony. The 1930 songs are performed at a somewhat slower tempo than the 1927 songs, and the instrumental backing from 1930 substitutes the mandolin for the fiddle as the lead instrument. Of course, this could all be accounted for if Phipps had assembled a different band. The lead male vocal on the 1930 sides could very well be from Phipps, and the subject matter of the songs and the accents in the voices on the latter recordings certainly resemble the earlier sides. A different group of Kentucky Holiness singers, though, having heard Phipps's Bristol records, could have performed the 1930 songs mimicking Phipps's musical style. A perplexing element on the 1930 sides is the interjected shouting on both songs. During the mandolin breaks on each song, the singers, seemingly on cue, shout "Glory to God," "Praise the Lord," and "Hallelujah." Unlike Phipps's 1928 Bristol sessions, which feature driving, fervent worship songs, the shouts on the 1930 sides sound staged. This may be why Wolfe dismissed this music as "definitely not that of Ernest Phipps." Granted their arrangements, Phipps's 1927 and 1928 sides feel authentic, as if they were recorded in the hills of eastern Kentucky at a Holiness service. The 1930 recordings by the Kentucky Holiness Singers, though, sound affected and self-conscious.

However, according to W. R. Mays, who has a copy of the very rare Vocalion 78 of the Kentucky Holiness Singers, the lead singer on those two 1930 recordings is "absolutely" Ernest Phipps.[49] Outside evidence suggests that it could be. According to Wolfe, many of the performers for the 1929 and 1930 Knoxville sessions came from Kentucky and even Cincinnati.[50] The 1929 sessions were booked ahead of time, like the 1928 Bristol sessions, but an article in the August 27, 1929, *Knoxville Journal* explaining that records were being made in the St. James Hotel would have sounded familiar to Phipps, who, given his experience and success, might have arranged for his group to record in Knoxville in 1930.[51] Wolfe notes that because of the timing of the Knoxville sessions, at the outset of the Depression, many of the Knoxville recordings were not widely distributed, and some were not released at all.[52] This may explain why the relatively unknown sides by the Kentucky Holiness Singers were never researched or discussed in the context of Phipps's career. The Vocalion records from the Knoxville sessions were not widely distributed and are now among the "rarest of old time discs."[53] W. R. Mays now has a copy of the Kentucky Holiness Singers record given to him by his brother; the record was originally owned by Ernest Phipps, who had a very limited collection of 78s. It is very possible, if not highly likely, that Phipps had that rare record because it contained *his* music. By the early 1940s, he did not even possess copies of his Bristol-recorded Victor sides.[54]

If the Kentucky Holiness Singers' 1930 Vocalion record is the last Ernest Phipps recording, what does that say about who he was and where he was headed as a musician? Perhaps by continually trying to record music in the studio that captured the sound and feel of a Holiness service — which certainly would have featured shouting — his role as a preacher overwhelmed his role as a musician. It is hard to imagine (in his effort to make records in the studio that reflected the spirit and drive of Holiness music) how Phipps could have topped his 1928 Bristol sides. And one cannot help but wonder why in 1930 he would not have traveled to Knoxville with the various people with whom he had made records in Bristol in 1928. Not having a larger group at the recording session in Knoxville would have limited Phipps's ability to re-create what had happened naturally at the 1928 Bristol sessions. Perhaps the problems on the 1930 Kentucky Holiness Singers' recordings (assuming that they feature Phipps) are more a result of decisions by the producer at the Knoxville sessions. If he was concerned with matching the energy of Ralph Peer's Bristol recordings, Richard Voynow may have encouraged the Kentucky Holiness Singers to add shouting to suggest the Holy Spirit was moving in the recording studio. Regardless, those 1930 sides (again, if they are by Phipps) illustrate the end of a creative arc that began in 1927 and peaked in 1928.

The years of the Great Depression were personally difficult ones for Ernest Phipps. His recording career was over, and his marriage to Minnie was ending. Sometime between 1928 and 1933, the couple separated. Minnie moved to Knoxville, leaving Charles and Helen with Ernest.[55] The cause of their separation is not known, and there are conflicting reports, ranging from Ernest "backsliding" to Minnie drinking heavily and running off with a man to Knoxville.[56] None of these claims have been substantiated, and the people who might have known the actual situation are dead. According to W. R. Mays, Ernest hated the idea of divorce and put it off as long as possible. The court record of their divorce does little to explain the cause:

> Ernest Phipps
> VS:
> Minnie Phipps
>
> The plaintiff has taken no proof to sustain the allegations of his petition. The defendant has answered, set up counter-claim, and fully established her grounds for divorce, by proof. It is made known to the court that property rights are settled and no children are born of the marriage.
>   It is the judgment of the court that plaintiff's petition be and it is dismissed and he will take nothing by it and that defendant is entitled to the relief sought. The parties hereto are hereby divorced from each other and the bonds of matrimony entered into between them is dissolved. Defendant is adjudged her costs and this case is stricken from docket.[57]

Ernest seemed a reluctant plaintiff, not supporting his allegations, and Minnie, proving her allegations, seemed eager to dissolve the marriage. The court mistakenly reported that Ernest and Minnie did not have children. From a legal standpoint, Minnie got more of what she wanted out of the divorce than Ernest, who likely wanted no divorce at all.

The divorce was hard on Charles and Helen, who continued to live with their father when their mother moved to Knoxville.[58] Tere Patierno, Charles's daughter, remembers that while Charles and Helen remained close siblings, they had a difficult relationship with their mother for many years.[59] Charles joined the army as soon as he could.[60] Helen married young and moved to Ohio. By the time he was 40, Ernest was living alone.[61] Moving out of Gray, he rented a room from friends on Kentucky Street in Corbin.[62]

In 1943, at the height of the United States' involvement in World War II, the 43-year-old Ernest Phipps was drafted into the army.[63] According to W. R. Mays, who would later serve in the army himself, Phipps was drafted at the time because he was under the cut-off age of 45 and had no dependents. Had his children been at home, he could have deferred, but as a single man with no children at home, he was eligible for the draft. For about a year he was in the army at the same time as his son, Charles, who would make a career out of the service. Ernest served in the Fifth Army Corps, which had its headquarters in Fort Hayes, Ohio.[64] He received some hospi-

Ernest Phipps, with his daughter Helen Eulene and his son Charles, circa 1941. Courtesy Randall and Claretta Sue Mays.

tal training and then was shipped to Washington State, where he worked for a few months in an army hospital.[65] Ernest's tour of duty was cut short by the end of the war. For a man whose life had been lived mostly in and around Gray, Kentucky, the train ride out west to Washington must have been a great adventure, and W. R. Mays remembers Phipps telling often the story of his train trip across the country. By 1945, Phipps was back in Corbin, living at a friend's home on Kentucky Street, driving a coal truck and preaching and singing.[66]

Personally and professionally, the last 15 years of Phipps's life were happy and successful. The last chapter of his life began in the summer of 1949 when he married Zola Mays, formerly Zola Sallins, a widow whose late husband, Lester Mays, had been a carpenter at the nuclear facility at Oak Ridge. Zola had two sons, 16-year-old W. R. and 11-year-old Randall. Ernest drove a coal truck to a coal tipple near Zola's home. Randall Mays recalls how the two first met:

> We think the Lord shows us visions and dreams. She says she was going to the post office, and she didn't really know this man, she just saw him

coming toward [her] in the coal truck, and she said the Lord just spoke to her and said "You're going to marry that man." And she didn't even know him, but later on he started stopping by. I remember when I was a kid he would come all cleaned up in the afternoon in his white shirt and his straw hat, especially in the summertime. They'd sit under the shade tree and talk, and she'd always send me somewhere to do something.[67]

A photo of Ernest and Zola Phipps taken on their wedding day shows the two standing in front of Zola's twin sister's home, where they had stopped to drop off Randall before leaving for their honeymoon. In the photo, the new Mrs. Phipps, wearing a light-colored dress with a dark stripe across the bottom, a corsage and a dark hat, is looking up and smiling at her six-feet-plus husband, in his white panama hat, white shirt, white slacks, and wide 1940s leaf-print tie. Phipps is smiling back at her.

After marrying Zola, Phipps moved out of the room he rented on Kentucky Street in Corbin and into Zola's home, a four-room house on two acres that had been the Mays' family home in Place, Kentucky (part of the Gray community).[68] Randall Mays recalls that his stepfather was a good provider, and Mays believes that Phipps "probably would have done more if Mom would have let him. She had her traditions also, you know."[69]

Phipps was in a position to be a good provider because by 1948 he and his brother Howard were into the coal business for themselves. Leasing several hundred acres in the Gray community from the Black Star Coal Company, the brothers started their own business, the Phipps and Phipps Coal Company.[70] According to W. R. Mays, who worked for the company for about three years, the Phipps brothers began with very little, but it was a good time for the coal business. Within a few years, they had many people working for them, mining and driving trucks. Howard Phipps managed the office, while Ernest Phipps drove a truck and worked in the field. All mining in the area at that time was deep mining; strip mining would not come to the region until the early 1960s. W. R. and Randall both remember their stepfather driving the coal truck all day and then sweeping out the back so he could use the truck to pick up people and take them to a revival or a midweek church service.

The mine boss, Harold Steele, was a good friend and a regular fishing partner of Ernest Phipps. W. R. Mays would eventually marry Harold's daughter Wanda. Ernest Phipps always enjoyed hunting and fishing, and he was a particularly good fisherman. W. R. and Wanda recall a few fish stories involving Phipps from these years. W. R. and some friends had gone up into the mountains to fish one weekend, and Phipps planned to meet them up there on that Saturday afternoon. The fishing had not gone well, and when

Ernest Phipps fishing off of the dock at Cherokee Lake, near Corbin, Kentucky, circa 1953. Courtesy Randall and Claretta Sue Mays.

he arrived, the group had not caught a single fish. Phipps, not knowing about the lack of fish but thinking that the boys might be getting hungry, rolled into camp Saturday afternoon with bags of groceries. He also brought along his fishing gear and told the boys that while he was there, he would catch them some fish. Sure enough, within a few hours, Phipps had caught enough fish for dinner. After bringing the groceries and catching the fish for the hungry young fishermen, he got back in his truck and went home.[71]

The other story W. R. and Wanda remember about Phipps would sound even more outrageous if it were not for the photo that survives to prove it. Ernest and Harold Phipps were fishing at Cherokee Lake in June 1957, and it was getting dark. Harold Phipps was ready to quit for the day, but his brother wanted to stay, saying he knew that there was a big fish waiting to be caught that day. Then, in a few minutes, Harold caught a large catfish, and, satisfied, told his brother that he was now definitely ready to leave. Ernest Phipps replied that if there was one fish that big in the lake, there had to be a bigger one. They stayed a little longer, and Ernest Phipps soon caught a catfish that was just as big. When they got back to weigh the fish, Harold Phipps's weighed eighteen pounds, and his brother's was a half pound more. In the photo the two men are standing side by side, wearing work clothes and caps, and holding their fish, tails to the ground and mouths up. Ernest Phipps is standing taller, and it certainly appears that he is holding the bigger fish.[72]

Ernest Phipps had stayed active in ministry as an evangelist and singer, but in 1960 he pastored for the first time in his life, at the Rossland Holiness Church in Gray, Kentucky, one of the oldest Holiness Churches in the U.S.[73] In his later years, Phipps and his sister, Hazel Champlin, sang together, with Hazel accompanying them on the piano.[74] As late as the early 1950s, Ethel Baker, who played piano on Phipps's 1928 Bristol recordings, would accompany him.[75] Randall Mays, today an Assembly of God minister in Corbin, Kentucky, knew Phipps not just as a stepfather, but also as a mentor in the ministry. As a young man and a young minister, Randall paid special attention to Phipps's preaching style. Mays remembers that his stepfather was a voracious reader and student of the Bible despite his limited formal education. By the time he came into Randall's life in 1949, Ernest Phipps was drawing his sermon material from the newspaper as well as from scripture, according to Mays:

> In his time he was a prophetic preacher. Even though he would drive an old coal truck — sometimes early in the morning — and wouldn't get back until after dark, he would always buy a *Knoxville News Sentinel* paper. That was the only daily paper we had back then, and he would always

read all the headlines and what was going on. Then he would get his Bible and he would spend every night, an hour or two, reading.... He could take the newspaper and read it right through all the latest news, and he would go to the Bible and look up references and scriptures.[76]

According to Randall Mays, Ernest Phipps believed that Israel's becoming a nation in 1948 was a fulfillment of Biblical prophecy and signaled the apocalypse, the return of the Lord.[77] The return of Christ and the preparation for that return was certainly an important theme in Phipps's songs. Mays also remembers Phipps's preaching style, and the unusual way he integrated scripture into the sermon:

> When he'd go to church he didn't take any outline. He knew what he was going to ask to be read. And if he was in a service with his brother-in-law Johnny Champlin, he would ask Johnny to read for him. And Johnny might read a verse or two of scripture, and Ernest would say, "stop there, stop there," and he'd preach on that scripture for a period of time. And then he'd say, "Go on, Johnny, read more, read more," and Johnny would read another portion, then he'd say "turn over to Daniel," or wherever, and he'd read that. So he had readers, he would make people read.[78]

W. R. Mays, a retired Baptist minister, was likewise impressed by Phipps's knowledge of the Bible. "He was well, well read in the Bible and had an awful lot of it memorized," recalls Mays. "He could quote the scriptures right down the line."[79]

Johnny Champlin, Phipps's best friend and brother-in-law, became seriously ill in the late 1950s, and the story, remembered by Randall and W. R. Mays, illustrates the faith of Ernest Phipps and the different perspectives of his two stepsons. Champlin, seriously ill with a bleeding ulcer, was bedridden for weeks and losing weight rapidly. Because of his faith, Champlin refused to be treated by a doctor, believing that the Lord would heal him. People throughout the community were praying for him, but Champlin's condition continued to get worse. Eventually his son went to the doctor, and gave the medicine prescribed by the doctor to his father. According to Randall Mays, the medicine was too little, too late, and Champlin's health continued to deteriorate, almost to the point of death. Phipps, hating to see his friend suffer, went to Champlin's home one day in the middle of the week. Standing at the head of the bed, Phipps prayed, "God, this is the day, and I pray that you either take Johnny home or you heal him. And I don't intend to leave here until you do something because he has suffered long enough."[80] Within a few hours, Champlin became seriously ill, and vomited profusely. When he had finished, he asked his wife to bring him clothes, and he got out of bed for the first time in several weeks and began a rapid recovery. That Sunday, Champlin gave his testimony at the Gray Pentecostal Church homecoming service.

In W. R. May's version of the story, Johnny was sick, refused to go the doctor, but finally relented, received medication and blood, and through that was healed. As Wanda Mays says, "Ernest believed in healing," but, adds W. R., "he believed you ought to go the doctor, too."[81] This story highlights the difference in style, but the similarity in substance, of faith in Phipps's two step-sons. W. R. — who was older when his mother, a practicing Baptist, married Ernest Phipps — remained a Baptist, and became a Baptist minister. Randall Mays was younger and more influenced theologically by Phipps and became an Assembly of God minister, holding to many of the charismatic beliefs of the Holiness church.

In late 1961, Phipps gave up pastoring and driving a coal truck after he suffered a serious heart attack. He was told by a doctor to give up working and to drastically cut down on physical activity if he wanted to live much longer. Selling the Phipps and Phipps Company and leaving his pastor position at the Rossland church, Phipps continued to preach and sing. According to W. R. Mays, "He was going every day right up 'til the day that he died."[82] On April 17, 1963, two weeks shy of his sixty-third birthday, Phipps suffered another heart attack. W. R. Mays drove him to the hospital, but Phipps died in the car just as they reached the hospital. The two men had talked all the way there, and Phipps tried to convince Mays to take him back home. He had a fishing trip planned for the next day.[83]

When asked what would motivate 27-year-old Ernest Phipps to travel the long road to Bristol to make recordings, Randall Mays says he thinks Phipps would have "wanted to seize the opportunity ... to do evangelistic work and ministry."[84] Mays believes Phipps had an unfulfilled vision for the "depth and outreach of his ministry."[85] We cannot say whether Phipps believed that recording his music was part of some personal mission to carry the gospel outside the Corbin, Kentucky, area, or whether he thought that making records was just another way of leading folks to God. We can say, though, that in Bristol, Tennessee, Ernest Phipps, a Holiness preacher from Knox County, Kentucky, was present at an early confluence of evangelism and mass media, overseeing the birth of a new genre of commercial music — Southern gospel music.

Discography[86]

Ernest Phipps and His Holiness Quartet: Ernest Phipps, vocal. Roland N. Johnson, fiddle. Ancil L. McVay, guitar. Possibly Alfred G. Karnes, harp guitar.

Recorded 26 July 1927, Bristol, Tennessee:

Song	Catalogue number
I Want to Go Where Jesus Is	39710–1-Vi 20834
Do, Lord, Remember Me	39711–2-Vi.20927
Old Ship of Zion	39712–2-Vi 20927
Jesus Getting Us Ready for That Great Day	39713–3-Vi 21192
Happy in Prison	39714–2-Vi 21192
Don't Grieve After Me	39715–2-Vi 20834

Ernest Phipps and His Holiness Singers: Ernest Phipps, vocal. Minnie Phipps, vocal. Nora Byrley, vocal. A. G. Baker, vocal. Roland N. Johnson, fiddle. Ethel Baker, piano. Ancil L. McVay, mandolin. Eula Johnson, banjo. Shirley Jones, guitar.

Recorded 29 October 1928, Bristol, Tennessee

If the Light Has Gone Out in Your Soul	47237–3-Vi V40010
Went Up in the Clouds of Heaven	47238–3-Vi V40106
I Know That Jesus Set Me Free	47240–2-Vi V40106
Shine on Me	47241- -Bb B-5540

Recorded 30 October 1928, Bristol Tennessee

Bright Tomorrow	47243–3-Vi V40010
A Little Talk with Jesus	47245- -Bb B-5540

Kentucky Holiness Singers: Possibly Ernest Phipps, vocal. Unknown, guitar. Unknown, mandolin.

Recorded 29 March 1930, Knoxville, Tennessee

I'm on My Way	K-8031 Vocalion 5439
I Will Not Be Removed	K-8032 Vocalion 5439

Notes

1. A. L. Phipps is a more popular gospel singer from the Corbin, Kentucky area. For many years, A. L., a Baptist, led the Singing Phipps Family, a gospel act heavily influenced by the Carter Family. I began my research into Ernest Phipps by calling Phippses in the Corbin area. Nearly all were related to A. L. and none were related to Ernest. Phipps is a common name in Eastern Kentucky, and Ernest and A. L. are probably related, though to name their common ancestor, one would have to dig into the life of A. L. Phipps as well, a search not in the scope of my research.

2. Charles Wolfe, liner notes to *Ken-*

tucky Gospel: Complete Works of Alfred G. Karnes, Ernest Phipps, McVay and Johnson in Chronological Order, 1927–1928. DOCD-8013. Document Records, 1997.

3. All information on Ernest Phipps's life before his first marriage comes from Lillian McDaniel. Interview by author, 13 May 2001, Corbin, Kentucky. Mini-Disc recording.

4. Ibid.

5. Ibid.

6. Marriage certificate on file at Knox County Courthouse, Barbourville, Kentucky.

7. W. R. and Wanda Mays, interview by author, 16 May 2001, London, Kentucky, cassette recording.

8. Marriage certificate on file at Knox County Courthouse, Barbourville, Kentucky.

9. Ibid.

10. "Gray," *Corbin Times Tribune,* 1 July 1927.

11. Robert V. Droz, *Old US 25E: Crossing the Cumberland Gap,* 20 June 2002, www.us-highways.com/cgap00.htm (15 January 2003).

12. James R. Goff, Jr., *Close Harmony: A History of Southern Gospel* (Chapel Hill: University of North Carolina Press, 2002): 114, 120.

13. Ibid., 113.

14. Ibid., 111, 117.

15. Ibid., 121.

16. Ibid.

17. Ibid., 118.

18. Ibid., 121.

19. Ibid., 121.

20. Charles Wolfe, "Ralph Peer at Work: The Victor 1927 Bristol Sessions," *Old Time Music* 5 (Summer 1972): 11.

21. Ibid.

22. "Record Engineers Locate in Bristol," *Bristol Herald Courier,* 24 July 1927, 3.

23. Wolfe, "Ralph Peer at Work," 11.

24. Ibid.

25. For sources, other versions, and histories of the songs Ernest Phipps recorded, see Guthrie T. Meade, Dick Spottswood, and Douglas S. Meade *Country Music Sources: A Biblio-Discography of*

Commercially Recorded Traditional Music (Chapel Hill: University of North Carolina Press, 2002) 585, 587, 591, 597, 600, 603, 652, 665, 666, 680, 681, 694. Meade's book opens up a world of questions regarding sources and possibly how Phipps's music influenced others (many of the songs he recorded first were recorded in the late 1930s, though you'd have to track down all the versions to make a case). It is, at least, a great resource for tracking down other versions of the songs Phipps recorded.

26. Wolfe, liner notes.

27. Donald Lee Nelson, "The Life of Alfred G. Karnes," *JEMF Quarterly* 8, no. 25 (Spring 1972): 32.

28. Deborah Vansau McCauley, *Appalachian Mountain Religion: A History* (Urbana: University of Illinois Press, 1995), 82.

29. Capwell Wyckoff, *The Challenge of the Hills* (Philadelphia: Department of Sunday School Missions of the Board of National Missions of the Presbyterian Church in the U.S.A. by the Presbyterian Board of Christian Education, 1931), 17.

30. Troy D. Abell, *Better Felt Than Said: The Holiness Pentecostal Experience in Southern Appalachia* (Waco: Baylor University Press, 1982): 125.

31. Wolfe, liner notes.

32. "Victor Machine Company's Recording Crew Arrives in Bristol to Make Records," *Bristol Herald Courier,* October 1928.

33. Ibid.

34. Wolfe, liner notes.

35. Ibid., Randall Mays remembers that Ethel Baker was originally Ethel Hicks.

36. This is not a scientific observation, but by the 1970s it would seem that the two separate strands of early Southern gospel, the four-part harmony school and the "mountain" school, would meet in groups like the Oak Ridge Boys that had tight singing over a driving rhythm section. Further, contemporary groups like the McKameys, a family quartet with male and female singers, are not so far in spirit

from the fervency of the Phipps recordings.

37. Randall and Claretta Sue Mays, interview by author, mini disc recording, Corbin, Kentucky, 13 May 2001.

38. Wyckoff, *The Challenge of the Hills,* 19–20.

39. W. R. Mays, interview by author, mini-disc recording, London, Kentucky, 16 May 2001.

40. Ibid.

41. Randall Mays, interview by author.

42. Wolfe, liner notes.

43. Charles Wolfe, "Early Country Music in Knoxville: The Brunswick Sessions and the End of an Era," *Old Time Music* 12 (Spring 1974): 28.

44. Ibid., 22–23.

45. Ibid., 19.

46. Ibid.

47. Ibid., 20.

48. Ibid., 30.

49. W. R. Mays, interview by author.

50. Wolfe, "Early Country Music in Knoxville," 22.

51. Ibid.

52. Ibid., 19, 26.

53. Ibid., 22.

54. Randall Mays, interview by author.

55. Tere Patierno, interview by author, email, 8 May 2002.

56. No one survives who can say why Ernest and Minnie separated, and these are the only two answers submitted as possibilities. Tere Patierno remembers Minnie drinking heavily, and another close family member who did not want to be interviewed said there were rumors of Phipps "backsliding" at the time. These conjectures are only included because the end of their marriage seems to mark the end of a successful period commercially and artistically for Phipps's music, and the end of his young family's time together.

57. Knox County Courthouse record, Barbourville, Kentucky. Again, it is only included because this was the end of an important time in Ernest's life, and insights into this period could do much to explain his life and career as a whole.

58. Tere Patierno, interview by author, email, 6 June 2002.

59. Ibid.

60. W. R. Mays, interview by author.

61. Ibid.

62. Ibid.

63. Ibid.

64. This information was put together with Ernest's dog tag number and the helpful web site "US Army WW2 Dog Tags." This was necessary because on July 12, 1973, a fire at the National Personnel Records Center in St. Louis destroyed approximately 16 to 18 million Official Military Personnel Files, including 80 percent of the veterans discharged between 1912 and 1960. Further information is available at the web site for the National Archives and Record Administration located at http://www.archives.gov/.

65. W. R. Mays, interview by author.

66. Ibid.

67. Randall Mays, interview by author.

68. Ibid.

69. Ibid.

70. W. R. Mays, interview by author.

71. Both of these "fish stories" were told to the author by W. R. and Wanda Mays.

72. Randall Mays, interview by author.

73. Ibid.

74. W. R. Mays, interview by author.

75. Randall Mays, interview by author.

76. Ibid.

77. Ibid.

78. Ibid.

79. W. R. Mays, interview by author.

80. Randall Mays, interview by author.

81. W.R. Mays, interview by author.

82. Ibid.

83. Randall Mays, interview by author.

84. Ibid.

85. Ibid.

86. Discography information comes from the CD *Kentucky Gospel: Complete Recorded Works of Alfred G. Karnes, Ernest Phipps, McVay and Johnson in Chronological Order, 1927–1928,* CD DOCD-8013. Document Records, 1997; and from Charles Wolfe's "Early Country Music in Knoxville: The Brunswick Sessions and the End of an Era," *Old Time Music* 12 (Spring 1974): 28.

Works Cited

Abell, Troy D. *Better Felt Than Said: The Holiness Pentecostal Experience in Southern Appalachia.* Waco: Baylor University Press, 1982.

Droz, Robert V., *Old US 25E: Crossing the Cumberland Gap*, 20 June 2002, www.us-highways.com/cgap00.htm (15 January 2003).

Goff, James R., Jr. *Close Harmony: A History of Southern Gospel.* Chapel Hill: University of North Carolina Press, 2002.

"Gray," *Corbin Times Tribune*, 1 July 1927.

Kentucky Gospel: Complete Recorded Works of Alfred G. Karnes, Ernest Phipps, McVay and Johnson in Chronological Order, 1927–1928. CD Number DOCD-8013. Document Records, 1997.

Kentucky Holiness Singers: I'm on My Way/I Will Not Be Removed. Record Number 78 5439. Vocalion, 1930.

Mays, Randall and Claretta Sue Mays. Interview by author, 13 May 2001, Corbin, Kentucky. Mini-disc recording.

Mays, W. R. and Wanda. Interview by author, 16 May 2001, London, Kentucky. Cassette recording.

_____. Interview by author, 15 May 2002, London, Kentucky. Mini-disc recording.

McCauley, Deborah Vansau. *Appalachian Mountain Religion: A History.* Urbana: University of Illinois Press, 1995.

McDaniel, Lillian. Interview by author, 13 May 2001, Corbin, Kentucky. Mini-Disc recording.

Meade, Guthrie T. Jr., with Dick Spottswood, and Douglas S. Meade. *Country Music Sources: A Biblio-Discography of Commercially Recorded Traditional Music.* Chapel Hill: University of North Carolina Press, 2002.

Nelson, Donald Lee. "The Life of Alfred G. Karnes," *JEMF Quarterly* 8, no. 25 (Spring 1972): 31–36.

Patierno, Tere. Interview by author, 8 May 2002, email.

_____. Interview by author, 6 June 2002, email.

"Record Engineers Locate in Bristol," *Bristol Herald Courier*, 24 July 1927, 3.

Steinert, David, "US Army WW2 Dog Tags," 7 December 2002, http://home.att.net/~steinert/us_army_ww2_dog_tags.htm.

"Victor Machine Company's Recording Crew Arrives in Bristol to Make Records." *Bristol Herald Courier.* October 1928.

Wolfe, Charles. "Early Country Music in Knoxville: The Brunswick Sessions and the End of an Era." *Old Time Music* 12 (Spring 1974): 19–31.

_____. "Ralph Peer at Work: the Victor 1927 Bristol Sessions." *Old Time Music* 5 (Summer 1972): 10–15.

_____. Liner Notes to *Kentucky Gospel: Complete Works of Alfred G. Karnes, Ernest Phipps, McVay and Johnson in Chronological Order, 1927–1928.* CD Number DOCD-8013. Document Records, 1997.

Wyckoff, Capwell. *The Challenge of the Hills.* Philadelphia: Department of Sunday School Missions of the Board of National Missions of the Presbyterian Church in the U.S.A. by the Presbyterian Board of Christian Education, 1931.

Zwonitzer, Mark, with Charles Hirshberg. *Will You Miss Me When I'm Gone? The Carter Family & Their Legacy in American Music.* New York: Simon and Schuster, 2002.

8. The Life of Alfred G. Karnes

Donald Lee Nelson

To collectors of old-time hillbilly music recordings, Alfred G. Karnes is known as the musician featured on four Victor 78s released between 1927 and 1930—all powerful renditions of religious or nostalgic songs, backed up by a distinctively emphatic guitar accompaniment. Little had been said of Karnes's life and background before the publication of the following account in 1972. The contents of this article were gleaned from a five-hour interview graciously granted the author by A. G. Karnes' oldest son, Alfred James Karnes of Lancaster, Kentucky, in July 1971, and from lengthy correspondence with Rev. Oscar F. Davis of Cookeville, Tennessee. The generous assistance of numerous other ministers and long-time citizens of the area around Corbin, Crab Orchard and Lancaster, Kentucky, is also acknowledged.

Alfred Grant Karnes — gospel singer, composer, multi-instrumentalist, Methodist minister, farmer, barber, sailor, Baptist minister, patent medicine manufacturer, instrument maker, and evangelist (but not necessarily in that order)— was born on February 2, 1891, in Bedford, Virginia. His mother, Maggie Grant Karnes, died at his birth, and his father, Alexander Hamilton Karnes, left him and his two brothers, William and Maynard, in the care of his Aunt Neely and Uncle Cap Harrington.

Even as a boy Karnes had two unyielding urges: preaching and music. He recalled in later years how he would go out into a large field of daisies with a violin he had fashioned from a cigar box. Using a horsehair bow on

Reprinted from *The JEMF Quarterly* 8 (1972): 31–38. Used by permission of the author and that periodical's editor Norm Cohen.

the instrument, he would play for a while and then mount a stump and preach. He left the Harrington farm when he was fourteen, having received only a third-grade education, and two years later was married to a woman several years his senior. The couple had two daughters, but the marriage ended in divorce.

Karnes enlisted in the United States Navy in World War I, and served as both gunner's mate and as a lookout on a submarine chaser. Upon his discharge from the service, he went to Jellico, Tennessee, where he entered the barbering trade. It was near there, at Gray Station, that he met Flora Etta Harris of Corbin, Kentucky. The couple was married in 1920 at London, Kentucky, and two years later the first of their seven children was born.

The barber shop of the post–Great War days was a social gathering place where quartet singing was still as popular as it had been during the "Gay Nineties." Because of his rich baritone voice, Karnes was in great demand among the quartets near his home. He often recalled "singing until I could see the sun come up." It was probably here that his fondness for the song of the same name earned him the nickname "Red Wing." He was also an accomplished instrumentalist, particularly on fiddle and banjo.

Although born in Virginia, a state rich in tradition and grandeur, Karnes always considered himself to be a Kentuckian. Upon moving there permanently after his marriage, his fascination with the "Bluegrass State" increased, and in spite of sojourns in other states, Karnes was never to remain away any great length of time.

A calling to the ministry, which he had always felt, finally overpowered the young barber, and in 1925 he graduated as a Methodist minister from the Clear Creek Mountain Preacher's Bible School. Some months later, Dr. Kelly, a Baptist of the Clear Creek School, asked Reverend Karnes to debate the merits of the two sects; Kelly converted his recent pupil to the Baptist persuasion. Upon hearing this, Mrs. Karnes, a devout Methodist from birth, threatened to join the Holiness Church in protest. She did not, however, and eventually embraced her husband's newly adopted faith.

The Karneses, who were then living near Corbin, experienced the frequent troubles of an Appalachian minister's family. Although rural communities were made very distant by the bad roads of the day, Brother Karnes felt that the faithful in the isolated regions of eastern Kentucky should not suffer the privation of religious solitude. He therefore pastored as many as four churches in widely separated communities at one time, devoting a quarter of his energies and time to each. That he was able to maintain this rigorous schedule in addition to his duties as head of a growing family is tribute to the depth of his convictions.

During his time in Corbin, Karnes became acquainted with Ben W.

Davis, a local druggist, and brother of Reverend Oscar F. Davis, a minister with whom Karnes had been ordained in the North Corbin Church. Karnes introduced his "Relax Rub," a compound for external application to relieve muscle tensions and soreness, to the apothecary Davis. The mixture was a successful seller, and old timers in the area still attest glowingly to its powers.

Just how Alfred G. Karnes and the Victor Talking Machine Company got together is not known; perhaps a local citizen, or group of citizens, impressed with Karnes's musical prowess, arranged for him to travel to Bristol in July 1927 for an audition. Rather than bring a fiddle or a banjo, Karnes took a $375 Gibson harp-guitar to accompany his singing. It was on this instrument that Karnes produced his distinctive bass runs. On July 29 he cut six sides, five of which were released by the Victor Company. "Called to the Foreign Field," his own composition and most popular song, was among those he recorded that day. Another Corbin resident, banjoist B. F. Shelton, recorded on the same day. Doubtless they knew each other, but what connection there was in their both recording for Victor that day is not known.

Certain serious students of music suggest that Karnes also appeared, sans credit, on recordings made three days previously by Ernest Phipps and his Holiness Quartet. Phipps, also from the general vicinity of Corbin, was a Holiness preacher. Although Karnes had no vocal part on the Phipps recordings, the sound of the guitar accompaniment is highly suggestive of Karnes's playing.

Reverend Davis wrote of a 1925 incident that gives evidence of Karnes's musical acumen. They had gone together to conduct morning services in a neighboring community:

> At the close of the service we were taken to a home nearby for dinner. While enjoying a conversation on a shady lawn while the dinner was being prepared, a member of the family brought out of the house an old harp of some kind. It had been there many years and idle for lack of anyone to play it. It was handed to Brother Karnes. After removing some of the dust from it with his handkerchief, he began to tune it, and he did not tune it with another instrument. I gazed with amazement while he tuned the strings. Finally I said, "How can you tell when a string is in tune or out of tune? I can't tell the difference." He was slow to answer, and finally said, "I can't recall the day, even early in life, that I could not tell when a string was in tune or out of tune. God gave me something that He did not give you.'"

In October 1928, Karnes retraced his steps to Bristol for a final session with Victor. He recorded four sides on October 28, and returned the fol-

Alfred G. Karnes, a Baptist preacher and gospel musician, probably traveled to the 1927 Bristol sessions from his home in Corbin, Kentucky, with his friend B. F. Shelton. At Bristol, Karnes primarily sang well-known gospel songs, yet his Bristol recordings continue to garner attention because of Karnes's progressive singing style and his skilled accompaniment of his singing on the harp guitar. Courtesy Birthplace of Country Music Alliance.

lowing day for three final songs. Only three of the seven numbers were released, and the recording career of Alfred G. Karnes had ended. The Phipps group also recorded at that session, and quite conceivably Karnes appeared, uncredited, with them.

As Karnes left Bristol for home, his harp-guitar nearly cost him his life. Returning along the James River with the instrument in the back seat of his car, he approached a ferry boat landing, where he would be carried across the water. Two carloads of men in large Buicks spotted the guitar, and seeing it in the possession of a lone man, decided to rob him. The three cars, Karnes's 1928 Chevrolet and the two Buicks, were ferried across at the same time. On the other side, one of the Buicks pulled ahead of Karnes on a dirt road that wound and twisted high above the river, while the other stayed behind. Coming around a turn, Karnes saw the lead Buick pull sideways across the road, blocking him. He swerved his auto around the obstacle and accelerated. The hoodlums gave chase with their more powerful but less maneuverable cars. Figuring he could not outrun them, Karnes pulled into the garage of a small lodge and closed the door just as his pursuers roared past. Not long afterwards the men returned, apparently figuring their prey had pulled off onto a side road. Only after they eventually abandoned their search and left the vicinity did Karnes continue on his journey.

Karnes continued his ministerial duties, also establishing churches at Turkeytown, Kentucky, and Jacktown, Ohio. In addition, he visited prisons and jails to hold services for inmates, gaining many conversions.

With the election of Franklin Roosevelt came the re-evaluation of certain governmental pensions to war-wounded servicemen. Karnes had been receiving $18.00 per month, with which he was paying for a home for his family at Roundstone, near Renfro Valley. The nature of his disability is not known, but the pension was stopped. The family faced a housing crisis, and Reverend Karnes took temporary leave of his loved ones with the assertion "I'm going to get a home." He located the ideal spot on six acres of land at Crab Orchard. Parishioners cut wood and built a home for their new minister and his family. It was taken over on the "squatter's rights" doctrine, and remained his residence for many years. His children still remember working to clear the land, and the one-and-a-half-story house of which they were so proud.

At this time, Alfred Karnes reached the prime of his life, both musically and professionally. He had formed a family band, consisting of his sons Alfred J. (called James) on guitar, Claude on bass (which A. G. himself made), Tom on guitar, Jack on mandocello, and daughter Doris on mandolin. Karnes himself played the fiddle — in a manner likened by those who heard him to Slim Miller (this was apparently the supreme compliment a Kentuckian could give to a fiddler). Doris Karnes was such an accomplished musician that the Finley Davidson Company of Middletown, Ohio, presented her with a Gibson mandolin.

The family gave four "courthouse steps" concerts every Sunday. They would travel early in the morning to Mount Vernon, then on to Brodhead, back home for lunch, and at 1:30 to Lancaster, and finally to Stanford. A neighbor of James Karnes recalled the Lancaster gatherings: "When they came in front of the courthouse there were only a few people around, but by the time they had done three or four songs the square was so full of people you could hardly drive through." A service station owner in the same town, who had been a little boy at the time, remembered, "I've seen old men who'd never been in church in their lives, sometimes so crippled they could hardly walk, but they'd come to hear 'em." The theme of the family band was "This Is My Day, My Happy Day," and was one of their most requested offerings.

Only once after taking up the ministry did Alfred Karnes return to the barber's trade, and then for only a short time. The reason is unknown, but after a futile attempt at the haircutting business, he told his wife, "It's no use, I can't make it as a barber." This, in spite of the fact that he is remembered as a good barber.

Karnes had a gift for painting described as "genuine" by those who have viewed his works. However, only three of his works are known to exist. He painted "The Gateway Home," his childhood impression of the Blue Ridge Mountains of his native Virginia, on a plywood canvas. He also painted Washington's home at Mount Vernon from a photograph. Karnes's only other existing work is a painting from his boyhood of his Virginia home.

He pastored Gilbert's Creek Church, a house of worship from colonial times, and the Ottawa Baptist Church, renowned in the area for its outstanding choir. Although the majority of his musical material was sacred in nature, he was fond of playing such fiddle tunes as "Eighth of January" and "Wednesday Night Waltz." He enjoyed doing the Charleston, and kept himself in fine physical condition through strenuous gymnastics. At fifty years of age, he was still able to ride a bicycle on one wheel.

In 1944, Karnes's beloved wife Flora passed away, and the strain on Karnes, along with the years of hard work, finally began to show. Although he held revival meetings at Roundstone, much of his activity had to be curtailed because of failing health.

He married Flora Karnes's niece Beulah Hays, but she died of cancer within two years. Sorrow plagued Karnes further when his next wife, Maggie Bollanger of Middletown, Ohio, died after little more than a year. He made one final try at marriage, this time to a Mrs. Edwards. The couple moved to Starke, Florida, where Karnes held evangelical meetings, but the couple separated, and he returned to his Kentucky home.

In early 1957, Karnes suffered a stroke which left him partially paralyzed. He was, after months of effort, able to walk with the support of his son James. The following year Karnes had a second stroke, and on May 18, 1958, he died at the age of 67. His funeral service was conducted by his friend Reverend Oscar Davis; Karnes is buried beside his second wife at the McHargue Church Cemetery near Lily, Kentucky.

Considering the fact that only eight sides credited to Alfred G. Karnes were ever released, the number of people who remember him is surprising. Many older people living in the Lancaster area have a reverent recollection of the man and the minister. That he is well respected by country and blues record collectors comes as no surprise to the people who knew him. Admittedly, this region is known for its devoutly religious populace, but more citizens than just the churchgoers seem to recall the gospel singer and his family band; and though he is departed, the Karnes charisma remains in the memory of all who came in contact with him.

9. The Life of Blind Alfred Reed

The Rounder Collective
(Ken Irwin, Marian Leighton Levy, and Bill Nowlin)

Editors' Note: One of the most remarkable performers to record at Bristol was a blind fiddler, singer, and composer named Blind Alfred Reed, from Pipestem, West Virginia. Reed's archaic fiddling and strong singing are still appealing today, and many of his songs contain compelling historical and social themes. Reed was also one of the first lesser-known musicians at the Bristol sessions to attract serious biographical research. In June 1971, a group of young enthusiasts from Boston calling themselves The Rounder Collective (Ken Irwin, Marian Leighton Levy, and Bill Nowlin) visited Arville and Etta Reed, Blind Alfred's son and daughter-in-law, in Pipestem. This initial visit was followed by a second visit in August of that same year, when the trio had an opportunity to interview Blind Alfred's son Collins Reed and Collins's wife Madline. Irwin wrote, "We brought along a cassette with all of Blind Alfred's music on it; this was the first time in over thirty years that they had heard the recorded versions of his [Blind Alfred's] music." The following essay is based on information obtained at those interviews.

Blind Alfred Reed was born on June 15, 1880, in Floyd, Virginia, and died on January 17, 1956, at Cool Ridge, West Virginia. He is buried in an unmarked grave at Elgood. (Unless otherwise indicated, all place names are in West Virginia. The family moved frequently around the area of Princeton, Pipestem and Hinton, West Virginia, area.) The blind son of a farmer, Alfred Reed recorded 21 selections for Victor, and through music he was able to support himself, his wife Nettie, and their six children. According to his son Arville Reed (incorrectly listed by Victor as Orville Reed on the discs), Alfred wrote every one of his recorded songs, and he would often play and sing around the house. Several neighbors agreed that the favorite song he would perform around Princeton and Hinton area was "Always Lift Him Up and Never Knock Him Down." Stores in the area were unable to keep any of Reed's records in stock: they were always sold as soon as the stores received them. Several of the song texts were ordered printed up on pasteboard cards ("any newspaper publisher would print them") at the Princeton printing office, and Alfred would sell them for ten cents a copy. They sold very well. Most of Alfred's income came from playing at dances and meetings; in addition, he gave lessons to youngsters. The pay at public gatherings was either by the hour or by the evening, and it seemed to be usually on a straight pay basis (often about $15, to be divided among the members of the band) rather than any form of passing the hat.

"During the hard times when there wasn't much money to be made," recalled Collins Reed, his father would walk the three miles down to Hinton and play his fiddle in the park or on one corner where there were two or three seats; passers-by who stopped to listen would give what they could afford. Many times Alfred would walk all the way back home without having earned a nickel; on more successful occasions he would pick up some groceries on the way back. Six or seven cents was enough to buy a pound of bacon. In later years, as many street preachers and musicians found out, the police increasingly prevented musicians from playing on the street. Collins likened this use of the law to taking prayer out of the schools.

Blind Alfred used to get much of his music from the radio. Via that technology, he was able to hear some of his favorite musicians — Vernon Dalhart and Carson Robison, according to Arville and Etta — and also to learn the addresses of various songbooks, for which Nettie would send away. She would read the songs to Alfred, and he would copy them down in the New York Point System, a form of writing for the blind. The radio also provided news of the day. Alfred composed one of his ballads, "The Wreck of the Virginian," after hearing radio news stories about the May 1927 train wreck at Ingleside, only three or four miles from Princeton, where the Reed family lived. Alfred learned further details of the fatal accident as his wife read him the newspaper accounts. Word of Alfred Reed's song reached Ralph Peer, the talent scout for the Victor Talking Machine Company. Peer, who wanted to record and issue the song right away, sent for Alfred. Arville was not at home — he was out working on the railway. On July 28, 1927, Arthur Wyrick drove Alfred to Bristol, Tennessee, to make recordings for Victor; consequently, "The Wreck of the Virginian" does not feature Arville's guitar on it as do Alfred's later recordings. When released, "The Wreck of the Vir-

Blind Alfred Reed (center) was a remarkable singer, songwriter, and fiddler. He composed and recorded a number of the most powerful protest songs from the early years of the hillbilly music industry. Having learned of one Reed song by word of mouth, Ralph Peer invited Reed to record that song — a topical ballad called "The Wreck of the Virginian" — at the 1927 Bristol sessions. Playing with Reed in this late-1920s photograph (featuring a hand-painted sign with misspellings) are fiddler Fred Pendleton and guitarist Arville Reed, Alfred's son. Courtesy *Goldenseal* magazine.

ginian" became one of the biggest sellers among all the Bristol sessions recordings. On its other side was a gospel song, "Walking in the Way with Jesus," an original of Alfred Reed's. The two other songs recorded by Alfred at the session in Bristol were another original, "I Mean to Live for Jesus," and "You Must Unload," an old homily written by evangelist Charles Stanley in 1902 and recorded by several early country musicians.

People soon recognized Blind Alfred Reed's talent for composing songs and sought him out to make up songs for various functions. For this reason, he often played at meetings as well as at dances and church services; like Fiddlin' John Carson, Alfred was known to have played at a Ku Klux Klan meeting (in Princeton), but this was for pay. (A feeling we encountered was that the Klan was made up "of better people then.")

One meeting for which Alfred was called on to play was to protest the proposed move of the courthouse from Princeton to Bluefield. "Chap" Hubbard, a local politician, hired him to compose a song on the subject, which may have helped the protest achieve its goal. Arville and Etta Reed agreed that there was a "big demand for him to come around to meetings," perhaps due to his attacks on the exploitation of poor people, most evident in "Money Cravin' Folks" and "How Can a Poor Man Stand Such Times and Live?" Despite his popularity at meetings, Alfred did not get politically involved; he would vote, and play when called, but wouldn't get involved in politics. Although a Republican, he greatly admired for Franklin D. Roosevelt.

Neither his mother nor his father played music, but Alfred, who started on the fiddle (which remained his favorite instrument), could also play guitar, banjo, and mandolin. He was born blind, as was his sister Rosetta. Alfred played frequently with other blind West Virginia musicians, including Harry Fulton of Romney, who played a tater-bug mandolin. Arville used to guide Alfred as well as Richard Harold, who lost his sight in the mines — each man would place a hand on one of Arville's shoulders. Harold, who recorded for the Columbia label, played both fiddle and guitar, and was Alfred's frequent traveling companion.

Blind Alfred Reed was a deeply religious man, and throughout his life, he played much of his music at churches. An ordained Methodist minister, he often sang and played at services, and Nettie often sent off for religious songbooks. Alfred took his religion seriously, and bitterly berated those "preachers [who] preach for dough and not for soul / That's what keeps a poor man in a hole." (From "How Can a Poor Man Stand Such Times and Live?") This same sentiment appears again in "Money Cravin' Folks" and "I Mean to Live for Jesus."

After the success of Alfred's initial Victor recordings, Ralph Peer sent for him to travel by train to Camden, New Jersey, to record again. This time, in December 1927, Arville and fiddler Fred Pendleton accompanied him. The Reeds recorded for the last time in New York City, in December 1929. As before, they were sent train fare, had hotel expenses paid (at the Knickerbocker Hotel), and were given the standard fifty dollars per selection. They met Dalhart and Robison, who told them New York was a "pretty hard town to get around in." Arville says they were asked to stick close to the hotel because the Victor people were afraid they would get lost if they went out on the street. As it was ten degrees below zero when they got off the train, they were content to stay at the hotel.

As the Depression came, Blind Alfred Reed's musical career suffered, and Collins says that after 1937 or so, his father did not play much in public, though apparently he still often stayed up late composing songs, which he would write out in Braille. Whenever people came to visit the Reed house, Alfred would play. Often he would play music entirely for his own pleasure. Talking books and magazines for the blind were also a source of enjoyment for him; Arville remembered *The Christian Record* and *Ziegler's Magazine* arriving at the house regularly.

Arville eventually gave up playing the guitar. After leaving the armed forces, he went to work at a brick plant in Princeton, and eventually built a home for his wife Etta and himself in Pipestem. They gardened around the house, though Arville also cut down trees and worked in a sawmill to pay off some hospital bills. The Reed family stayed in touch, though spread from Ohio to New Jersey and Virginia, and they remained sufficiently aware of Blind Alfred's music to want to see it reissued. Collins Reed of Pipestem still possessed his father's fiddle, dated 1695, built by Giovan Paolo Maggini of Brescia, Italia. The fiddle itself has had some rough times. Once, while playing for a dance somewhere in Murphy County, Blind Alfred's fiddle was knocked out of his hand by an energetic dancer, and the head broke off. Another time, returning from playing at a school in Lashmeet, Blind Alfred was holding the fiddle while standing up in a boat. People rocked the boat, and in his fright he dropped the fiddle into the water. Someone fished the fiddle out and glued it back together; according to Arville, the only change was a better tone.

Peer International Corporation kept up yearly royalty payments on Alfred's compositions, but since Victor kept this material out of print for over thirty years, the payments amounted to only a few dollars a year. Sometimes they just sent postage stamps to cover the small amounts. They found out Alfred Reed had died when Arville returned a three dollar check one year with a note. Immediately on word of Alfred's death, the Peer Corporation prevailed upon the relatives to sign away all rights to the music for the sum of one dollar, though Arville reports they were never paid the dollar.

Editors' Postscript: *Rounder issued an LP of Reed's songs in 1971, the first in a long line of historical reissues the company would release in the coming years, and the preceding essay was first published in the brochure that accompanied that record. The Rounder reissue had a considerable influence on new generations of musicians: the New Lost City Ramblers recorded numerous Reed songs, and in the 1980s guitarist-singer Ry Cooder brought songs like "How Can a Poor Man Stand Such Times and Live?" to yet another generation. In 2000, the Austrian label Document Records released a compact disc of all Reed's recordings, and American labels like Yazoo and County have issued numerous individual tracks on CDs.*

10. The West Virginia Coon Hunters: On the Trail of a Lost Mountain State String Band

John Lilly

Not long ago, two men from West Virginia — both fine guitarists — were enjoying a visit to Nashville. During their stay in Music City, they browsed some of the big record stores, marveling at the wealth of country music LPs, cassettes, and compact discs offered for sale there — recordings that they could never find in the stores back home.

Robert Shafer, a national champion flatpick guitarist from Elkview, West Virginia, casually picked up a recording of vintage old-time music. On the back of the jacket, he was surprised to find listed a selection by a group called the West Virginia Coon Hunters. He alerted his friend, Darel Meadows, a resident of Lewis County, West Virginia — Darel's father, Clyde S. Meadows, a talented guitarist and singer, had been a member of the West Virginia Coon Hunters from the late 1920s until the 1940s. Clyde Meadows passed away in 1969, yet Darel still recalls stories that his father told him about traveling and playing with the group. Darel, though, had no idea that any recordings of the Coon Hunters existed.

More surprising to Darel was the fact that this rare recording of his father's music was part of the most significant country music recording event of all time: the famed Bristol sessions. Considered by some to mark the

Reprinted from *The Old-Time Herald* (Feb.–April 2003), vol. 8, no. 7: 12–13. Used by permission.
www.oldtimeherald.org

beginning of the country music recording industry, the Bristol sessions took place from July 25 until August 5, 1927, in the city of Bristol, straddling the Virginia and Tennessee state border. Those sessions were conducted by Ralph Peer for the Victor Talking Machine Company and resulted in the discovery of several important musicians, including Jimmie Rodgers (often called the "Father of Country Music") and the Carter Family (often referred to as the "First Family of Country Music"). The fact that his father had participated in this seminal event was exciting news to Darel.

The news was tempered, however, by Darel's discovery that his father's name was incorrectly listed on the recording as "W. A. Meadows." Disappointed by this error, Darel was determined to set the record straight. In the process, he began a challenging and often frustrating hunt for additional information about this nearly forgotten West Virginia string band.

The reissued recordings of the West Virginia Coon Hunters' Bristol sides list the group's personnel as "W. B. Boyles, fiddle; W. A. Meadows, comments; other musicians undetermined." Victor released two lively numbers from the group: "Greasy String" and "Your Blue Eyes Run Me Crazy." The fiddling is clear, unadorned, and forthright on both numbers. Meadows' "comments" on "Greasy String" are in fact sparse interjections, in a spoken style commonly heard on string band recordings from that era. On "Your Blue Eyes Run Me Crazy," Meadows reveals he was a strong and accomplished singer. That song is a variant of the traditional number also known by such other names as "Fly Around My Pretty Little Miss," "Western Country," and "Blue-Eyed Gal."

Darel is certain that he hears his father's voice in the recordings. "I heard him sing for years, and I'd recognize it anywhere," Darel says. Determining the identity of the remaining musicians, however, is a bit trickier. Darel has several aging, but clear, promotional photographs of the West Virginia Coon Hunters taken on October 14, 1927. In one photograph — the only one specifically labeled as being of that group — there are a total of nine musicians. The young men in the photograph are dressed alike in clean work clothes. They are all well-groomed, and each player is holding what appears to be a high-quality musical instrument. Included are three guitars, two fiddles, a mandolin, a banjo-mandolin, a tenor banjo, and a five-string banjo. Other photographs in Darel's collection, apparently taken on the same day, depict the same musicians in a variety of smaller groupings.

Notes on the backs of the photographs, in Clyde Meadows' handwriting, provide the actual names of the musicians in the West Virginia Coon Hunters. Fiddler W. B. "Bane" Boyles appears in a number of the photographs, as does guitarist Clyde Meadows. The other fiddler is Fred Pendleton, and the two additional guitarists are Fred Belcher and Jim Brown. Clyde

The West Virginia Coon Hunters, as they likely appeared at the 1927 Bristol sessions, on August 5, 1927. Standing, from the left, are guitarists Fred Belcher and Clyde Meadows. Seated are fiddler Wesley Bane Boyles and banjo player Joe Stephens. It is possible that multi-instrumentalist Vernal Vest also recorded with the group at Bristol, playing the ukelele on at least one recording by the West Virginia Coon Hunters. Courtesy *Goldenseal* magazine.

Meadows' notes identify the group's mandolinist as Vernal Vest, the banjo-mandolin player as Regal Mooney, the tenor banjo player as Dutch Stewart, and the five-string banjo player as Joe Stephens.

According to Darel, the group was based in Bluefield, West Virginia, located in the southernmost part of the state. Clyde Meadows hailed from Bluefield, and fiddler Bane Boyles had moved there from Bland County, Virginia, in the early 1920s. Fred Pendleton was a well-known fiddler who had lived in nearby Princeton, West Virginia, for many years. Darel has had little success establishing the personal histories of the other musicians, but it is likely that the majority of the remaining group members lived in the vicinity of Bluefield in the late 1920s, on one side or the other of the Virginia — West Virginia state line.

How the West Virginia Coon Hunters found themselves in Bristol on August 5, 1927, the final day of the famed session, remains a matter of speculation. It is interesting to note that Blind Alfred Reed, also from Princeton and the only other West Virginia musician to participate in the Bristol sessions, made his Bristol recordings several days earlier — on July 28. Fiddler Fred Pendleton was well-acquainted with Alfred Reed and Reed's son Arville, and actually did some recording for Victor with the pair (as the West Virginia Night Owls) later in 1927. While it is quite possible that the Coon Hunters undertook the journey to Bristol after hearing positive reports about Ralph Peer's sessions there from Blind Alfred Reed, it is unclear why those musicians took the trip without fiddler Pendleton. Ironically, Fred Pendleton was personally invited by Peer to come to Bristol for a follow-up Victor session the next year. On November 3, 1928, Pendleton recorded two sides with Clyde Meadows on guitar, entitled "The Last Farewell" and "The Young Rambler."

Other details of the West Virginia Coon Hunters' brief 1927 recording career are equally sketchy. Although it is difficult to tell exactly how many instruments created the group's driving rhythm, careful listening suggests that considerably fewer than nine musicians were involved in making these recordings. Who, then, did Peer record in Bristol as the West Virginia Coon Hunters?

Darel feels certain that his father played the guitar on the Bristol recordings in addition to singing and adding "comments." "Your Blue Eyes Run Me Crazy" features a five-string banjo played in a clawhammer style. This fact, along with photographic evidence, suggests that Joe Stephens made the trip to Bristol, since he is the only member of the group shown with a five-string banjo in any of the pictures.

The recording of the tune "Greasy String" does not include a five-string banjo, but it does feature at least one guitar and one or more strummed rhythm instruments (in all likelihood one of these is a ukelele).

One photograph from Darel Meadows' collection stands out as a possible portrait of the particular combination of musicians that might have appeared in Bristol 75 years ago. The photograph shows Bane Boyles on fiddle, Joe Stephens on banjo, and Fred Belcher and Clyde Meadows on guitars.

A recently published discography of Fred Pendleton's recordings reveals that "L. Vernal Vest" played ukelele in Pendleton's West Virginia Melody Boys during the early 1930s. It is probable that this is the same Vernal Vest shown with a mandolin in the West Virginia Coon Hunters' 1927 photographs, and it is certainly likely that Vest also made the trip to Bristol with the latter group and recorded at least one song there, playing the ukelele.

Clear as mud? Perhaps, but at least we are now able to put names and faces to these previously obscure historic recordings. And, much to Darel Meadows' satisfaction, the record has been set straight regarding his father Clyde S. Meadows's correct name and his small but very real contribution to the history of old-time and country music.

PART III

Remembering the Bristol Sessions

11. Discovery of the First Hillbilly Great

Ralph Peer

Ralph Peer was among the most important A&R directors (artist and repertoire directors: that is, those entrusted with discovering new recording artists and guiding them in their choice of material to record) of the 1920s and 1930s, first for OKeh and then for Victor. Below, he recalls his discovery of Jimmie Rodgers.

The best things in life seem to occur by pure accident. We strive to accomplish something worthwhile; success finally comes to us, but usually from an unexpected source.

In 1927, after serving as an executive of OKeh Records for a number of years, I decided to go into business for myself as a music publisher. At that time a business alliance was started with the Victor Talking Machine Company, which continued for many years. The arrangement was that I would select the artists and material and supervise the hillbilly recordings for Victor. My publishing firm would own the copyrights, and thus I would be compensated by the royalties resulting from the compositions that I would select for recording purposes.

During the spring of 1927, I made a survey of various Southern cities and determined to make initial recordings for Victor in Atlanta, Savannah,

Reprinted from *Billboard* magazine, May 16, 1953. Copyrighted 1953 VNU Business Media, Inc., and used with permission.

Bristol, Tenn., and Memphis. A recording crew of two men was assigned to me, and I set about the business of finding talent and repertoire.

In Bristol, the problem was not easy because of the relatively small population in that area. The local broadcasting stations, music stores, record dealers, etc., helped me as much as possible, but few candidates appeared. I then appealed to the editor of a local newspaper, explaining to him the great advantages to the community of my enterprise. He thought that I had a good idea and ran a half-column on his front page. This worked like dynamite, and the very next day I was deluged with long-distance calls from the surrounding mountain region. Groups of singers who had not visited Bristol during their entire lifetime arrived by bus, horse and buggy, trains, or on foot.

Jimmie Rodgers telephoned from Asheville. He said that he was a singer with a string band. He had read the newspaper article and was quite sure that his group would be satisfactory. I told him to come on a certain day, and promised a try-out.

When I was alone with Jimmie in our recording studio (a very old warehouse which had not been in use for many years), I was elated when I heard him perform. It seemed to me that he had his own personal and peculiar style, and I thought that his yodel alone might spell success. Very definitely he was worth a trial. We ran into a snag almost immediately because, in order to earn a living in Asheville, he was singing mostly songs originated by New York publishers — the current hits. Actually, he had only one song of his own, "Soldier's Sweetheart," written several years before. When I told Jimmie what I needed to put him over as a recording artist, his perennial optimism bubbled over. If I would give him a week he could have a dozen songs ready for recording. I let him record his own song, and as a coupling his unique version of "Rock All Our Babies to Sleep." This, I thought, would be a very good coupling, as "Soldier's Sweetheart" was a straight ballad and the other side gave him a chance to display his ability as a yodeler. In spite of the lack of original repertoire, I considered Rodgers to be one of my best bets.

He was quite ill at the time, and decided that instead of trying to return to Asheville he would visit a relative in Washington, D.C. The money was enough to pay for this trip.

Talent Obvious

A few weeks later, when I heard the test recordings made in Bristol, it was apparent that Jimmie Rodgers was tops as a yodeling singer, and I arranged to have his record issued quickly. The dealers ordered heavily and then reordered. It was obvious that Jimmie Rodgers was the best artist uncovered by the Bristol expedition. I had already written Jimmie about getting more new material ready, but had received no reply. Consequently, I located him by telephone and was pleased to have his assurance that he had a wealth of new songs. I arranged a recording date at the Victor studios in Camden. Jimmie and I met for the second time when he stepped off the train in Philadelphia.

We worked hard far into the night getting enough material in shape for the first recording session. Actually, we did not have enough material, and I decided to use some of his blues songs to "fill in." When we recorded the first blues I had to supply a title, and the name "Blue Yodel" came out. The other blue yodels made at the same time had titles suggested by the words, but when I witnessed the tremendous demand for the original, I decided to change these names to "Blue Yodel No. 2," "Blue Yodel No. 3," etc.

From this time until his death he was able to lead a new life because of his income from recordings and copyright royalties. Unfortunately, he was generous to a fault, and when he received a large check he shared it with friends and relatives. The best doctors told him that he would not live because his tuberculosis was incurable. As a result of his fast-selling Victor records, Jimmie Rodgers quickly rose to the top as an entertainer. He began to earn good money working in night spots, traveling shows, etc., but his bad state of health was a great handicap.

This man really had "guts." He was fired with a great ambition to be successful, both as an artist and financially. Eventually he headed his own traveling show. As a guitarist he was an individualist;

Recognizing their potential for achieving wider success after first hearing them in Bristol, Victor producer Ralph Peer nurtured the careers of Jimmie Rodgers and the Carter Family after the 1927 Bristol sessions. Collection of Charles K. Wolfe.

that is, he had his own way of selecting his chords, and was what can best be described as a "natural" guitar player. I remember that another artist, during the year 1931, spent a great deal of time learning one of Jimmie's "wrong" chords. Whatever he used always sounded right, but upon examination it was quite often not the chord which would ordinarily have been used. This provided individuality for all records in which his guitar playing predominated amongst the accompaniment, but quite often it was a problem to find musicians and other artists able to fall into the spirit of his recording style.

His recording of "Blue Yodel" skyrocketed Jimmie to fame in the amusement business. The once-poor Mississippi brakeman became the idol of the Southern and Western states. His fame developed through his record fans. Broadcasting stations were then comparatively infrequent, and only the radio chains had sufficient power to create nationwide propaganda. They adhered closely to a policy of using live artists, and almost invariably artists popular in the New York and Chicago areas. Jimmie was practically unknown north of the Mason-Dixon Line, but within a year he became the most important recording artist in the region where hillbilly music has always enjoyed [the] greatest popularity.

If his health had permitted, Jimmie would have become a top name in the theatrical world, but routine work on the stage was bad for him. His copyright royalties began to pile up, and eventually Victor gave him a royalty contract on a basis similar to a grand opera star. In an effort to extend the Rodgers popularity to our Northern states, I booked him on the Radio-Keith-Orpheum Circuit. He was to appear as a single act in most of the leading vaudeville theaters. The salary, $1,000 weekly, was considered high at the time. Jimmie became ill, however, and we had to cancel the project.

Rodgers liked working in "tent shows." He felt at home in the informal surroundings and greatly enjoyed his contacts with other performers. One of the highlights of his career was a tour through north Texas and Oklahoma as part of a charity Red Cross drive in which he was starred alongside of Will Rogers. They became fast friends.

In the spring of 1933, Jimmie and I corresponded about the possibility of additional recordings. Victor had about a year's supply of material already on hand. The record business in general was not good, and they did not think it wise to be too far ahead of the market. Jimmie Rodgers by this time had become "standard." There were one or two masters to be remade because of technical defects. There was also the necessity to negotiate a new agreement between Victor and Rodgers. Working with all of these factors, I arranged matters so that Jimmie could come to New York for a series of recordings, and after the first two dates it seemed best to delay further activities. He died May 26, 1933, in his hotel bedroom. It became my painful duty to send him back home to Meridian, Mississippi, for burial.

Today his distinctive style remains a goal for all new recording artists. Many of the compositions that he wrote wholly or in part have become perennial standards. His fame has spread to all countries of the English-speaking world. The impetus which he gave to so-called hillbilly music, in my opinion, set in motion the factors that resulted in making this sector of the amusement business into a matter of world-wide importance and a source for a high percentage of our popular hits.

12. My Husband, Jimmie Rodgers

Carrie Rodgers

Chapter XIX

"I'm going to pack my grip —
"And head that way —
"You'll see me hangin' 'round — some day —."

When Jimmie Rodgers had flung back his cavalier salute of farewell to Asheville and had crooned his mournful bit of song, he added: "Gosh, I sure hate to leave that town. Swell folks there."

Asheville had been neither glad nor sad to see us go, but why should it be either, anyway? How could Asheville suspect that "genius had strolled among them"? Particularly, when not even the genius, himself, suspected it? Well, Jimmie knew he was no genius, then or ever. All he knew was that he had done his best to make good with what humble gifts he possessed; although he was confident that he had "just sort of happened" on an unusual method of expressing the music that was in his Irish heart, and he was shrewd enough to gauge its potential value. If enough folks could hear him, and would approve, as he was convinced they would, it would mean for himself and "his two" that longed-for and very necessary security: rest, freedom from petty, irritating worries. In Asheville, at WWNC, he had been so sure he all but had it. But — he'd been wrong.

So — we drove away; the young tubercular ex-brakeman and his wife

Reprinted from the book *My Husband, Jimmie Rodgers* with permission from Jimmie Rodgers Properties, Inc., and the Country Music Foundation, Inc.

and child, with the three young musicians who, with Jimmie Rodgers, made up the humble hillbilly ork, The Jimmie Rodgers Entertainers.

On the road. Wildcatting. Barnstorming. Playing the sticks, the tanks, the jerkwaters, the turkeys. These, I learned, were the professional showman's terms when small "amusement enterprises," such as The Jimmie Rodgers Entertainers, moved about from small town to village to crossroads, stopping to "show" wherever they could; whenever and for whatever they could get.

Humble itinerant musicians though they were, Jimmie included, they spoke now always in terms of "the profession." (To a showman there is only one profession!) They observed, too, with much care, the time-honored traditions of the show world; especially its superstitions. Often I just didn't know what it was all about! But I was beginning to get my first glimpses behind the scenes of that most fascinating world, a world I was to know quite well indeed, in the very near future.

Once, moved to song, I began humming gaily, "Home, Sweet Home"— but such wails and howls instantly assailed my ears that I was not only mystified, but fairly horrified; until it was explained to me that it meant we'd all be going home! I didn't say so, but I couldn't help thinking that would be no great calamity.

When I asked: "Why? You boys play it every night, nearly — at the end of a dance; all orchestras do!" they assured me: "That's different. It's okay to use it as a dance-tag number, a chaser. But — no other time."

Several times I heard one or another of them yelp vigorously at some poor unsuspecting kid, who hovered near, wistfully watching and idly playing a mouth-harp. That, it seemed, would "queer the house, sure."

And once I heard a yowl: "Who threw whose hat on the bed? Betcha we don't make the nut tonight!" If we didn't get the nut — the overhead — didn't make expenses, I knew quite well that Jimmie Rodgers' "two" would be left "in soak" — left in town with all the personal luggage as security for hotel bills, while the breadwinners hustled on to some other "spot" to try to collect enough to "lift us out." And if they didn't get enough? — Ever?

But we were young, life was good, and we could manage, somehow, to see the humorous side of everything — even an old sedan with four flat feet! The mountain air was sweet and cool; crackers and cheese by the roadside can be ambrosia fit for the gods; and hot coffee out of a cheap vacuum bottle, nectar fit for goddesses.

I had been so sure this sort of life on the road, through the mountains in summertime, would be good medicine for an eager, ambitious young husband, with wasting-away body and sick lungs; but Jimmie had now so little time to give that body needed rest and no chance at all, it seemed, to rest his mind. He couldn't catch up with his big worries; there were too many small immediate worries to pester him. Securing bookings; consecutive dates. Getting the "tonighters," the heralds, printed, and saving out money to pay for them. Even when he could find a few free moments, he was too exhausted to even reach for his guitar and tease "his two" with phrases from his rowdy songs; too tired to yodel a gay retort or to pull my hair or tweak Nita's ear and "whoo — whoo — oo."

Happy and carefree as he'd always been; now tired and sick, it seemed there were so many annoying little things constantly happening to distress him. Mostly he was patient and cheerful; but I didn't like to see him push his plate of restaurant food away, frowning at it. There was no other food to be had; no delicacies for a sick boy. There was seldom time to wait for a special order, and even if there had been, there was no money.

No matter how carefully he prepared his copy for the printers, they'd make annoying mistakes. Jimmie Rodgers was, all through his professional life, much distressed by the misspelling of his two names and of the word "yodel," with its variations.

On this barnstorming tour, having his very first publicity, cheap though it was, one of the very first printing jobs delivered to him had his first name spelled J-i-m-m-e-y. Others would persist in omitting the "d" from Rodgers. Small matters? Not to a professional artist whose name is his trade mark. And even if Webster does give "yodel" as a secondary spelling, Jimmie preferred and insisted on "yodel"; but in spite of all he could say or do about it, sometimes his manager or his agent, or some one, somewhere, would overlook that, to him, most important little detail. To Jimmie Rodgers "yodler" was "yoddler." As he grinned once, somewhat disgustedly: "Hang the luck! I don't yoddle!"

Just then his yodels weren't putting us on top of the world; nor did it seem likely that they ever would. But at least they were helping to keep us from starving. At every little concert, in wayside school auditoriums, Jimmie's solo numbers stopped the show, even without his yodeling. But — when he gave them his yodels —.

Once, after a performance, Jimmie said to me: "Mother, I don't know if they were kidding me or not; but [it] kind of sounded to me like they ovationed me!"

They weren't kidding. I sat among them and heard their eager comments; saw the delight in their eyes, the pleased smiles on their lips. I heard one girl at a mountain resort tell her escort: "Boy, can that fella yodel! I'll say! Listen to the blues when he sobs those yodels!"

Her companion said: "That's a new way to spill your blues. Yodel 'em! That blue yodeler's there!"

Blue yodeler! Of course! Why hadn't we thought of that before? That would be a keen way to bill himself, I thought.

But Jimmie was loyal to his boys; his hillbilly ork. He was pleased that his solo efforts were so well accepted; but he refused to give himself individual publicity. So, on all billing matter, consisting solely of those minute hand-bills which showmen term "tonighters," printed on slips of red, blue, green, yellow, pink and lavender paper, appeared simply the professional title of the little band of musicians: The Jimmie Rodgers Entertainers.

Blue yodels. That's what they were; those heartbreaking yodels he'd first flung out over the Texas plains, testing his lungs against the Texas winds as we drove gaily westward in our decrepit little Dodge; westward to Arizona, to Tucson. Blue yodels. We'd both decided then that they were "pretty good." Now other folks, lots of folks, were liking them, too. And they liked also that amazingly natural mellow train whistle he'd perfected on that very same trip.

The going, that July of 1927, was, as the boys said, "plenty tough." If they could have worked every night we would all have gotten by, very nicely. But it seemed impossible to arrange bookings for more than two or three consecutive nights. Yet, when we "laid off," of course our expenses went on just the same.

Therefore, the inevitable day came when Mrs. Jimmie Rodgers and little Miss Carrie Anita Rodgers were left "on the lot," with the luggage, while the bread-winners hurried on, not knowing when they could return with sufficient cash to get us "out of soak." Tomorrow, of course — sure — if possible. If—

Idling around in the little general store I lingered in the radio and phonograph department, since my husband, Jimmie Rodgers, was now a popular radio artist. At least, so the tonighters stated — and as those bundles of fan letters seemed to prove. And there I had my first thrill of being recognized by a "towner" as a trouper.

The man said: "O — you're one of the radio entertainers that showed here last night, aren't you? I wanted to go — but our baby was sick."

I told him: "Well, I'm with them, but not one of the artists. My husband, Jimmie Rodgers, is."

The man showed eager interest. "Is that so? I heard him over WWNC a while back. He's sure good. Folks keep asking me for his phonograph records, but they don't seem to be listed in any catalog I have. Maybe he's with some group, though — like the Southern Fiddlers, or something. What company's he with?"

I said, as calmly as I could: "Well, he's had correspondence with the Brunswick folks and with the Victor people, but he hasn't decided yet. He's waiting until we get up near New York."

Then the man told me: "One of our local singers was telling me a while ago that a talent scout for Victor is bringing portable equipment down to Bristol and will give auditions. I wonder if your husband knows? It might save him a trip to New York — unless he's going there, anyway."

Did that blessed man suspect the truth? I believe he did.

But — where in the world was Jimmie Rodgers? I was frantic to spill the grand news. Where — where — was he? And where was Bristol? As far as I was concerned, it wouldn't be on the map officially until the Victor talent scout was actually there and my Jimmie was actually proving to him what The Jimmie Rodgers Entertainers could do.

As far as I could learn from the road map, Bristol was in Virginia — or Tennessee — or perhaps both. You could take your choice, it seemed.

I just couldn't sleep. Until after three in the morning I wrote letters, mended, embroidered, did everything, trying to still my frantic wish to get the news to my boy.

And — in he came! Not looking tired at all, nor even worried: but happy and confident.

In a rush I began: "Jimmie, there's a —."

My young husband laughed softly, put his hand over my mouth, and chuckled:

"Throw your things together, kid. Soon's it's daylight, we're leaving here for — Bristol."

CHAPTER XX

"Once I had a sweetheart —
"A sweetheart brave and true —."

We couldn't get to Bristol in a couple of hours, as I wished; nor in a couple of days. For a time it seemed that we were unlikely to make it in even a couple of weeks!

We had to barnstorm our way, stopping wherever the boys could get a chance to earn enough for beds, gas, oil and such food as we simply had to have; all the time hoping and praying that the old sedan wouldn't go hay-wire and that we wouldn't have to lay out cash for even used tubes or casings.

But — at long last we did drive into Bristol. Bristol Town, which very magnanimously gives itself to Virginia and Tennessee, half and half, with the State Line serving as its main street, State Street. Bristol — where fortune or misfortune awaited us.

And I wailed: "O dear; I do hope that Victor man is still here! But what would he think if he could see us now! This tired, dirty, crumpled bunch of tin can tourists coming to town, depending for their very dear lives, almost, on just a word from him."

Jimmie grinned: "Shucks, Mother, why should he care one way or the other? If we can show him the goods, that's all he's looking for."

Our small daughter, Miss Anita Rodgers, spoke then:

"Yes, but Daddy! Maybe he doesn't know who we are."

Jimmie said solemnly: "Nope, don't reckon he does. Just who are we, anyway? Anybody 'round, here know?"

"Why, Daddy. We're national broadcasting artists!"

So — tired, dirty, crumpled and laughing — we drove straight to a modest little cafe on State Street to "coffee up." Often you can get all the information you need while coffee-ing up.

Yes, the Victor man was still there. Second floor over that brick, down a block and across the street — on the Tennessee side.

We bustled out, bent on a frantic cleaning up for this most important occasion. But first, rooms! Jimmie Rodgers and family considered themselves lucky, indeed, to find a pleasant room up over a bakery; a front room in Virginia from which we could stare across, above the "traffic" of State Street, to the tall windows of that glamorous "second floor over that brick" in Tennessee, where the talent scout for Victor was making magic for a few lucky unknowns.

It was still early in the day when Jimmie, with his hillbilly ork, all hurriedly pressed, clean-shirted, freshly-barbered, went hurrying across from Virginia to Tennessee to learn their fate.

An account in a magazine of national circulation, some time ago, stated that Jimmie Rodgers approached his man sick, unshaven, unkempt. Jimmie was indeed a sick man. But personal neatness and cleanliness were to him, always, among the very essentials of existence. No other condition was to be endured. He had a gift for wearing clothes, even though shabby and threadbare, so that he appeared always well dressed. So on this occasion, while he was threadbare, perhaps, he was otherwise as natty as he could make himself.

When Jimmie came back to me, that day in the beginning of August, in 1927, his step jaunty, his eyes shining, I knew that he had good news.

Yep, the man had consented to give them an audition! And if he approved of the hillbilly ork, the Jimmie Rodgers Entertainers, he would make a test record. And if the Victor folks at the factory in Camden, New Jersey, liked their efforts — well.

And then Jimmie told me: "You'd never guess what the man's name is. Peer!"

"Yes?" Just what of it, I wondered.

"Well, Hon — don't you see? He's working with the Victor people."

"Yes, I know, of course — but —."

"Well, gosh, Mother! Victor — Peer. Sort of looks to me like those two names would be pretty nice for me to be connected with. A victor is a winner, isn't he? And a peer is the top of the heap."

I laughed and teased: "Then maybe you'd better change your name to something like — Jimmie Starr!"

"No sirree! Jimmie Rodgers is my name, no matter what happens. Good enough for me."

"But," I demanded impatiently, "When, Jimmie — when?"

"Huh? O — be ready for us in just a little while. 'Bout an hour, he said."

All the way into Bristol there had been lively argument as to just which numbers in the repertoire of the Jimmie Rodgers Entertainers it would be advisable to offer the Victor man — if he consented to listen to them. Not "T for Texas," of course, as that was one of Jimmie's solo numbers; nor "The Soldier's Sweetheart," nor any of his own compositions.

I was wishing it would be possible for Jimmie to show the man how he could put over a solo; one of his crooning lullabies, or even one of his rowdy novelties. But of course, I knew he couldn't and wouldn't. Because the hillbilly ork was a group, working together: all for one — one for all.

I wondered then, however, just where the boys were. Usually they were right at Jimmie's heels. But — where were they — in an exciting time like this?

Jimmie told me they'd gone down the street "to see a guy they knew." And he added, grinning: "They'll meet me up there, don't worry. They'll be there right on the dot."

So I told him: "Good luck, darling," and he gave his straw hat a still more jaunty tilt and hurried out, his guitar under his arm. But as I heard him hurrying, happily confident, down the stairs just beneath our room I heard also — that pitiful cough. And I prayed: "Please, God —. Please!"

When I hurried to look out the window I couldn't see which way he'd gone. Across the street, at the entrance of that two-story brick, that "magic land," I could see no one I knew. Others, coming and going; but not one familiar figure; not one of the hillbilly ork, neither Jimmie nor any of the other musicians. Perhaps, during that moment I'd closed my eyes, looking to God, the four of them had met and hurried on up, out of my sight.

But then I heard — a pitiful cough — and stumbling feet — coming back up the stairwell!

The door opened slowly. My boy came in, a tired, wistful, heartbreaking little smile on his lips; but none at all in his brown eyes —.

I got to my feet, shaking; but found I had no words to say, nor voice to say them.

Jimmie laid his guitar aside, slumped his long frail body tiredly into a rocker, his back to the window that looked on Tennessee. I saw his fingers trembling as he lighted a cigarette.

Again I prayed to God — to tell me the right thing to say. He must have told me: Say nothing, child.

Suddenly Jimmie got to his feet, flinging his cigarette aside. He told me, his words tumbling over themselves:

"The boys have made arrangements with Mr. Peer to make a test record — without me!"

For a moment he looked at me like a hurt little boy, puzzled over why somebody should have injured him unexpectedly, then continued:

"I guess I don't blame them. If they go over — if they click — they'll get more. Dividing by three is more per each than dividing by four. And it's like they told me: They worked as a trio before they met me, so they're used to it. They know just what they have to offer. They've already had an audition, so it's all set for them. They're to record in the morning."

My thoughts were wild. How could they? O — how could they treat him so? I wanted to protest, to hold him close in my arms, to speak my sympathy, assure him of my love and loyalty. But — he knew those things; and I saw that, just then, he didn't need them!

Jimmie Rodgers was taking his uppercut, his sock on the chin, gamely, as always. He was busy — fighting through; puzzling out the next move; how to tear down that block others had raised in his alley.

After all, though, it seemed simple — or was it? Anyway, my Jimmie suddenly clenched his fists, drew a big breath, and told me: "Mother, I'm going over and camp on Mr. Peer's trail — until I make him give me a chance to show him what I can do — alone! Look for me — when you see me coming. And, Mother — wish me good luck again, for God's sake!"

The pleading, the earnest prayer in my young husband's voice was heart-breaking, but I told him again, smiling, in words husky with tears: "Good luck, darling!" And as I heard his determined steps going down the stairs, I added: "And God bless you, my beloved."

And some way I just knew Mr. Peer would listen; would give my boy — his chance!

And I thought: "Oh, I do hope Jimmie will play and sing 'T for Texas,' if Mr. Peer will listen."

Suddenly I went scrambling through our luggage for all those blessed fan letters! If only Jimmie had taken those with him! Then Mr. Peer would see!

I didn't know just what to do. Should I "take my nerve with me" and venture over there to that "magic land" with my Jimmie's fan letters from his pitifully few broadcasting appearances over WWNC? If I did, what would Mr. Peer think? And maybe I'd make an entrance on the wrong cue — and queer my Jimmie's chances!

Undecided, yet filled with frantic longing to help, I glued my nose to our window in Virginia and my eyes to those magic windows over in Tennessee. And could see nothing.

But I heard — once again — determined footsteps on the stairs — coming back up. The door opened and Jimmie stepped inside, a curious light in his brown eyes; an almost mischievous little quirk trembling on his lips.

I have a few superstitions of my own. Now, with a small chill, I gasped: "Darling — if you forgot something — sit down quick — and count ten!"

Surprised, Jimmie protested: "Aw, shucks, Mother!" But he sat down obediently. Got up again and hurried to the door, his hand on the knob — and stood there, chuckling. He told me: "I didn't forget anything, though. I just came back to tell you I remembered something! Or maybe — just for a minute — we both forgot something. Forgot to remember — to take it with a grin!"

The fan letters! Laughing, I poked a bundle of them into his coat pocket. And I was alone. But added to the muffled sound of those eager, receding footfalls, I heard a subdued plinking and a softly caroled: "He said goodbye, little darling — to France I must go —."

CHAPTER XXI

"Will the hobo ride with the rich man —
"Will he always have money to spare —?"

A simple matter to heave that block aside? Not if you view it in the right perspective.

R. S. Peer was — and is — a business man. A busy man could scarcely be expected to listen to the troubles and yearnings of every Tom-Dick-and-Harry who swarmed through that temporary studio in Bristol that first week in August, 1927, each individual convinced that all he or she needed to become famous and wealthy was to persuade or trick "the Victor man" into lending them his ear.

Moreover, it was, of course, absolutely necessary for Mr. Peer to adhere strictly to the number of test records he had set as his limit for submission to the factory at Camden. The Victor officials had faith in his good judgment; but nevertheless, each and every record he submitted to them was his gamble. If they turned it down he was out both time and expense. When he picked a loser, that was his hard luck; but when he did discover a winner, all concerned, including the artist, were to the good.

The deciding board at the factory did not always see eye to eye with Mr. Peer — nor hear ear to ear with him. They were bound by no contract to pass favorably on all tests he submitted. And even those they okayed did not always click with the public.

After all, it was the men and women who shelled out their six bits each for those black discs — throughout this land and foreign countries — who could, and sometimes did, decide thumbs down on a solo artist or a group of artists.

Thus, artists desiring fame and fortune, or even something like security, had to please not only Mr. Peer, but also "Mr. Victor," and then, having done both, could be knocked into a cocked hat by Mr. and Mrs. Public.

That day, when Jimmie left me, intent on camping on Mr. Peer's trail until he could make him listen, I reminded myself that a conservative business man is not likely to be overpleased, having made a business agreement with a group of four, and later consented to deal with only three of them, if — still later — the fourth member of the group comes trailing back, whining his troubles. He is, I thought, more likely to throw the whole matter out of the window and forget it.

One thing was certain. The Jimmie Rodgers Entertainers, as an organization, was definitely in the discard. Jimmie had not put it there, but even though I sensed how this scrapping of his beloved little hillbilly ork had hurt him, still I was glad. Jimmie Rodgers was now, once again, completely on his own. I knew well enough the difficulties he would have to overcome to "make Mr. Peer listen" — but I had supreme faith in his succeeding, eventually. He had to! Everything, just everything in the world, for us, depended on it! He would. That bulldog tenacity of his, combined with that wistful charm, would win for him — where others might fail.

And suddenly, my nose pressed against the screen of our window in Virginia, my eyes glued to those mysterious windows in Tennessee, I thought: "O, if I could just have given my poor sick boy a son! A son, soon to grow into manhood, to stand by his father, to think for him, to give him man-person companionship. Some one to depend on. Some one sturdy and strong and determined — instead of 'his two' — a weak, shy woman and a small girl-child."

I visualized, then, our beloved and idolized Carrie Anita, with her hair of gold and eyes of deep blue, and her vigorous, lithe little body. And I thought, even prayed: "Give her time. She'll be a son-daughter for my Jimmie!"

Staring intently at those inscrutable windows in Tennessee, visualizing the man-child, stalwart and strong, I so wished I could have given my husband, quite suddenly I caught my breath. Was it my imagination — that apparition over there in one of those windows? It might have been Jimmie Rodgers' own son, that tall, lithe body, the face too white, but so youthful of line, the lips wide over white teeth in an unmistakably boyish grin.

He was making, for my benefit, curious motions, guarded — but insistent.

A match! He wanted a match for his cigarette!

Not bothering my head with silly questions as to why he could not borrow a match or a light from somebody over there in that fascinating place, I snatched a penny box of matches from the dresser, opened the door — and ran smack-dab into our greatly excited girl-child, clinging to the hand of an equally excited visitor — Lottie Mae Rodgers!

Without even so much as a "Howdy," I gasped: "Jimmie! He's over there! He wants a match!"

Lottie Mae, who had come hundreds of miles to see us, had long ago ceased to expect anything approaching sanity where we were concerned. She merely said instantly: "Let's go."

Together, then, the three of us went scurrying breathlessly from Virginia to Tennessee, to carry Jimmie Rodgers the momentous gift of a match.

Lottie Mae, now Mrs. Lawrence C. Mixon, of York, Alabama, was Jimmie's half sister, but Jimmie and I, both, always spoke and thought of her as our sister. Jimmie's father had gotten his daughter a pass to visit us in Asheville, but I'd had to send her word about our leaving, and when I knew about Bristol I sent her further word, telling of our hopes. And here she was — to help if she could. Kindly, sympathetic, sensible, as always.

After all, though, there was little for us to see — up there in that mysterious place. Nothing particularly exciting or out of the ordinary, I mean. A well-dressed, pleasant-faced man was sitting by a desk, speaking into a telephone. Somewhere behind him — and what really astonished us — was our Jimmie, impudently greeting us by waving a lighted cigarette.

He leaned forward then and whispered to me: "I just wanted you to be here to watch me make my first record."

His first record! It might easily be his first, last — and only. But at least, it would be his first! He knew, whether or not he ever made another, this moment of watching him make his first would be, for me — for us all — a pleasurable thrill which could never be duplicated. Thoughtful Jimmie always remembered to include me in the little excitements and adventures that played so important a part in our lives.

Just being there was, for me, one of the big moments of my life — even though watching him make his first record was, in itself, no more than look-ing at him while he confidently strummed his guitar and sang into a little microphone. It was a grand moment for Lottie Mae, too; and something for our daughter, young as she was, to remember.

But — Jimmie had already given to that little "mike" his first number — before we could get up there. So, our first real thrill was hearing the "play-back."

And through that very same little "mike" which appeared, to our unso-phisticated eyes, so incapable of anything, came Jimmie's voice! So clear and sweet; every word so distinct! There beside me sat my boy — smiling. And why shouldn't he be smiling with satisfaction — when every one of us, Mr. Peer included, realized that, without doubt, Jimmie Rodgers had a perfect recording voice?

Still — I found myself not a little dismayed. It was seldom that I ever criticized or questioned my husband's judgment, but this occasion was, I felt, of extra importance. So, when I realized he had used for the first of his two numbers — and with only two allowed him — that thousand-years-old lul-laby "Sleep. Baby, Sleep," I was decidedly uneasy.

Surely, though, for his second number he would use something — well, something bright and lively, or something quaintly humorous, like "Way Out on the Mountain" perhaps, or even "T for Texas." But — would he dare confide to that august deciding board at the Victor factory the details of his troubles with poor Thelma?

Anyway, the listeners-in had liked it — over WWNC.

Before I could make up my mind what to say or do about it, or ask Lottie Mae what she thought about it, I heard Mr. Peer saying to Jimmie: "Haven't you any of your own compositions you can use? You'll get extra royalties, you know."

I settled back at ease. Now, I thought, Jimmie will give his mournfully rowdy "T for Texas."

But — he was plinking his guitar softly and singing; and I was glad he could not see the consternation in my eyes nor hear the little choked gasp in my throat.

Standing there before that microphone, one foot on a chair, his eyes closed, Jimmie Rodgers was singing as if he'd forgotten everything and every-body in the world — except a boy who'd gone to "that awful German war" — and a girl sobbing in heartbroken agony: "My darling dear was dead —."

CHAPTER XXII

"I like Mississippi"
"I'm a fool about Tennessee—

I must have been in some sort of a daze; because, before I realized it, Jimmie had finished and was talking quietly with Mr. Peer.

My ears were still hearing his song, but I was remembering also a child-hood phrase; a rueful or taunting saying used when it was too late to cor-rect an error: "The train's gone."

Here was Jimmie Rodgers staking his future, perhaps, and our future as well — Nita's and mine — on an old-timey lullaby and an out-of-date war ballad, pathetic in its very simplicity. These — when he had a daring nov-elty like "T for Texas," with its blue yodels those city people at the moun-tain resort had so raved about. "T for Texas"— that had so delighted, because of its very audacity, all those listeners-in over WWNC.

I found my breath; stirred myself to action, and deliberately dug into my husband's pocket for the selected few, out of all those wonderful letters, which I had given him such a little while ago to help him sell himself.

With these in my hands I said to Mr. Peer: "O, please — please let him make another record. He didn't give you 'T for Texas'— and that's the one everybody's so crazy about. It shows what he can really do! These two he's just given you — why, almost anybody could do those. Please let him make one more."

Mr. Peer was interested, kindly — but very, very firm. "I never make more than one test record for anybody. That's an ironclad rule. Sorry."

Maddeningly — Jimmie just smiled — a small, pleasant smile.

Woman-like, I persisted: "But, Mr. Peer. Just everything in the world depends on this! You don't know! Give him a chance to show how he can yodel the blues. He's different!"

Mr. Peer said patiently: "If this first one clicks he can do his blue yodel number for his second recording. Sorry — but that's all I can do, Mrs. Rodgers."

The train has gone! How could there be any possibility for his second recording if there wasn't even a fair chance for his first to get over?

Jimmie was, just then, trying to control a little spasm of coughing. I saw Mr. Peer glance at him — pityingly. Lottie Mae gripped my hand. And I wished I could rid myself of that sobbing phrase: "My darling dear was — dead —."

But I had been permitted to watch my husband make his first record. And I could see how happy he was: supremely content. So I put aside my worries. And I put aside my chills of foreboding. The thing to do now was congratulate him with happy smiles; assure him of my stout belief in his ultimate success.

Something whispered to me: "You ought to be ashamed of yourself! Even this much of a chance doesn't come every day to an ex-brakeman with sick lungs. Be glad! Don't just act glad: Be glad!"

So — I was; honestly glad, thankful that, at least for the moment, my boy was happily content, secure in his belief that at long last his eager feet were firmly planted in his own private alley.

Then came something which astounded me; something which even yet I must confess I don't quite understand. I was too happy over it all, too excited, to ask questions, then or later. But — I saw that Mr. Peer was explaining a paper to my husband and offering it to him for his signature. A contract!

I saw that Jimmie was quite as surprised as I was! Then, after Jimmie had put his name to the dotted line, Mr. Peer was, I realized, doing another amazing thing. Opening his billfold, he selected a gold-colored piece of currency and put it into Jimmie's hand. And Jimmie was saying:

"Gosh, that's fine! Thanks, Mr. Peer. We sure need that twenty right now."

Twenty dollars! I had almost forgotten there was so much money in the world — all in one place.

Was that Mr. Peer's customary procedure when, as a talent scout, he'd approved of some unknown musician and had decided to make a test record for submission to the Victor factory? Or was it that, on this occasion, satisfied that he'd made a "find," he was willing to take more than his usual gamble? I don't know. All I know is that he gave Jimmie Rodgers a much-needed and appreciated twenty-dollar bill.

He gave him, also, a contract which, although it was really nothing more than a sort of short-time option on his services, subjecting him to a call for a second recording — if it ever came — was still "a contract."

As we were leaving, Mr. Peer suggested that it would be wise for us to locate somewhere within easy reach of Camden. When Jimmie received his "call," he told us, all expenses would be met by the Victor Company, including transportation and hotel bills.

And was it a big relief to know that!

Through it all our small daughter had been unusually quiet, taking it all in, in wide-eyed interest, asking no questions — for once — but, we knew, storing them up by the dozen for future airing. She was not frightened by the strange surroundings. Not our little Carrie Anita! Poor child, she'd never known anything much but strange surroundings.

However, just at the last, she did ask a question; just one. As Jimmie reached for his old guitar — which had that day, unsuspected by any of us, already started on its own path to fame — Nita sidled close to her father and loud-whispered: "Daddy, when are you going to phonograph?"

Jimmie gave his guitar into my keeping, took his child up in his arms, and loud-whispered back to her, solemnly: "Daughter, your honorable father, Jimmie Rodgers, has already phonographed."

To which she wailed: "Daddy! I wanted to see you!"

Grinning, he whispered: "Hush, darling. Your parent is now a Victor recording artist."

As we hurried, an excited, elated group, back across State Street to our room in Virginia, Jimmie said: "Gosh! I sort of hate to leave Tennessee."

Then he added: "Nothin' more there for me, I guess. It's all in Camden now."

We had so suddenly become personages of such vast importance — to ourselves — that it seemed strange nobody on State Street was paying the slightest bit of attention to us! It didn't seem possible that such an upheaval could occur in the lives of two struggling, puzzled human beings — and the world go right on about its business unheeding — and uncaring.

Back in Virginia, Lottie Mae had something to say to us.

"Listen, children. I'm going to take Nita home with me for a little visit and we are going tonight. You kids must locate somewhere near Camden, and you will need time to get set and get on your feet again. It'll be quite a while, you know, before you can expect any hard cash in hand from your records, Jimmie. Mother Rodgers and I will enjoy having her, and I know Nita wants to see her Grandpa! If you like, we can start her in school there in Geiger, or we can take her to your mother, Carrie, and she can go to school there in Meridian. Then, when you get set and want her, we'll all see that she gets to you, wherever you are, all safe and sound and sweet as ever."

Well — I had, in Asheville, made secret plans along that line; yet now, right along with Jimmie, I found myself rebelling. Of course, we deeply appreciated the kindness and thoughtfulness which had prompted the offer — yet — it seemed we just couldn't bear to let our baby go away from us.

Jimmie looked at me pitifully and said: "Mother!"

But — quite suddenly I could see into the future. Not far: just a little way. Lottie Mae was right. We'd need time to get set; to get on our feet again. Where we were going to be, or for how long in one place, or what we were going to use for money to buy food and shelter through the coming winter, time alone could tell. If the deciding board — if the old-time lullaby and "Soldier's Sweetheart" — if — if — IF — .

All we could have, even if his record went on the market and clicked, for several months perhaps would be whatever dates Jimmie could manage to book as a single entertainer. But — where? Who'd want a sick boy with a bad cough? A threadbare, gaunt-cheeked young fellow whose only accomplishment was an ability to strum steel strings and pour out his heart in lonesome-sounding blue yodels?

Well, maybe he could get on, somewhere, with some other radio station. And even if his first record never got on the market, still — he had that contract! Even if it didn't mean much, it was something to show proudly; proof of — something or other.

At last Jimmie gave in to us, Lottie Mae and myself, and agreed that it was for our baby's good. Her grandfather, Aaron Rodgers, adored his Jimmie's child, and kindly Mother Rodgers, together with Lottie Mae, would give our Nita the very best of care. Most important of all, either there in Geiger — or in Meridian with my folks — our little daughter could be getting her education. Very soon, now, school would be starting.

So — it was decided that our little Nita should take the train for Alabama that very night!

Having made up our minds to let our baby go, there was, of course, much hurried unpacking and repacking to be done.

And right in the midst of it came a messenger boy with a telegraphed money order from my sister Annie, in Washington, D.C. More money! Fifty dollars! In our possession now were seventy whole dollars!

To Annie I had explained our being headed for Bristol, and why; and had intimated, quite plainly, our desperate circumstances, in spite of our good hopes. So she wired us, urging us also to come to Washington, saying she was sure we could both get work there; she'd help us find it. Both? Yes, she knew, of course, of my short business course, and in my letter I'd told her of my determination to hunt work somewhere, whether Jimmie consented or not.

What we needed, what we had to have, regardless of what Bristol might mean to us, was some regular cash coming in every single week, if only a few dollars. Just something we could depend on. None of us had warm winter clothing. So — I was going to get a job. Mrs. Jimmie Rodgers was going to work; anywhere, doing anything, just so it was honorable — and meant cash. Now, my sister, Mrs. Alex Nelson, of Washington, was going to stand by us. She would help me persuade my stubborn, darling husband that it was wise and right for me to be a working partner in the firm of Jimmie Rodgers and Family.

Seventy dollars! Train for Washington — when? Early tomorrow morning. Train for Alabama — tonight. We were almost too breathless with hurried plans and excitement to think of grieving over the approaching break-up, even if only temporary, of our little family. Just the same, every moment Jimmie spent hovering over his baby, but being careful not to be sad. She shouldn't take our tears with her.

Suddenly, astoundingly, Jimmie said: "Throw your things together, kid. We're leaving here — for the big hotel!"

I stopped throwing my things together, looked at my husband and gasped. A room at the "big hotel" would cost us almost as much for one night as the one we now had would cost for a whole week! And we would be here only one night. Why move?

Jimmie's eyes and mouth were just a little stubborn, a little guilty, as he turned to look through narrowed eyes toward those windows in Tennessee.

Suddenly I knew; knew exactly how he felt. At first this room had seemed pretty grand, after the cheap, shabby holes we'd endured "on the road." Now it was — depressing, somehow; made you feel cheap, frustrated, in prison: just a window, a door, four walls —.

Before I could say anything Jimmie turned back to me, saying a bit defiantly: "I want to feel like somebody — just once more!"

Lottie Mae stared at the two of us, as suddenly I declared gaily: "Okay darling. You're the boss! Gangway — let's get going!"

"Well, my goodness! You kids!" said Lottie Mae Rodgers.

But — we were alive tonight; we had money! Seventy dollars! Never again, maybe, would we have that much, all at one time. Winter clothes? Perhaps we wouldn't need them. Perhaps we wouldn't be here. Who could tell? Who knows what will happen — tomorrow? But if a swell room, with private bath, in a nice hotel, could help my boy celebrate this momentous day, then that's what he should have!

And in the lobby of that lovely hotel I knew that not for one moment would I ever regret what that move had cost us — in dollars. At a time when, quite literally, we didn't know where the next dollar was coming from.

Watching my Jimmie, swaggering a little, but looking the picture of health, I was completely happy. His straw hat was worn with an air! His step was firm and confident. His eyes were bright. Yes — too bright, and his cheeks too flushed. Danger signs, I knew, yet happy signs, too. Few could guess, I knew, watching him ever so closely, that the lungs under those bravely erect shoulders were so ravaged. Few could surmise the wasted-away body under that threadbare, yet somehow smart, summer suit. Happy! Just then, that was what mattered! I was frantic for him to be happy, content, just every possible moment of every day. There might not be very many of those days.

Yet, however content, neither of us could forget for one moment that our baby was leaving us — in just a little while now. And — when would we see her again? Ever?

We had no time then to dwell on that, nor even to enjoy the lovely room, so soul-satisfying after the one we'd just left. A door, windows, four walls — but what a difference! It had not only spaciousness and comfortable, even luxurious furnishings; it had — well, an air. You knew that it had welcomed nice people; people who were accustomed to nice surroundings.

Somehow, a room like that can give a "lift" to the wanderer; especially to penniless vagabonds weary of heart as well as in body.

But — there's always the business of eating to be attended to. Back again we went to the modest little cafe on State Street where we'd coffee-ed up and asked about "the Victor man." The owner, to our delight, "made over" our child when he learned she was leaving that very night. He gave her candy bars and her favorite chewing gum, in return for which she informed him:

"Daddy phonographed today for Mr. Victor."

He pretended great surprise. "Is that so. Who is your papa? Do I know him?"

Miss Carrie Anita Rodgers replied importantly: "There he is. He's Jimmie Rodgers, national broadcasting artist! And he's my Daddy!"

Through her laughter Lottie Mae told Jimmie: "You'll never need a press-agent; not as long as she's on the job."

The depot! Never, whenever we had occasion to be in a railroad station, did Jimmie Rodgers fail to show eager interest. Unless too weak to walk alone, his step quickened, his very being seemed to expand with joy. His eyes would narrow with wistful longing to be not merely an onlooker, but once again a part of that surging movement. To be one of those blue-garbed figures, alert, vigorous, laughing or hurrying homeward after their day's work. The great, throbbing engines. The lights. People. People laughing — or crying; weeping with joy or sobbing, brokenly in grief. People confused or people sturdily confident. And people waiting; just waiting.

Soon now that southbound train would go speeding through the night toward Alabama, taking away from us — just about everything. Tumbled hair of gold, eyes deep blue and, almost always, filled with teasing laughter; tight-clinging jealous little arms; sturdy little whirlwind feet.

In the days that followed it seemed that our little family was continually having these enforced separations, but we, all of us, did our best about our goodbyes. We tried to make them gay, but —.

So, this night in Bristol, waiting for that southbound train, Lottie Mae and I watched Jimmie and his little daughter together; Nita clinging tight to her worshipped and worshipping Daddy's slender, too-white fingers; Jimmie proudly, pathetically loading her with fruit, candy, toys, story books — Jimmie Rodgers and his baby girl — pretending to be gay.

As the train pulled slowly away from us we hurried frantically along beside it, following "her" window, and — just at the last — Jimmie crooned mischievously to his idolized little daughter and his well-loved sister: "You may see me — walking down the railroad track — You may see me — Oo-de-lay-ee Whoo-whoo-oo —."

So, laughing back at us, waving, they vanished into the night. And we were alone. My feeble efforts at bright chatter met with but little response. Anyway, I didn't feel like talking, either —.

A real train had gone; quite different from the one that had so worried me — and still did — and this one bore precious freight —. Laughing words from Jimmie's long-ago railroad days came to me: "That old eight-wheeler may take a notion to leap the rails —."

I clutched my husband's arm and demanded: "Darling, sing! Sing to me as we walk along. Sing."

Before I could think what I'd like him to sing, he was crooning so softly that not even the passers-by could hear:

"Sleep — baby — Sle-e-p-."

13. Before the Myth Was Born: Claude Grant of the Tenneva Ramblers Remembers Jimmie Rodgers

Richard Blaustein

Claude Grant, who was born on April 17, 1906, in Bristol, Virginia, and died in his hometown in October 1975, was the last surviving member of the Tenneva Ramblers, a trio of young professional musicians and entertainers from that city. The Ramblers — Claude and Jack Grant and Jack Pierce — toured briefly with Jimmie Rodgers during June and July 1927, but ended their affiliation with him the first week in August — the night before they were supposed to record as a group for Ralph Peer and the Victor Talking Machine Company in Bristol, Tennessee. Growing up in a prospering southern railroad and mill town not unlike the piney-woods railhead of Meridian, Mississippi, where Jimmie Rodgers spent much of his youth, the Grant brothers and their neighbor Jack Pierce had absorbed a variety of popular musics before they formed the Tenneva Ramblers.

Although viewed as country music pioneers today, the Tenneva Ramblers and Rodgers were in fact struggling small-time vaudeville entertainers whose musical tastes were not particularly rustic or folksy. The Ramblers and Rodgers, however, learned to perform "rube" comedy and play hillbilly music for audiences on the school house and coal-camp circuit during the early 1920s.

Claude and Jack Grant's parents — who had given up sharecropping

*in Chilhowee, Virginia, to find factory jobs in Bristol—were devoted
gospel singers who frequently sang with relatives at home. Claude and
Jack's grandfather Dave Grant was an old-time banjo picker. The following is from a videotaped interview with Claude Grant, recorded at
his residence on May 13, 1975, five months before his death.*

I can just barely remember my grandfather playing. I was about six
years old, something like that. He played "Furniture Man," "Bile Dem Cabbages Down"…gosh, I don't know, I can't remember all that stuff; it was so
far back. But every evening after supper, he'd get out his old homemade five-
string banjo — didn't have any frets on it, and how he played it I don't know.
I guess he slid up and down the neck like you do on a fiddle. I think he
frailed the banjo.

We started organizing our band, the Tenneva Ramblers, about 1924. A
boy who was just learning the fiddle, Jack Pierce, got together with us every
day and every night, to play and practice. It was just us three to start with.
We went to parties and luncheon dates and stuff like that. We finally got
pretty good. Of course, we played old-time music, but we played other stuff,
too. Say, for instance, we'd perform for a Kiwanis luncheon or something
like that: we had to have something besides "Sally Goodin" to play. Jack liked
popular music, you know.

There was this fella in Bristol back then named Fred Roe. Fred and
Henry Roe made a few records for somebody, but they left here. They went
to Washington, both of them, to work in the post office. The Roes were good;
they mostly played popular music. Fred could play old-time music, too, and
he was really good on the fiddle. He used to play with us, for square dances.
We played the Belmont Hotel up there in Abingdon [Virginia] one year all
winter long. And we performed at a tea room down at Greendale once a week.
There was a night spot over close to Plastico [Virginia]—we were playing
for square dances there about four nights out of the week.

Well, we played some in Kentucky, but mostly in Tennessee and Virginia. We played all over Tennessee; in Virginia we played mostly high
schools. We played the old opera house, in Abingdon, where the Barter Theatre is. We played there three solid nights. We had a good crowd every night.

We played towns close by — Marion, Saltville, Chilhowee; we'd go and
come back. We played high schools in Haysi, Duffield, Clinchport, and the
way we'd do, we'd go out and book maybe a two weeks consecutive run. We'd
just go in and see the principal. Those country high schools like that, you
brought them some recommendations, and told 'em what you had, what
kind of show. And they were always wanting to make money in those places;
you'd tell 'em what you'd do it for, 70 percent–30 percent or something like

that, sometimes 75 percent–25 percent. We'd furnish everything — the tickets and the show; all the principal had to provide was his building … furnish the advertising, hand bills and circulars, and stuff like that.

I learned to play guitar at the age of fourteen and began working with a traveling medicine show at seventeen. My brother Jack joined me the following summer. He didn't even play a mandolin at that time. I had just been banging around on a guitar, you know. A "doctor" named Doc Pagett needed somebody to make some noise for a medicine show. I could sing a little, you know. So he offered me a job, and I took it. I started out at fifteen dollars a week. He paid for our room and board. 'Course, he had to take us with him, 'cause he wouldn't have had a show if he hadn't. He gave us transportation.

We went into a town with a medicine show and set up outside on a platform, and we would ballyhoo all over town with a black face sitting on the hood of a car, and we'd play as loud as we could. We'd tell folks there was a "free show tonight," and people would just come out to hear us. If we were in a town and business was good, why, we'd stay maybe two weeks. Doc would leave with a suitcase full of money, and we'd get eighteen dollars a week!

He was educated, a real good medicine man. You know, back in those days people thought that a medicine show man was a hustler and a chiseler. But he made some good tonic. And he had a thing he called "King of Burns" made out of pine oil, and I used to demonstrate its use onstage; I'd light a match and burn my hand. A burn blister would raise up, and I'd put that "King of Burns" on it. My hand didn't hurt anymore.

We played every place around in this vicinity. From Norton, Virginia, to Mountain City, Butler, Rogersville, Lenoir City — just everywhere in East Tennessee. We'd go into those towns and set up for about a week, usually in buildings. We were on a street that fronted the Tennessee River in Lenoir City; we had a lot of fun there. There were guys working lumber barges going up and down the river, so they'd come to the show every night. And there was this one little fella, a mountaineer; you could tell by looking at him. He said, "How would you like to come to my house? We'll have us a good time. We'll throw the furniture out the door and have us a dance all night; we'll square dance. I make some awful good home brew." My brother said, "It has been a long time since I had some home brew." And so we made arrangements with the man to pick us up after the show — I believe it was on a Saturday. The show went on to 9:00 P.M., 9:30 P.M., something like that. Then the man took us down there and put us on a barge. I don't know how far we went up that river; we landed somewhere on the other side. When we got there, he and another fella who was with him reached down alongside that barge and came up with two tote sacks full of jars of homebrew where it had been getting chilled. And they had a whole big round of this cheese, and a little barrel of crackers, and they ate crackers and cheese and drank homebrew all night. Oh, those people come out to dance. We played "Sally Goodin," "Bile Dem Cabbages Down," "Old Joe Clark," and "Black Eyed Suzie." They were the best people; there never was a cross word out of any of them.

Finally, my brother got to fooling around with the mandolin, and he picked it up right off the bat. And then he went with us a while, while Doc Pagett was still living. Then, after Doc Pagett died, a guy named Doc Kerr came through here. He was from South Carolina and he had two of his sons with him, and they had candy rights on the medicine show. You know what candy is on a medicine show? Well, there was a place in Chicago where you could buy a shipment of candy — 330 boxes of candy for $13 — and then they'd send you prizes: silk bedspreads, silk pillows, everything. Of course, the winning tickets were separate, and we'd put them in there ourselves. You know, just one to a case. Comedians usually worked the crowd when they had a candy sale. They had a box around their neck, so we'd put maybe two prizes to a box, one close to the top, one down to the bottom, or middle or something like that. They usually made expense money. Medicine show candy, they sold a gang of it.

> *By May of 1927, when the Tenneva Ramblers met Jimmie Rodgers, they had become adept at a variety of musical styles, including Hawaiian, blackface minstrel, and gypsy music, as well as popular dance tunes and songs accompanied by diverse string instruments, particularly the tenor banjo, ukulele, and mandolin.*
>
> *The Grant brothers and Rodgers initially worked well together because of their shared musical eclecticism and cosmopolitan tastes, but their partnership was short-lived, according to Claude Grant, because of Rodgers' egotism and focus on solo stardom. Even though Rodgers was scuffling to make a living in Asheville, he already envisioned himself as a star, a view shared by no one at the time except his devoted wife Carrie Cecil Williamson Rodgers.*
>
> *In his introduction to Carrie Rodgers' ghost-written tribute, My Husband, Jimmie Rodgers (originally published in 1935, reprinted in 1975 and in 1995), Nolan Porterfield contends that "rarely has the truth suffered more from our natural compulsion to mythologize our heroes than in the case of James Charles Rodgers, the Singing Brakeman, America's Blue Yodeler, pride of Meridian, Mississippi, 'father' of country music" (1995: ix). Carrie Rodgers glossed over many details of her famous husband's early life, particularly the time he spent in and around Asheville from January through July, 1927. Claude Grant's personal rec-*

ollections of that period confirm Porterfield's contention that Carrie had good reason for not wishing to dwell upon what was clearly one of the low points in her marriage. According to Porterfield, "Clearly, there were other fables, some not so beautiful, which Carrie Rodgers did not want messed up with the truth" (1995: xviii).

Although he claimed to be a "special detective" for the Asheville police force, Jimmie Rodgers in truth had no regular job and was swapping his services as a janitor for the rental of a scantily furnished cottage. He spent a lot of his spare time "making the rounds," which included visiting music shops where he purchased instruments on credit which he then pawned for cash (Porterfield 1979:58). Rodgers had just signed on with radio station WWNC in Asheville when he somehow managed to land a playing job at a Kiwanis picnic in Johnson City, Tennessee, where the Tenneva Ramblers, from nearby Bristol, were also on the bill. Claude Grant vividly recalled this fateful meeting with Rodgers:

I don't know how we got that job, but they had a platform built outside for special entertainment. An event was sponsored by the Johnson City Kiwanis Club at the ballpark. And so they hired us to entertain, and of course we took Smokey Davis with us, for blackface comedy. The event was in the daytime, so naturally we did not do any blackface acts or skits, just jokes. We'd play awhile, and then Smokey would come out and he'd do a few jokes, and we'd play some more and sing. And Jimmie was there, over from Asheville. He was doing special entertainment. I don't know how they ever got a hold of him, but we got to talking to him and got acquainted with him. He said, "I like the way you fellas play, and I can get us a spot on WWNC anytime you want. If you really want to make some money, why don't you come over to Asheville and go around for a while with me?" I said, "I don't know, we're playing just about every night." He gave us his telephone number and said, "Well, think it over. We can play every town within a hundred miles of Asheville and make real good money."

So we talked about it for about a week and finally decided to go on over there. Jimmie had said he'd guarantee us that we wouldn't lose anything. So I called him and asked him if he was still in the mood, and he said, "Yes, come ahead."

There was a little guy here who played guitar named Otto, but we called him Peanut—Peanut Shelton. His daddy was a contractor, so Peanut borrowed his daddy's old Reo Speedwagon and said, "Here, I'll take you to Asheville. I'm going on down to Statesville; I've got some people there." Well, we hadn't gone a hundred yards on the Bluff City highway when we had a flat. We got out and fixed that flat.

I said, "You sure that tire's all right? It's a long way across that mountain." We went on, and just before we got into Bluff City, BLOOEY! there she went again. I said, "Great day in the morning, man!" I'm telling you the truth: it seemed to me like we had a flat tire every hundred yards. We'd fix 'em ourselves, and if there was a service station anywhere along the way, we'd stop and fix 'em at the service station. Didn't have much money, though.

We left here about 2:00 P.M. in the afternoon and got into Elizabethton about dark. We went into a restaurant in town and ate supper. I said, "Boys, we're going to have to have some money. Let's go down to the pool hall and play some music." So we went down to the pool room, and asked the guy there, "How about if we play a little music in here?" He said, "Go ahead." Back in those days, they didn't care. You couldn't do that now; the law wouldn't let you. And so we picked up a little money there. Some guy came over and said, "How'd you like to come to my house and play a little? I'll pay you." I said, "Well, I don't know; we've got to be going along."

But, we went anyway. The man lived in a nice house, and there wasn't anybody there. He had a nice car, everything. He said, "You guys afraid I'm not going to pay you?" I said, "No, I'm not afraid." And we went on up there and sat around and played awhile, and he was drinking pretty heavy, you know. I finally told him that we just had to be going and asked him to take us back to town.

He said alright, so we went and got in the car, and we started back to town, when all at once he pulled over to the side, and he leaned across the back of the seat for what was the biggest automatic gun I had ever seen. He swore that we had robbed him, and my brother Jack said, "That fella, he's drunk or something." I said, "No, he's crazy." And the man got Jack's mandolin — he had a tater bug model — and said, "Here goes your mandolin." Jack said, "No, I wouldn't do that." Jack soft-talked him, you know.

Finally, the man took us into town. We got out, went directly to the sheriff's office, and told him what happened. The sheriff said, "Do you know his name?" I don't remember it now, but we told him who he was. He said, "That man's only been out of the asylum three days." I said, "We ran a pretty good chance of getting hurt, didn't we?" He said, "Don't let just anybody pick you up that way; you never know." I said, "Well, now, if he's still mentally disturbed and is that sort of a person with a tendency to violence," I said, "Why don't you lock him up?" He said, "You want to file a complaint?" I said "No, I want to go to Asheville."

So we started out and got to the top of the Blue Ridge; our car had had so many flats on the way that we were running on the rims when we got to the top. We found one of those wide places to picnic, one of those parking places, and we parked that thing and started walking. And some guy in an old T-model Ford came along and picked us up; he was going to Asheville.

He pointed out the landmarks to us. Jack got scared to death. Going down around that mountain, that guy would just flip around the curves, while pointing over there. He'd say, "Now, down there so many hundred feet...." Jack said, "Let me out of here!" I finally told the man, "Hey, mister, hadn't you better watch that road a little bit?" He said, "Why, I know this road better than I know my backyard." I said, "Yeah, but I would rather be driving around in your backyard."

He let us off at Biltmore, about a mile and a half from town. We went up there and got a street car and went up to where Jimmie lived. Jimmie brought us to Pack Square to a place called the Western Hotel. We stayed there, I guess, five, six weeks, and when we left, he paid off the hotel owner in instruments. He had guitars and banjos and ukuleles.

We played on WWNC every night at 8:00 p.m. for four or five weeks. And we performed in shows around Asheville. They'd go all right if you could get the crowds out. And Jimmie, he was doing the booking and the advertising and stuff like that. We'd go in places sometimes where you wouldn't have a dozen people.

We went to Hendersonville one time, and Jimmie booked the high school auditorium for that night. I said, "Man, you can't get a crowd in there in that length of time." "Ah," he said, "You watch me, George!" He called everybody George.

So Jimmie made the arrangements and ran into the little printing shop there, got 500 little handbills printed, and got a couple of kids to give 'em out. He went into the drugstore and talked to the man; so we went into the drugstore to play that afternoon. They even wrote "Jimmie Rodgers Special" on the mirror as if he was a big star. See, a chocolate soda then cost you a dime, but they wanted fifteen cents for it because Jimmie Rodgers endorsed it. And nobody knew of him then!

We played music in the drugstore all afternoon, and we went up to the high school that night around 7:30, with the door supposed to open at 8:00. We waited until 8:30 or about a quarter 'til nine, and I never did see anybody but the janitor. I said, "Jimmie, this is sure some big crowd!" He said, "Let's get out there and play some!" I said, "I know you're crazy now." Yeah, Jimmie would have got right out there on that stage and played to an empty house. There wasn't a soul in that auditorium.

When we performed with Jimmie, we put on the show, the actual entertainment part. All he did was play and sing. When we went into a high school auditorium, we would never have less than an hour and a half to perform. If we had a real good crowd and they were receptive, then we stayed in there for two hours, you know. We liked that.

My brother Jack was a blackface comedian, too. He was good. Now,

In the months preceding the 1927 Bristol sessions, Jimmie Rodgers and Claude Grant performed together in and around Asheville as two of four members of the Tenneva Ramblers. Having left that group by early August 1927, Rodgers recorded as a solo act at Bristol, on Thursday, August 4, 1927; the three remaining members of the Tenneva Ramblers, who were all natives of Bristol, recorded together in Victor's temporary Bristol studio that same day. Courtesy Richard Blaustein Collection, Archives of Appalachia, East Tennessee State University.

Smokey Davis was a big, long, tall guy, and his appearance would make people laugh. But my brother was the sorrowful kind. Good, though — he could
get the laughs. Smokey wasn't with us in Asheville, but Jack had done comedy, and I had done straight. Jack Pierce and Jimmie, they'd take part in the
skits. There was a gang of them: "Butcher Shop" and "Haunted Hotel" ...
slapstick comedy; skits like Red Skelton used to do.

We left Asheville for Bristol because Jack Pierce and Jimmie wanted to
obtain a car. They decided to see if Jack's daddy Mr. Pierce, who owned a
barber shop on Fifth Street in Bristol, would get them the car. Ralph Peer,
the Victor man, happened to be at the barber shop. Mr. Peer told Jack and
Jimmie to bring us on over to make some music; he'd see what we had.

When they came back to North Carolina, we were at the North Fork
Mountain Resort. We played there, oh, five, six weeks playing every night
on the veranda; the resort had a screened-in veranda all the way around the
dining room. Nice place. Big parties would come out from Asheville for
supper, and we'd sit on the veranda and play a lot of Hawaiian music and
sing a lot of Hawaiian songs while they were eating. We played songs, you
know, that were popular at the time. After they'd eat, they'd usually dance —
round dancing; they never square danced. I could double some on tenor
banjo; Jimmie, of course, played guitar; Jack, my brother, played mandolin;
and Jack Pierce, fiddle.

When we came over here to Bristol, Jimmie said, "Well, if we get to
cut any records, I've got a sister in Washington, and whatever money I can
get out of making the records, why, I'll just take my family with me on to
Washington."

Jack Pierce and Jimmie came to Bristol with us, and they went over to
Jack Pierce's mother's boarding house. Of course, she put 'em up. We went
up to practice that night, and Jimmie and my brother got into an argument
of some kind. Jack came back here and told me: "Claude, I'm not going to
make any records with him."

He had fallen out with Jimmie, you know.

And I said, "Don't make any difference to me; I don't care whether we
make them or not." Young as we were then, we didn't realize the potential
that might be in it. And so I told Jimmie, "Jack says that he doesn't want to
make any records with you." See, I believe in coming out with anything and
not beating around the bush.

Jimmie said, "Well, I know Jack don't like me very much."

I said, "Well, Jimmie, you do some things that we're not quite ready to
accept. Jack Grant will not do anything that's the least bit shady. And I
think the argument that you had with him was the straw that broke the
camel's back."

Jimmie said, "All I know to do then is try to sing one or two by myself and get the money and then go to Washington." So I went to see Peer and told him that we were splitting up. He said, "Okay, I can make some records with you boys; I'll try Jimmie by himself." And Jimmie recorded "Sleep, Baby, Sleep," and "Soldier's Sweetheart," just singing, playing guitar, and yodeling.

Mr. Peer was recording in an empty building; it used to be the Cox Hat Company. He had rented the second floor and was using it for a studio. It was roomy and airy. I never did see what kind of machinery he and his engineers used; they had it off in a little room. They had a microphone set up in the studio, but the machinery was in the back. The machine, whatever it was they were cutting the records with, had a little red light and a buzzer. So, when we [as the Tenneva Ramblers] were going to record, why, Mr. Peer would place us the best he could around the mike, and he would go on back there. I guess he was doing the work; I never did see anybody else. And so the light would come on and that meant "get quiet," and "bzzzt" [imitates buzzer] meant "go." And if he wanted you to stop for anything, to readjust, why, he'd just buzz the buzzer a couple times to stop. He had to stop us two or three times; I was too loud on guitar once, and he had to move the banjo back, you know, to get everything balanced.

After the Victor sessions in Bristol, Jimmie went on to Washington, and it was several years before I saw him again. That was in Johnson City at a tent show. I didn't talk to him much.

Claude Grant's Bristol recording dates do not coincide with those in Carrie Rodgers' My Husband, Jimmie Rodgers *or Nolan Porterfield's* Jimmie Rodgers: America's Singing Brakeman. *Accurate with so many other details, Grant perhaps needed to believe that he and his brother Jack Grant — who had balked at the prospect of losing the familial and regional identity of the Tenneva Ramblers by becoming known as the Jimmie Rodgers Entertainers — were the very first country music pioneers, despite what the rest of the world had come to believe.*

After brief careers in show business, Claude Grant and the other Tenneva Ramblers would marry, settle down into regular jobs, and spend the rest of their lives in obscurity, living where they were born. In the six years remaining to him during his tuberculosis-shortened life, Rodgers would rise to meteoric fame and fortune, ultimately achieving mythic immortality as country music's first superstar. Interweaving diverse strands of American vernacular music, Rodgers' soulful sound is still vital and moving over 75 years after that recording session on the Tennessee side of State Street in Bristol, now considered as one of the major events in the history of American popular culture during the twentieth century. But, of course, no one knew that at the time, least of all the people who were there when it happened.

References

Interview with Claude Grant, Bristol, Va., May 13, 1975 (transcribed from audio dub of video tape).

Nolan Porterfield, *Jimmie Rodgers: The Life and Time of America's Blue Yodeler*. Champaign & Urbana: University of Illinois Press, 1979.

Carrie Rodgers, *My Husband, Jimmie Rodgers*. Introduction by Nolan Porterfield. Nashville: Country Music Foundation Press, 1995 (1975, original 1935).

14. I Remember Daddy

Gladys Carter Millard

On April 15, 1891, A. P. Carter, my daddy, was born to Robert and Mollie Bayes Carter. He grew up with his four brothers and three sisters — Jim, Ezra, Vergie, Etta, Grant, Ermine, and Sylvia — on the side of Scott County's Clinch Mountain in a little country village known as Maces Spring, Virginia. In later years, Maces Spring was known all over the world due to Daddy's singing and playing with my mother, Sara, and Aunt Maybelle.

In his early life, he helped his father on the farm, and, as soon as he was old enough to start earning a little money of his own, Daddy started selling fruit trees, helping at a sawmill, cutting timber, and he took up the carpenter trade. He often told us how he made his first day's wages of one dime working for his uncle Elish Carter all day in the corn field. Daddy kept adding to the dime until he had enough to buy a pig, which he later traded for a cow, and kept exchanging until he finally had enough to buy a small tract of mountain land, which was to be his first home for him and his bride.

His first desire in life was for a small farm of his own, as his father had always had to rent a lot of extra land to make enough to keep his family going. Daddy never did care much for farming the ground, but he wanted to have one of his own. He would much rather sell to the people or do anything to be with them. He loved to work in timber and always said he enjoyed making a dollar with a sawmill better than anything he ever made a dollar with in his life. Believe it or not, he made up several of the tunes he wrote to the hum of a sawmill sawing logs.

Originally self-published by Gladys Carter Millard. Reprinted by permission of the author's daughter, Flo Wolfe.

Daddy started singing when he was a very small boy. He would sing in church with his two uncles, Flan and Will Bayes, with his oldest sister, Vergie, joining in by the time they were of school age. The neighboring churches for miles around would send for their help in all the revival meetings.

Grandpa and Grandma Carter, seeing Daddy was so fond of music, decided to give him and his brother, Jim, a fiddle between them. There were never two happier little boys. Grandma said that before the first day was over, Daddy could start several tunes, and though Uncle Jim had a wonderful voice, he never could master a tune on the fiddle. Grandma and Grandpa were very religious, and Daddy never played a jig around the house as a young man. As a promise to his mother, he refused the first recording offered him and Mama. It was for Brunswick Recording Company. They sang "Little Log Cabin by the Sea" and "Poor Orphan Boy," and Daddy sawed away on a few favorite fiddle tunes. The recording company wanted to call him Fiddling Doc — Doc was his nickname. They wanted mostly square dance tunes at that time. Daddy refused the offer, but the recording company told them that with voices like theirs, there was no need to worry about getting to make records, for someone would be sure to want them, and there was no need for them to be poor folks with voices like theirs.

Anyway, I am ahead of my story. Daddy was on one of his fruit tree selling trips when he met my mama. She was also getting up an order in a book of some kind to get herself an autoharp. When this nice-looking young man sold her uncle Mil Nickles some fruit trees, she sold him an order for a set of water glasses. After one glance at this beautiful young woman, Daddy fell head over heels in love and said, "If I thought I had a chance with you, I'd take the whole book." Well, the trips over the mountain came more often, and the pathway grew a lot less grass on it; and in no time at all, on June 18, 1915, Daddy hitched his horse, Dan, to his one-horse wagon and went for his bride.

I know that it was a wonderful trip home. Daddy always walked over the mountain as it was so much closer to go courting, but now he was bringing her home with her harp, all of her fancy crochet pieces, quilts, and a few dishes; and Aunt Nick had picked her out twelve of her nicest pullets and a rooster and put them in a coop on back of the wagon. They had about 20 miles of dirt roads to travel, and had to cross many ruts and creeks. They would be settling down with their horse, a milk cow called old Brin, two good squirrel dogs (which was a must for every family in those days) named Top and Brownie, a twelve-gauge shotgun, their chickens, a step stove, a table, four cane-bottom chairs, two iron beds, and a new dresser with a big mirror in it (very rare in those days). Daddy's brothers, father, and all the neighbors had pitched in to build a little two-room log cabin for the new couple as soon as Daddy had told them that he was going to bring his bride home in so many days. He had to have a house on his own little tract of land.

In those days, almost everyone built cabins in the mountains or near the foot of the mountain. There was always a good mountain spring to furnish water, and they could have a good spring house to keep milk and vegetables cool in the summertime.

Everyone heated their house with wood then, mostly in open fireplaces; people also cooked on wood stoves, so it was natural to move where the wood and water was. Strange as it may seem, we still get our water from the same mountain spring, and several of our neighbors are blessed with running water and bathrooms in their houses, all from Daddy's first mountain spring.

There was scarcely any money anywhere in those days. They both worked hard tending the ground. When they had laid by the crops, Daddy would sell fruit trees, work at a sawmill, or help build a house if there were any to build. Of course, all during this time they sang at churches, family get-togethers, schoolhouses, and ice cream suppers — not dreaming they would ever make a record or be known outside their community.

The first song my mother ever sang solo in public was in Bland County, Virginia. She was there with Daddy and Uncle Flan Bayes, at a singing convention. They asked if anyone else would volunteer for a song; so, my mother took the harp and sang, "The Wandering Boy." She said that the people came around and gave her several dollars, and one man gave her a five-dollar bill and complimented her on her wonderful voice. One of the first schools they ever played was near Charlottesville, Virginia. They had been there visiting Mama's sister, Mae, while Daddy was selling fruit trees. When they started home, the car tore up, and it took all the money they had to repair it. Daddy said, "Sara, I don't know what we will do for money." Mama said, "We'll sing." There was a little country store nearby; they told the man their circumstances and that they could play and sing. He sent Daddy to the schoolhouse to ask the people there if they could put on a musical entertainment. The man at the store told every one he saw, and the show went off good, so they got enough money for the trip home.

I was born after they had been married four years, and four years later Janette came along; then, four years later, came Joe. By this time, Mama's first cousin, Maybelle Addington, had married Daddy's brother Ezra. They were expecting their first child, Helen, when the word came out in the Bristol newspaper that there was to be a recording man in Bristol, a Mr. Ralph Peer. Well, why not try for it? Mama and Daddy had already made one try and hadn't liked the type of music the man wanted them to play. Since Aunt Maybelle had joined the group, and they were singing the songs they loved best, and all the neighbors loved their music, they agreed they might as well try to make a record.

Uncle Ezra thought Daddy was crazy to try such a thing, and he didn't think Maybelle should do such a task with her baby due in a month. Daddy pleaded with his brother to let Maybelle go, promising to clean out for him a new ground of corn that the weeds had almost taken. Uncle Ezra finally agreed for Maybelle to go. On July 31, 1927, Daddy loaded up the old A-model automobile with the guitar, autoharp, Mother, Maybelle, my seven-month-old brother Joe (who was on Mother's breast), and me, a little eight-year-old girl to mind the baby. With the best wishes of all the neighbors, we all took off for Bristol, with Janette left safe in Grandma Carter's care. It took us almost the whole day to get the 25 miles from our house to Bristol. There were dirt roads all the way and many creeks to cross; and poor Daddy had three flat tires. It was so hot that the patches melted off almost as fast as he could put them on the tubes. Mama and Maybelle were dead tired and sore from all the bumps. Joe was cross as a bear, and I was thinking I had gone to the end of the world, as it was my first trip to Bristol. We got to Aunt Vergie's house about dark. She lived in Bristol. That would give them the night to rest, and time to tune the instruments, rehearse the songs, and walk the floors and wait for daylight and the big day.

Bright and early on August 1, 1927, they were at the recording studio with several other musicians also trying out. Jimmie Rodgers and the Carter Family were the only ones chosen out of the whole group. Where was I? Out on State Street trying to keep quiet the maddest baby in Bristol. Mrs. Peer fed Joe ice cream until he was about to burst, as it would have to do until his Mama finished singing. There was no loose trash on State Street that day. It had all been pitched in Beaver Creek, which flows through the town, trying to keep one little boy quiet, while his parents became the number one singers of the country.

The recording session was finally over. A tired, worn-out bunch of people with enough money to buy a tire went home with very few dollars in their pockets and a hope that they were good enough musicians to sell records on the market. The first record finally came out, bringing a few dollars of royalties, and a demand for more music from the Carter Family. New songs had to be found or composed. Daddy had to do about all of the song-getting as Mama and Maybelle were tied down taking care of their babies. I have often wondered how Daddy could know if a song was suitable to sing. Most of the ballads he found were from country folks who lived in the most out-of-the-way places, whether up mountains or in hollows. Nobody hardly

The Carter Family, featuring husband and wife A. P. (right) and Sara Carter (center) and Sara's younger cousin Maybelle Carter (left) who was married to A. P.'s brother Ezra. Recordings made by the Carter Family at Bristol in early August 1927 were not among the earlier ones to be issued commercially, though after they were released on records at the request of the Victor dealer in Bristol, songs by the Carter Family soon became popular nationally. Peer rushed the group to Victor's studios in Camden, New Jersey, to make more recordings, launching the Carter Family's career as professional musicians. Collection of Charles K. Wolfe.

ever knew a complete song, just a part or a chorus. If Daddy, Mama, or May-belle ever thought of a tune or heard one, it was no problem to make the words. They just seemed to slip in with the tunes. Daddy, Mama, and May-belle made most of their songs themselves.

As the records began to sell, they began to book a few more schools and churches to sing in. Daddy had to arrange all of this as there were no radios in those early days, no television, no one to sponsor a program. The roads were almost impassable. If they got a $20 or $25 house, it was a big turnout, with an admission fee of 15 cents or 25 cents. The advertisement was often a little circular nailed on a tree or left in a country store window. No one in those days had much money. Daddy, knowing everybody was just like him, would usually let all the children in free or would just charge one member of the family. Lots of times, there was hardly enough money to get enough gas to come home.

We had moved off the mountain by this time, into a little four-room house down in the valley. Maybelle had two babies now, Helen and June. Daddy's brother, Grant, and younger sister, Sylvia, filled in for Mama or Maybelle if there was a new baby or a sick child. Maybelle's brother, Doc Addington, and good friend, Carl McConnell, helped too in the later years.

The farming had to go on, and Daddy had a sawmill now so he could pick up a few extra dollars. The farm had to be paid for, and children had to be sent to school; with the Depression getting worse all the time, fewer jobs brought less pay. The Carter Family had made four or five records by this time, and they had had to go to the bigger towns to do so. I usually went along as Maybelle, like Mama, had her babies on the breast, and they had to be tended to until the Carter Family got through singing. I used to be so afraid being with a crying baby in those big hotel rooms. I was just sure the colored maids would carry me off, but they all turned out to be the sweetest people on Earth.

I'll never forget the first time the Peers came to visit us. The letter came that they would be here in two days to arrange for a recording, spend the night with us, and eat supper. How in the world did poor country people like us entertain rich people from New York? Mother and Maybelle cleaned the house, killed chickens, baked cakes, and made every country goodie that could be thought of. All the straw ticks had to be filled, and the feather beds sunned. That is what everyone used; no one ever heard of a spring mattress. And because there was no electricity or running water, no one ever heard tell of a bathroom in Poor Valley in those days. Daddy had to get a garage up quick, as it would never do to let a big Cadillac sit out overnight. There weren't over six cars in the whole valley, and every one of them was a T-model, an A-model, or a truck. Daddy got the four corners up, a tin roof, and braces around the side, and a handmade door with a big Yale lock on it. Bless our wonderful neighbors, they all pitched in to help. The garage was a little boxed house, and all the cracks had little narrow strips on them to keep out the wind. Daddy bought a gallon of blue paint to cover the front of the garage, and it sure looked cute. There were but two other houses in the valley then with paint on them. The Peers finally arrived in their big car around the middle of the afternoon, and, what do you know, Daddy had made the garage two feet too short and the doorway too narrow. He couldn't see why it didn't work, because it fit the T-models fine. It never fit the rest of Daddy's cars either; so our new garage was never used as a garage, it was turned into a cowshed.

We decided to fix supper for the Peers at Maybelle's house, as she had an extra room with a big long table in it away from the hot stove. She was the only one with a matching set of dishes — a little china tea set, service for four, that Ezra had just given her. She loved those dishes and wished she had a china closet to set them in. She kept them on a little shelf on the wall, and nobody but her could wash and take care of them. Anyway, you never saw such a supper. Not only were Mama and Maybelle tops in singing, but two better cooks were never on earth. The Peers learned what red-eyed gravy was, and they loved our country hams. They loaded us kids down with toys and those fancy chocolate candies, which we only had at Christmas. The only kind of candy kept at Neal's store was peppermint sticks.

The Peers left with country ham and dewberry jelly. The Carters were left with a new recording date, and the most money they had ever received at one time in their lives. We children were all left with chocolate-smeared faces, and, bless Mrs. Peer, her pretty new dress had chocolate smears and little fingerprints all over. She always loved us kids to pieces, as she never had children of her own. Who wouldn't love us then? Joe and Helen were both just walking. June had one big tooth and one curl. Janette and I were little barefoot girls.

Our wonderful neighbors all got on the scene that day. They had saved their eggs and chickens so they could have an excuse to pass by the store. No one in Poor Valley had seen a Cadillac before, and certainly not a New Yorker. I guess the scene was just as strange to the Peers. All those people with a curious look in their eyes passing on horseback, with baskets of eggs on their arms, and some with dogs and guns or fishing poles.

Anyway, after the Peers left, Daddy bought our first new car. He wanted to book concerts at some schools in North Carolina and find some new songs. The next recordings were to be made in Louisville, Kentucky, with Jimmie Rodgers. Daddy booked schools, located songs, and also found a real buy in a sawmill boiler, a great big steam engine. Getting it home 200 miles over those North Carolina mountains was no problem to Daddy, for he had a Chevrolet that would pull anything. You weren't required to have a driver's license, and anything that could roll had a right to be on the highway without a sticker either. You didn't worry about a patrolman stopping you; they were too glad to see any kind of a car on the road to try and stop it. About dark one night, we heard the most unusual noise coming up the road, and it looked like a Texas dust storm blowing in. Mama said, "It can't be ... surely Doc wouldn't pull that thing with our new car." But it was Daddy, all smiles, with his purchase. The old Chevrolet was a little hot from going up hills. It would sure make these television commercials of today look silly, showing what cars can do. I guess Daddy's was the only car in history to pull a sawmill boiler 200 miles up mountains and over dirt roads.

Time went on. The Carter Family's recording with Jimmie Rodgers was a great success, and plans were made for more with him. However, Jimmie soon died in New York at a recording session. It was a great loss of a dear friend — not only to the Carters and Peers, but to the whole world.

Times began to get a lot better for us. More records were sold, more concerts were booked. Maybelle had a new baby, Anita. An upstairs was added to the house. Joe was helpful in building a new porch. Daddy and two other men worked all day and until twelve o'clock that night before they got the cement poured. All the cement had to be hand-mixed. We drove the car up in the yard for light. Mama made lots of sandwiches and coffee. It was four o'clock in the morning when they finally got it smoothed and finished. Poor Daddy and one of the men, W. T. Barker, had just got the kinks out of their backs and had begun to sleep when Daddy woke to this strange squeaking noise. He hollered, "Hey Sara, what is that I hear? Where is Joe?" Four-year-old Joe on a new tricycle at the crack of dawn was trying out his first concrete highway. The concrete was just starting to set up good, yet the tricycle was buried up to the hubcaps, with little tracks from one end of the concrete to the other. Daddy was ready to bust his hide, and Joe looked up with that little innocent look and said, "Daddy, I helped you fix the road; I put the little tracks in it." I guess Joe thought they were supposed to be there. All the roads back then had big ruts in them. Well, Daddy and his helper had another couple hours of work, smoothing down the little tracks in the concrete.

It was about this time that the Carters made their first trip to New York. They were to record at the Victor studio in Camden, New Jersey, and then get to a broadcasting date in Radio City, New York. Radio had just begun to come out. The Peers had promised to show them the city. Everyone was so excited over the trip, and what a trip we had. I was going to have my fourteenth birthday, and it was to be my first trip that I didn't have to babysit. They were finally all weaned from the breast.

Mama and Maybelle got new outfits, and I especially remember the big fox fur pieces they wore around their necks. Minks were the style, but we couldn't afford them, so I guess foxes were the biggest things Mama and Maybelle could get for their money. Their big dream was a new dress and hat from a big New York store, and they had even promised me one as a gift from Aunt Maybelle for all my faithful years of babysitting. Well, it didn't turn out that way. The car tore up in New Jersey the day before they were to get paid. When the car was paid for, only 35 cents remained. Gone were the dress money and my savings of $5.20 that I had saved for almost a year. My dear parents and Aunt Maybelle would have starved before they'd ask for their money and let the Peers know they were flat broke. Starve we almost did. Mr. Peer got called away on a business deal that night, so he sent his chauffeur to take us to the hotel he had selected, and he also sent tickets to a big Broadway show. It was all so beautiful—we had never been in rooms like in that hotel, or seen a Broadway show. Yet, Mr. Peer didn't send a bit of food along. The next morning Daddy, Mama, and Maybelle walked to a little cafe on the corner. Coffee then was 5 cents a cup and doughnuts were 5 cents each, with no tax. That left 5 cents for me to buy a doughnut. They knew Mrs. Peer would feed me as she was going to show me the town while they broadcast, and the coffee and doughnut would last them until dinner, even though they had had no supper and only a sandwich the day before. The problem was, these New York people, who we were hoping would treat us to a dinner at noon as we like to eat, had their dinner from nine o'clock at night to midnight.

The next day, Mrs. Peer came early with the chauffeur. It would be one-and-a-half hours before the Carter Family went on the air, and Mrs. Peer wanted to help Mama and Maybelle select hats. Of course, they went along with Mrs. Peer and tried on the most beautiful hats in the world, and they had to find faults with them all, as there wasn't a red cent in anybody's pocket. That was a miserable hour for them to pass, and I guess Mrs. Peer thought she would never take hillbillies on another shopping spree. They left for the radio station, and I was on my own with Mrs. Peer, starved to death; I was wearing my first pair of high heels, and my feet were killing me. We took in the zoo, went up in the Empire State Building, went over to Coney Island, and even walked on the deck of the Queen Mary. Soon I had all the souvenirs I could carry for myself and the children back home. I'd have gladly exchanged them all for a bag of popcorn. It was then around five o'clock in the afternoon, time to pick up the rest of the Carters. Mrs. Peer said we would stop for a drink. It was the most beautiful place I was ever in, and I thought for sure she would get us a sandwich. She ordered up champagne, whatever that was, in a big long-stem glass. I hoped she would get me two or three of them, but I was served a big glass of lemonade instead.

The Carters got paid and said their goodbyes. The chauffeur was to drive us through the big Hudson tunnel and get us on the right road home before dark. All this had to be done before we could eat. Daddy told him to stop at the first hamburger joint across the river. I can only imagine what the chauffeur thought of us, the way we ate. Soon we were on our way home without dresses and hats, and we never were so glad to get out of a town in our life.

Time passed about as usual for the Carters. Janette and Helen, two cute little girls, started singing a little, and they would sing once in awhile on stage, and Janette would dance sometimes. She sure could dance when she was a little girl.

Then, the Carter Family got their first real break: a radio job in Del Rio, Texas, over Mexican station XERA in 1938. It brought them high hopes for a better future and much sadness to have to leave home and friends. It meant new schools for the children. By this time, I had married and had had my first baby, their first grandchild. She was just ten days old when they left for Texas.

Mama and Daddy separated during this period, and she later remarried. They stayed the best of friends and worked together making records and appearing on radio until Daddy died. Why they chose separate lives, no one ever knew but them. Anyway, they were the best parents that ever were on Earth, and I feel we were the luckiest children in all the world.

The Carters stayed in Texas for three years. Joe was there until Christmas and then came home to stay with me. Janette remained in Texas the first year, then came home and married and had a family of her own. After the Carter Family left Texas, Mama stopped performing live; she only played with the other Carters for recordings. Daddy and Maybelle had quite a few show dates and worked together in Knoxville, Tennessee, and Richmond, Virginia.

Later, Maybelle and her girls, Helen, June, and Anita, started working together as Mother Maybelle and the Carter Sisters. Joe, in the meantime, married and settled in Poor Valley close to the homeplace. Daddy's health got bad, and he quit music altogether except for making records. He ran a grocery store for a while in his last years, and enjoyed his grandchildren and his farm. He always loved his cattle and horses. Although tractors and modern machines filled up the barn, Daddy never did without his horse.

New homes and electric lights filled the valley, and there were new highways and new ways of life. People no longer carried baskets of eggs and chickens to the store; but Daddy never changed much. He loved people better than any man I've ever known. He believed in a clean Christian life and always gave us children good advice. Many of his and Sara's children and grandchildren — and Maybelle's and Ezra's children and grandchildren — still pick and sing today. I know they will always remember their Daddy and Uncle Doc, who got them started in the music world.

15. My Memories of the Bristol Sessions

Mabel Phelps Morrell

It is a real pleasure and an honor to have this opportunity to tell the story of how my family and I became involved in the recording sessions that took place in Bristol, Tennessee, in 1927. I'll tell you how it was. Somehow my parents had learned about the auditions of musicians that would take place on State Street during July and August of that year; and since our family group — the Phelps Family — had been singing gospel music for several years, all over Bristol and the surrounding area, my parents decided that we should go for an audition.

So, while my mother tended our jewelry store on Front Street (now Randall Street) in Bristol, Virginia, Daddy took his three oldest children — Earl (then 13 years old), Ruby (almost 9 years old), and me (11 years of age) — to State Street. We crossed the street to the Tennessee side of town, and about midway down the block between 4th and 5th streets, we ascended a narrow stairway to the second floor of the Taylor Christian Hat Company. Back then, everybody wore hats when they went out, so this was a thriving business. We three children auditioned for Mr. Ralph Peer from the Victor recording company of New York. But, since we had no accompaniment to our singing, we were not chosen to make a recording. You can imagine what the voices of three little kids sounded like without accompaniment, even though we had real good harmony. We needed to add instruments to our singing, like the Carter Family and everybody else at the Bristol sessions.

But before Daddy and we three children left the upstairs studio, a church

Georgia Warren (left) and Mabel Phelps Morrell (right) were both children when they recorded at Bristol as part of a large church group from nearby Bluff City, Tennessee; this group, which Peer named the Tennessee Mountaineers, was the last act to record at the 1927 Bristol sessions, on August 5, 1927. In late July 2002, Warren and Morrell spoke publicly of their experiences at the Bristol sessions during a two-week-long program in Bristol celebrating the 75th anniversary of those sessions. Photograph by Jason Davis. Courtesy *Bristol Herald Courier.*

choir, consisting of approximately twenty people, arrived for a recording session. Some of the men in the choir knew my father, and they invited him and us three children to sing with them. And so we did, recording two songs with that group, "Standing on the Promises" and "Shall We Gather at the River?"—one song for each side of the record. So that's the way our family became involved in the recording sessions at Bristol, as part of that group.

Later, we obtained a copy of the recording we had helped make; it was labeled as being by the Tennessee Mountaineers. Our dear mother listened intently, trying to identify the bass voice of our father and the youthful voices of her children. But she was unable to hear any of us distinct from the chorus.

I shall never forget the many happy years our family members enjoyed singing together. There was always music in my parents' home. My father died in 1965, my sister in 1994, and my brother in 2000, which leaves me as the only surviving member of our family who auditioned for Mr. Peer. My participation in the 1927 recording sessions in Bristol has always brought me great pride.

PART IV

---

*Musicological Studies
of the Bristol Sessions*

16. Ernest Stoneman's 1927 Session: Hillbilly Recordings of Gospel Hymns[1]

Jocelyn Neal

Sunday Morning Hymns

Just before 11:00 A.M. on a windy spring Sunday morning, I drove down East State Street in Bristol, as church bells began to ring throughout this city straddling the Tennessee-Virginia border. Since it seemed the entire city's population was attending services that morning, I selected one of literally hundreds of churches in this Bible-belt community, joined the worship service, and picked up a hymnal with the rest of the congregation. Opening *The Baptist Hymnal* (1991) to #301, I saw the following lines of text: "I am resolved no longer to linger / Charm'd by the world's delight."[2] Three-quarters of a century earlier, a few blocks away in a warehouse on that same street, Victor Talking Machine Company producer Ralph Peer set up a temporary recording studio, where, on a Monday afternoon in late July, Ernest Stoneman and the Dixie Mountaineers opened a paperback hymnal and sang those very words as they recorded the hymn "I Am Resolved."[3]

Ernest Stoneman recorded six gospel hymns that afternoon, after an equally busy morning in the studio, and with that day's work, launched the now-famous Bristol recording sessions, which would signal a coming of age in the history of country music.[4] I had gone to Bristol in search of those hymns' origins, both in print sources and in the cultural context of that region's religious history. I found the roots of those hymns in the paperback hymnals that had flooded the area during the Revivalist Evangelical and Pentecostal fervor at the turn of the twentieth century, as well as in the formative experiences of Stoneman himself, who was not only the son of a preacher but was also married to a church organist, and was living in the midst of Appalachian religious culture.

That those hymns have persisted in Southern Protestant musical traditions tells much about their continuing importance and prominence within Appalachia, yet they were so much an ingrained and assumed part of the musicians' lives that they have received little attention. More than being mere reflections of the religious musical traditions prevalent in the 1920s, those six hymns offer a particularly revealing perspective into the blending of formal, published musical sources with oral tradition; the derivation of secular entertainment from sacred repertoire; and Ernest Stoneman's performance practice and individual musical identity. The portrait that the hymns paint of Stoneman and the Dixie Mountaineers is a complex one. Their self-constructed image as hillbilly musicians working in a folk tradition was a contrast to their performances, which borrowed heavily from published musical sources and more formally composed musical traditions.[5] The group's reliance on printed musical sources complicated their various business dealings because they did not possess their own copyrights. Finally, those six sacred recordings offer insight into Ernest Stoneman's musical identity and provide possible reasons why his initial commercial success was eclipsed by other musicians' record sales in the wake of the Bristol sessions.

A Preacher's Son

It is not surprising that a boy from southwestern Virginia would learn hymns, but Ernest Stoneman's exposure to the music was inordinately intense. Born May 25, 1893, near Monarat, Virginia, Stoneman was raised by his strict and conservative father, Elisha Stoneman; his mother died when Ernest was only three years old.[6] Principally a farmer, Elisha was also a Baptist preacher who traveled throughout the area delivering sermons. According to Patsy Stoneman, Elisha's children would accompany him to his revivalist services, and Ernest, as the oldest child, held the responsibility of leading the singing.[7] Not only did he have to know the hymns, but he had to project his voice in front of the congregation and sing with sufficient enthusiasm to support the religious fervor of the service. Furthermore, the tradition of hymn singing in the region would have had the congregation singing in four-part harmony, but Ernest led hymns by singing the melody, a practice that he continued when recording the hymns later in his life.

Those popular hymns were part of the revivalist evangelical tradition that emerged in Appalachia during the post–Civil War era. Designed for communal singing, the hymns incorporated energetic rhythms, simple melodies, and rousing choruses (sometimes termed "refrains") following each verse. Musical devices used to make such hymns particularly suited for the fervor of congregational singing, these refrains were "enthusiastically received as an invaluable aid to soul-saving."[8] Repetition — both within individual compositions and across the hymn canon — embedded hymns in the community's collective memory. It is, therefore, not surprising that Stoneman drew on this repertoire for many recording sessions later in his life; yet, his early church experiences and exposure to sacred music has garnered little mention in historical accounts. For instance, Ivan Tribe's biography of Stoneman recounts stories of secular musical performances during the musician's youth, but Tribe mentions almost nothing of church music.[9] Most likely, the hymns were such an assumed, commonplace part of Stoneman's daily existence that they appeared literally unremarkable and thus went unnoticed.

In November 1918, Stoneman married Hattie Frost, a fiddler, banjo player, and organist who lived nearby. As a wedding present for his bride, Stoneman selected a beautiful parlor organ, no small gift for a young man working as a carpenter at the time.[10] The organ, manufactured by the Miller Organ Company in Lebanon, Pennsylvania, spanned five octaves and was housed in a rather ornate cabinet replete with decorative carvings and a mirror (figure 1). Parlor organs were reasonably common middle-class household items in the late nineteenth and early twentieth century — more than 250 American manufacturers produced these instruments, which were available for about one-third the price of an upright piano.[11] Although it was by no means the most expensive or elaborate model available at the time, an instrument like this would have cost Stoneman several weeks' wages. The presence of the organ in their household underscored Hattie's ties to a more formal church music tradition and symbolized the young couple's investment in their music.[12]

Although Hattie's contribution to Stoneman's musical output must not be overlooked, it was Hattie's little sister, Irma Lee Frost, who most strongly shaped his identity as a performer of gospel hymns. The two sisters connected Stoneman's folk tradition of hymn singing with the more formal world of published music, and their contributions to Stoneman's Bristol recordings helped define his signature sound.

Figure 1. Ernest Stoneman's wedding present to his wife, Hattie. Photograph by Jocelyn Neal.

Aunt Jack's Hymnals

According to the family's oral history, Irma Lee Frost was at one time courted by a suitor with the surname of Snow. As the children giggled about the budding relationship, "snow" and "frost" gave rise to the lasting nickname "Jackie Frost." Known as "Aunt Jack" within the family ever since, Frost's contribution to the Stoneman musical tradition was substantial: among the more formally trained musicians in the extended family, she was a talented organist and owned a large collection of hymnals. Her paperback hymnals, filled with scribbled teenage musings, handwritten notes, and the occasional doodle in the margins, became the central resource for Ernest Stoneman's gospel hymn recordings and a bridge between the oral tradition of hymn singing and the more formally communicated world of printed music.

Over a dozen of Frost's hymnals — all paperback shape note editions, published between 1890 and 1930 — are still in the family's collection.[13] Those sorts of hymnals, specifically gospel song collections from well-known publishers such as Robert E. Winsett, Charlie Tillman, and John B. Vaughan, were extremely popular, in part because they were accessibly priced. The earlier publications, like Vaughan's *Windows of Heaven No. 2* (1902), cost only $0.20 for the paperback shape note edition (editions containing texts but not music were typically about half that price), while later books like Winsett's *His Voice in Song* (1918) advertised a price of $0.35 on their covers. All of Frost's copies show evidence of frequent use: some of the books have her name and notes scrawled throughout them; many have shredded bindings; most of the covers have long since been torn off; and all are tattered and worn. The back covers of some of her books sport their owner's efforts at romantic poetry, and the margins feature scribbled names of suitors. Clearly, those books were treated as personal treasures and were kept close at hand for many years; Frost viewed them as being sufficiently private to serve as a makeshift diary, yet she also treated them with a casual practicality that permitted doodling and wear and tear. The hymnals' dog-eared corners and bookmarks indicate the pages of apparent favorites. The hymns that became part of Stoneman's recorded repertoire were the same ones that had been played and sung repeatedly from these very hymnals, as indicated by these folded page corners, bookmarks, and handwritten reminders.

A much-loved portrait of the Dixie Mountaineers from 1926 features Ernest Stoneman with his guitar, Hattie Stoneman with fiddle in hand, Irma Frost holding a mandolin, and Bolen Frost with a banjo on his lap (figure 2).[14] Standing in the rear at far right is the stately Walter Mooney, cradling an opened hymnbook the same way that the others are holding their instru-

Figure 2. The Dixie Mountaineers (from left to right): Bolen Frost, Hattie Stoneman, Ernest Stoneman, Irma Lee Frost, and Walter Mooney. Courtesy Patsy Stoneman.

ments. Such hymnals were as much a part of the ensemble's music production as the instruments: they supplied the musicians with crucial musical source material and lyrics; the hymnals also connected the musicians to their religion's musical history; and they provided useful information on hymns' songwriters and copyrights.

The published musical scores found in the hymnals, and the oral tradition of family gospel singing—so prevalent in the Appalachian region—equally influenced Stoneman's Bristol recordings. Many of the hymns that the Dixie Mountaineers recorded in Bristol were indeed family favorites passed on through an oral tradition; both Patsy Stoneman and her sister Donna Stoneman recall that the hymn "Sweeping Through the Gates" was often sung around their home when they were children.[15] Hymnals were certainly not necessary for singing favorite hymns, and even the participatory traditions of the Stoneman family's congregation seldom included books for everyone. Yet both Irma Frost and Hattie Stoneman, in their roles as church organists, helped the congregation learn new hymns, and they relied heavily upon published musical sources.[16]

There exists compelling evidence that Irma Frost in particular was fluent

INDEX

	No.
A Blessing at the Cross	30
A Circle for Jesus	107
A Glory Side to the Cloud	38
All is Well	18
Are You Seeking for the Fullness?	8
At the Cross	19½
Blessed Jesus, Thou Art Mine	66
Building on the Sure Foundation	105
By the Sea Shore	87
Calling for Reapers	34
Carry the Blessed Sunshine	108
Christ Does Redeem	73
Come To-day	71
Danger in the Border-land	12
Don't Go	35
Don't Let It Be Said Too Late	63
Dr. O. B. Joyful	2
Enough for Me	99
Forty Years Ago	93
Forward, Reapers	77
Forward, Soldiers	7
From Faith to Faith	88
From the Cross to the Crown	75
...ood-bye	102
...ospel Waves	54
...ave You Drifted Away?	95
...ear the Macedonian Call	3
Heavenly Land	29
Heaven's Joys Have Begun	59
He Knoweth the Way	67
...e'll Roll the Clouds Away	48
...'s Coming Again	55
...Come Again	65
...a Child	80

	No.
O Glory Hallelujah	
Onward, Christian Soldiers	
Papa's Last Farewell	
Perfect Trust	
Place My Name on the Roll	20
Pleasant Pathways	58
Pleyel's Hymn	53
Praise the Lord	109
Praise Ye Jehovah	111
Resting Sweetly	106
Rock of Ages	80½
Saviour, Like a Shepherd	33
Scattering Precious Seed	16
Send the Tidings	76
Shall I Meet You?	84
Shall It Be You?	14
Sinner, Come	104
Sweeping Through the Gates	110
Sweet Hour of Prayer	98
That City so Fair	27
The Army Moves Along	10
The Beautiful Life Beyond	37
The Coming King	6
The Day of Great Rejoicing	
The Dying Girl's Farewell	
The Gates are Open for Me	
The Miner's Song	
Then I Knew there was a W
The Precious Bible	
There Will Be Light	
There is Joy in My S
The Rifted Rock	
The Rock that is
The Shepherd's
The Story of t

Figure 3. This photocopy shows a torn fragment, which is all that remains of the index page from *Windows of Heaven No. 6*, owned by Irma Frost. Both margins show the handwritten song title in colored ink. This page was found tucked in the middle of the hymnal in Patsy Stoneman's collection. Photograph by Jocelyn Neal.

in musical notation. Stored among Ernest Stoneman's lyric sheets and other professional papers, all of which are tucked into an old pasteboard case, is a single piece of musical manuscript paper with the melody sketched out for "Till the Snowflakes Fall Again."[17] The handwriting appears to be Irma's, and the musical notation is clear and confident. This transcription confirms that these musicians were familiar with the hymnals' musical notation, not just the lyrics.

Furthermore, the well-used hymnals in Irma Frost's possession clear up romanticized notions regarding the origins of some of the songs the Stonemans recorded. For instance, published speculation credits "The Dying Girl's Farewell," the first tune recorded at the Bristol sessions on July 25, 1927, as the possible work of "a now forgotten Gilded Age composer or someone around Galax who was Hattie's kin,"[18] when, in fact, the published version of it sits in Irma's copy of *Windows of Heaven No. 6.* The song (by a professional songwriter with ties to a singing school in Georgia) is clearly marked by a folded page corner.[19] On the book's torn index page, the song's title is boldly written in blue ink on the top margin, and in darker blue ink on the side margin (figure 3), reminding any singer in the family that this favorite hymn could be found on page 28.

Although the hymnals were obviously a resource from which Ernest Stoneman learned hymns, he also appropriated favorite hymns into his personal repertoire by separately transcribing their texts. Over the years, he compiled a master set list in the form of song lists, lyric sheets, and scripts, both handwritten and typed, all of which he stored in a pasteboard case. The hymns appear in two guises within this collection: he made lists that simply indexed his favorites from the various hymnals, yet he also typed up separate lyric pages for some of the hymns. For instance, a page entitled "List of Sacred Selections" catalogs 20 different hymns, citing corresponding hymnals and page numbers. Conversely, Stoneman simultaneously distanced himself from those resources by transcribing the text for "The Hallelujah Side," even though it was in one of the hymnals.[20] On that particular sheet, no melodic or harmonic information appears other than the minimal indication of "Key of C"—the music itself resided in his memory.

Many accounts of early hillbilly recordings romanticize the roots of such recordings in the folk traditions of rural Appalachia and in the oral transmission of "mountain music," sometimes not recognizing other performance practices. That the Stonemans—unquestionably influential in the early hillbilly recording scene—were working with commercial, published sources and had the training to use notated musical sources should not be passed over lightly. In many ways, when recording gospel songs, The Dixie Mountaineers defied the common perceptions of the hillbilly music industry. It appears that the group entered the studio with printed music close at hand and produced a large number of recordings that were essentially direct performances from those songbooks and gospel hymnals; indeed, most of the hymns they did at any given session can be found clustered in one or two hymnbooks. Certainly, the Stonemans were not the only hillbilly musicians to be experienced in formal musical performance—Jimmie Rodgers' Aunt Dora Bozeman, for instance, had been a music teacher, and Rodgers's sister-in-law Elsie McWilliams likely had formal musical training through a sister's singing school lessons. The blending of oral tradition and formal musicianship, however, is particularly vivid in the Stonemans' work, and should largely be credited to Hattie Stoneman and Irma Frost.

The Recording Sessions with Mr. Peer

Details of the Bristol sessions from 1927 have morphed into legend for fans and historians of country music and need not be repeated here.[21] One detail, though, is worth noting: the recording studio was located just down the hill from the imposing Greek Revival architecture of the First Baptist Church (figure 4), a building symbolic of the importance of religion in Appalachia. The church had been built about fifteen years prior to the sessions, but in September 1926, the *Bristol Herald Courier* reported that "A huge crowd is expected to attend the dedicatory services at the First Baptist church" this week.[22] Evangelical revivalist enthusiasm was still strong within the region then, and whether in the smaller southwestern Virginia towns that were home to the Stoneman family or in larger cities like Bristol, people actively participated in the life of their churches.[23] The hymns that Stoneman and the Dixie Mountaineers brought to Bristol were not obscure or elaborate musical compositions; instead, they were the much-loved standards of that era, part of the worship traditions of Protestant congregations and fuel for people's daily existence. The Dixie Mountaineers made those recordings almost literally in the shadow of the First Baptist Church, and those recordings were figuratively an echo of the community's daily experience with sacred music.

Figure 4. The First Baptist Church, on a hill overlooking 408 State Street, Bristol. Photograph by Jocelyn Neal.

At 8:30 A.M. on Monday, July 25, 1927, Ernest Stoneman brought Walter Mooney and Kahle Brewer with him into Ralph Peer's temporary Bristol studio and spent an hour and a half recording "The Dying Girl's Farewell" and "Tell Mother I Will Meet Her."[24] The trio did two takes of the first song and three of the second, singing in close harmony to Stoneman's guitar accompaniment and harmonica introduction. The rest of the morning was spent on "The Mountaineer's Courtship" and "Midnight on the Stormy Deep." Early that afternoon, the Dixie Mountaineers, Ernest Stoneman's gospel hymn ensemble, consisting of himself and Hattie Stoneman, Irma Frost, Kahle and Edna Brewer, Walter Mooney, and Eck Dunford, returned together and spent the remaining hours of the day on six gospel hymns.[25] The first hymn, "Sweeping Through the Gates," was allotted three takes; the remaining five hymns were granted only two takes each: "I Know My Name Is There," "Are You Washed in the Blood," "No More Goodbyes," "The Resurrection," and "I Am Resolved."[26] Those hymns, plus the two songs from the morning session, came from four of Irma Frost's hymnals: *Windows of Heaven No. 2*, *Windows of Heaven No. 6*, *Waves of Glory*, and *The Revival No. 2*.[27] Those recordings, transmitted via ever-evolving technology to today's audience, are the only audible evidence we have of Ernest Stoneman's performance practice and of the group's methods of music-making that day.

What can be heard of those hymns on commercially available recordings differs considerably (in terms of pitch, timbre, and the balance of the ensemble) from the sounds the musicians produced that day. In particular, not only was it common for hillbilly musicians in the 1920s to tune their guitars to non-standard pitch frequencies, but the recording equipment Peer used at that session did not operate at the standard 78 rpm but rather at 76.5 rpm, and even that speed was variable.[28] According to Charles Wolfe and Richard Nevins, these differences result in only a slightly appreciable change in pitch — less than a quarter tone — when the records are played back on a 78 rpm turntable, but such differences substantially affect the underlying timbre of the music.[29]

Furthermore, the monophonic recording process and the physical spacing of the ensemble in the studio blend and disguise the contributions of individual musicians sufficiently so that the most thorough discographies cite the participants with the qualifier of "most likely" or "probably including"—and many of these lists differ as to which musicians might have participated in a session. In short, listeners today cannot hear all of what Ernest Stoneman and the Dixie Mountaineers did that day. A music aficionado investigating the intricacies of their Bristol recordings must acknowledge that today we can only hear an altered version of the original performance.

Ralph Peer's session notes for the Victor Talking Machine Company provide insight into the activities of July 25, 1927.[30] Peer jotted down detailed — if occasionally incomplete or inaccurate — copyright and song-book publication information for many of the hymns that the Dixie Mountaineers sang. The only one of the hymnals whose title appears in the session sheets is *Windows of Heaven*, but publishers are listed for each entry from the other books.[31] Peer was acutely aware that there was money to be made through owning publishing rights to songs, long before others in the music industry were paying much attention to that aspect of the business.[32] History has confirmed that one of Peer's savviest career decisions as a producer of recordings was to develop his music publishing company; not surprisingly, he sought out musicians with original, unpublished material to record, and he encouraged those musicians to publish their compositions through his new company.

Peer's notes about the composer and copyright for the hymns are the strongest evidence that songbooks were present at the actual Bristol sessions. The session sheets include more details than are found in any of Stoneman's notes. Peer, for instance, cites "Comp. J. L. Moore, Pub. Chas. Tillman. Copyr. E. T. Pound. 1890." for the hymn "Sweeping Through the Gates" (identical to the information printed in the hymnal). For those hymns without a specifically identified copyright notice, Peer wrote "Non Copyr. R. S. Peer." in his notes. The above example raises interesting questions about the producer's own thoughts and intentions in recording so many songs to which he could not get publishing rights. In many of his other recordings (including several at the Bristol sessions), Peer credited the musicians as songwriters, even in cases where they were bringing in either public domain material or songs derived from orally transmitted versions. That business plan netted him considerable profits, but in the case of the Stonemans, the presence of the published sources facilitated honest and accurate citations while eliminating copyright or publishing opportunities.

That Monday afternoon in late July 1927, Irma Frost set up her portable, folding pump organ in the studio, and Eck Dunford and Kahle Brewer brought their fiddles and Ernest Stoneman his guitar. Hattie Stoneman sang soprano, Irma sang alto, Ernest sang lead (doubling Hattie's melody down an octave), and the other men filled in the tenor and bass parts, with Walter Mooney's resonant voice supporting the low registers.[33] Singing one hymn after another, the Dixie Mountaineers performed each hymn in the same style, according to the same musical formulae and interpretations. On the one hand, they sang much of the music according to the published versions; on the other hand, they modified certain aspects of the printed versions in the consistent and predictable ways that marked their own style.

Arranging the Hymns

The Dixie Mountaineers' approach to these hymns focused on artful distribution of the vocal parts, with supporting instrumentation layered primarily under the verses. Opening the hymns were rousing introductions consisting of guitar, organ, and fiddles. Following that, each verse was sung with guitar (and occasionally with fiddle) accompaniment. Typically, only the guitar persisted through the chorus, where the intricate vocal parts of the group's members are enough to hold the listeners' attention. Generally, the hymn concluded quite simply with the final chord of the chorus. In several instances, the fiddles and organ joined the guitar for an instrumental interlude. Most of the singing, however, is accompanied only by guitar, so that the emphasis remained on the vocal harmonies.

Example 1. Ernest Stoneman's typical guitar figuration.

The most constant and audible identifier of the group's style is Ernest Stoneman's guitar playing, a steady pattern of bass notes plus strummed chords in a two-beat pattern (example 1). This limiting and nearly unwavering pattern keeps almost every hymn that the group recorded in simple duple meter and thereby modifies the rhythms and metric settings of hymns drastically from their published versions. The Dixie Mountaineers' other modifications of some hymns, though not as foundational, are equally predictable: melodic rhythms are smoothed over and simplified from their published patterns; harmonic progressions are simplified to accommodate a three-chord guitar accompaniment; small modifications in melodic contour sometimes occur; and metric adjustments allow expanded phrases with extra beats between them, letting the music breathe in a more narrative flow.

Stoneman was clearly concerned with arranging hymns suitably for recording purposes. In the margins of several hymnals are notations about the timing, the number of verses, and the placement of the chorus; one such indication in Stoneman's handwriting says "Cho twice only."[34] Twice through the chorus (using it only after verses 2 and 4, in that case) would keep that particular hymn under the allotted time limit for commercial recordings of approximately three minutes. These are the notations of a musician paying close attention to the professional constraints on the recording process, adopting practical approaches to making recordings, and using his hymnals as working scores.

Two Sacred Songs

The versatility and expressiveness of Stoneman's musical performances are best illustrated in the two sacred, somewhat maudlin songs that he recorded with Kahle Brewer and Walter Mooney. Both of these songs — "Tell Mother I Will Meet Her" and "The Dying Girl's Farewell" — were clearly Stoneman family favorites, made evident by the fact that the songs were worked in two volumes of *Windows of Heaven* by folded page corners, as well as handwritten reminders of their location in the books.[35] While a distinction is often made between "sacred songs" and "hymns," the primary difference in Stoneman's case is that the two sacred songs Stoneman recorded at Bristol were performed by the male trio, while the six hymns were performed in congregational style. Other than that, the sacred songs share many compositional similarities with the hymns, in that the published versions of both types of compositions appear in the same hymnals, notated in four-part chorale style, with lively choruses and dotted rhythms throughout the pieces. However, unlike the congregational approach to four-part harmony, which required no significant adjustment to the published hymns, the trio faced the task of deriving three-part vocal harmony from the four-part chorale-style printed versions, while relating the narrative of these plot-driven texts to the listener in a musically expressive way. These acts of musical arranging, which relied on the ensemble's creativity, provide evidence of Stoneman's musical identity and style.

The published version of "The Dying Girl's Farewell" features a four-part conventional hymn arrangement (example 2, transcribed in round notes).[36] Without the organ to tie the performance to the published key, the three musicians were free to migrate to a more comfortable key for Stoneman's guitar — in this case, A major (example 3). The version that the trio recorded combines Stoneman's typical guitar pattern with vocal three-part harmony, comprised essentially of the published tenor and bass lines, plus Stoneman singing the melody. The three noticeable adjustments these musicians made to the song's published version are indicative of their typical performance style: first, the rhythmic patterns are smoothed out throughout most of the song; second, the harmonization is simplified; and third, extra beats are inserted at the end of phrases to allow the music to breathe (example 4 contains an excerpt transcribed from their performance).[27]

A comparison of measure 4 in the published version (example 3) and the performed version (example 4) reveals the simplified harmonic setting that the musicians adopted — the secondary dominant progression is entirely missing. However, Mooney's bass line still follows the published version (the circled pitch in measure 4, example 4), resulting in an audible conflict between the vocal bass line and the guitar harmonization. This subtle clash is tangible evidence of the contrast between the printed music and the oral tradition of simplified harmonizations.

The ensemble's rhythmic normalization of the melody is clearly apparent in measures 2 and 4, while the phrase itself is expanded in measures 4 and 8 (transcribed as measures of 3/2 meter, these add an extra half bar to each phrase). These changes, specifically harmonic simplification and metric liberty, are not particularly drastic. The musicians' approach toward achieving a three-part vocal arrangement, borrowing the published tenor and bass lines to surround the melody, is quite conventional, and merits comment primarily because in some instances it results in open fifth voicings — incomplete triads that are atypical for three-part vocal harmony in early hillbilly music styles.

Example 2. First four measures of "The Dying Girl's Farewell," by Archer and Patton, as published in *Windows of Heaven No. 6.*

Example 3. First four measures of "The Dying Girl's Farewell," as published, transposed to key of A for ease of comparison.

Example 4. "The Dying Girl's Farewell," opening phrases, as recorded by Stoneman, Brewer, and Mooney, July 25, 1927.

Far more radical changes to a published musical score occurred in the second song that the trio recorded at Bristol. Like "The Dying Girl's Farewell," "Tell Mother I Will Meet Her" was performed in A major, allowing Stoneman to employ the same guitar chords and strumming patterns as before. Again, the trio took vocal harmonies from the published tenor and bass lines, but in a marked departure from the published version (example 5), the melody of the verse and the entire compositional structure of the chorus are changed. Beginning with the conclusion of the verse (example 6, measure 8 of the transcription), the singers greatly expanded the rhythmic setting of the song. The chorus itself bears almost no musical resemblance, melodically, rhythmically, or harmonically, to the published version, until the word "thro'" (measure 13, example 6). Thus, while the musicians could have used the hymnal as a source of that song, this performance of "Tell Mother I Will Meet Her" was most strongly tied to an oral tradition that recast the song with a new, expressive melody. The new setting of the text includes more descending melodic motives, evocative of the musical sigh that would match the tale of death and departure in the song. Furthermore, the drawn-out rhythms and expanded measures (metrically shifting into 3/2) capture the yearning tone of the song beautifully. The metric expansion of "In the land beyond the blue," and the repetition of this phrase in every verse, lend that line the flavor of a refrain — effectively inviting the listener to join in (either literally or figuratively) in preparation for the chorus.[38]

Example 5. Excerpt from "Tell Mother I Will Meet Her," by Tinsman, published in *Windows of Heaven No. 2*, transposed from A-flat major to A major for ease of comparison with the transcription.

Example 6. Transcription of excerpt from "Tell Mother I Will Meet Her," performed by Stoneman, Mooney, and Brewer, July 25, 1927.

These two recordings illustrate in detail the blending of published musical sources, oral traditions, and the standard arrangement modifications that Ernest Stoneman adopted in his work. The ever-present guitar pattern often involves simplification of harmonic progressions; minor melodic reworkings are reinforced by a general adherence to the published vocal parts; dotted rhythmic patterns are smoothed out into steady, evenly paced rhythms; and metric expansions are freely employed to allow the pacing of individual phrases to adopt a more natural, settled feel. Finally, the complete reworking of the chorus's melody for "Tell Mother I Will Meet Her" reminds the listener that the Stonemans were indeed drawing upon an oral tradition, and their own musical creativity extended beyond published sources. This notion ties in quite strongly to the general perception among early hillbilly recording musicians that ballads and sacred songs were part of an oral tradition, and that their melodies either were selected from a pool of known options or were newly conceived. This faith in the oral tradition takes on new meaning in juxtaposition with the trio's obvious attachment to published scores.

The Dixie Mountaineers' Performances

Most of the six gospel hymns that the Dixie Mountaineers recorded followed published versions, with only the basic stylistic accommodations just described. Three excerpts from those recordings characterize the musical breadth of the ensemble's performance style. "The Resurrection" contains a chorus with three independent texts in counterpoint; the recording captures the intricacies of this published hymn with almost no deviation from the printed score. The differences between published score and recorded version of "No More Goodbyes" represent the typical modifications that the ensemble employed in arranging the hymns. Finally, "I Know My Name Is There," one of most exciting and musically interesting of the group's recorded performances, links the gospel hymns that the ensemble sang that day to their secular musical traditions, apparent in the fiddling, rhythmic arrangement, and guitar styles present on that recording.

"The Resurrection" recording opens with an instrumental introduction, then proceeds through a sequence of four verses, two instrumental verses, and several iterations of the chorus. The latter part of the arrangement contains the most intriguing chorus, as it features three distinct texts in counterpoint, performed simultaneously with rhythmic independence, converging at a final cadence.[39] The Dixie Mountaineers' performance of this chorus adheres almost exactly to the published version, with all three texts and four independent harmonic lines present (Stoneman's lead doubles Hattie's soprano). The only adjustments are subtle: scalar bass passages that walk from one harmony to the next as well as the elimination of a few dotted rhythms in the bass.[40] What results (excerpt shown in example 7) is a rather complex ensemble passage, one which is musically sophisticated, yet which was undoubtedly quite fun to perform.

Example 7. Excerpt from "The Resurrection," vocal parts transcribed from the Dixie Mountaineers' performance. Stoneman's guitar is also present throughout this chorus.

"No More Goodbyes" illustrates these musicians' more drastic adjustments of both rhythmic and harmonic elements to suit their own performance style. The hymn appears in print in the key of E-flat major, notated in compound quadruple meter (12/8), and it follows the standard verse/chorus format.[41] The entire hymn employs the lilting rhythm of quarter-note, eighth-note, quarter-note, eighth-note (example 8). Given that Ernest Stoneman relied on his standard guitar accompaniment pattern (a rhythmic pattern incongruent with 12/8 meter), the notated rhythms for this hymn would have been continually syncopated against the guitar's chords. That consideration, combined with the simple fact that reading compound metric notation is more complicated than simple duple, probably led the ensemble to reach the compromise heard on the recording: all the uneven rhythmic patterns (quarter-note, eighth-note) are normalized into a simple quadruple metric setting (example 9).

This significant rhythmic and metric change in the recorded version of "No More Goodbyes" changes the entire feel and mood of the hymn. The published melody's dotted rhythms have an energy, brightness, and lilt. Thus, when Stoneman and the other musicians "straightened out" the rhythms into a constant pattern of eighth-notes in simple meter, the hymn lost some of its drive and rhythmic sparkle. What emerged instead was consistent with the other hymn recordings from the Dixie Mountaineers — the steady, plodding rhythmic motion being part of that group's characteristic style.

The harmonic setting of the chorus in the published version of "No More Goodbyes" features an applied dominant harmony, outside the diatonic realm of the hymn, leading to a half-cadence in the middle of the chorus (example 8). Other than this one chord, the rest of the hymn adheres to a standard three-chord harmonization: tonic, subdominant, and dominant. It is in the treatment of this one distant harmony that the distinct traditions of choral vocal harmony and guitar-accompanied folksinging again audibly meet.

In the Dixie Mountaineers' performance of "No More Goodbyes," the

Example 8. Excerpt from published version of "No More Goodbyes," by Latta and Fillmore, published in *Windows of Heaven No. 6.*

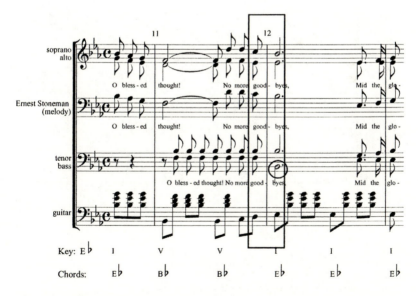

Example 9. First and second iteration of the chorus of "No More Goodbyes" as performed by the Dixie Mountaineers, illustrating simplified rhythmic and metric setting and reharmonization in measures 11–12.

only instrumental accompaniment through this section of the hymn is Stoneman's guitar, consistent with his usual pattern of bass notes plus strummed chords. Following a typical progression on his guitar, he changes the harmonization through this section to rely only on tonic and dominant harmonies (E-flat and B-flat), eliminating the more interesting, published progression from the second half of measure 11 into measure 12. The singers gamely adjust their parts accordingly, so that all meet on an E-flat-major chord in measure 12 (example 9). Although this harmonization works perfectly well with the melody, it interrupts the flow of the chorus by eliminating the presence of a half cadence in measure 12. As with the rhythmic normalization, this harmonic change strips the chorus of some of its color.

Walter Mooney's bass voice clearly is heard landing on the low "B-flat" in measure 12 (circled on example 9), hinting that the singers were still working from the printed version and trying to accommodate Stoneman's chord progression without complete success. That this was not a planned situation becomes evident in the third verse and chorus. Having sung the chorus twice with this conflict, on the third iteration of the chorus, Stoneman changes chord progressions ever so slightly, to reinstate the half cadence in measure 12 (example 10).

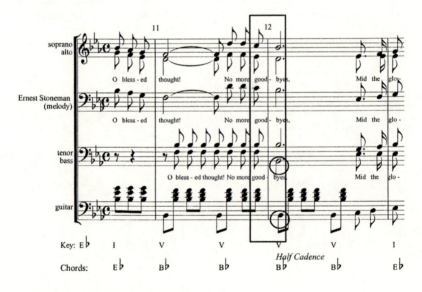

Example 10. Third iteration of the chorus of "No More Goodbyes," with a different guitar accompaniment in measures 11–12.

With this minor adjustment, Mooney's bass line and Stoneman's guitar line match, the presence of the half cadence in the middle of the chorus is restored, and the hymn continues to a resolved conclusion.

This situation illustrates another characteristic of the Dixie Mountaineers' approach to harmony: the group's version keeps within the scope of the standard three chords (E-flat, A-flat, and B-flat, in this particular key). Where harmonic simplification was required, it was employed. More crucial to our understanding of the musicians' methodology, however, was the fact that Stoneman changed his guitar chord pattern for the third iteration of the chorus. This reflects the spontaneous nature of the group's performance of the hymn (detailed chord progressions had not been worked out in rehearsal), underscoring the group's flexibility during live performance.

The only hymn from the Dixie Mountaineers' session in which the ensemble departs from Stoneman's regular, duple guitar strumming pattern is "I Know My Name Is There." The group's performance style of this hymn, which was released as the B-side to "Are You Washed in the Blood," most resembles the secular dance music and rowdy vocal numbers that the Stonemans also included in their musical repertoire. The lilting compound meter (6/8 time signature) echoes a fiddle player's waltz style. We need look no further than the introduction to find evidence of this: the second phrase of the introduction, transcribed in example 11, contains traces of waltz rhythms (measure 5), decorative ornamentation (the turn in measure 6 and the figuration in measure 7), and a sweet obbligato above the melody (measures 7–8), all of which render the recording different from the style of the other hymns.

Example 11. "I Know My Name Is There," fiddle melody (with obbligato in measures 7–8) in the introduction to the hymn as recorded by the Dixie Mountaineers.

For the vocal performance, the ensemble adheres basically to the published version of the hymn (example 12 shows the published version of the second phrase, which can be compared to the fiddle transcription in example 11). Yet the presence of the freer fiddle style and the rhythmic energy of this particular performance act as a musical bridge between the gospel performance styles that the Stonemans employ on the other hymns and the secular tunes that were an equally important part of their repertoire. Divisions between musically secular and sacred become blurred. Patsy Stoneman recalled rousing church services from her childhood when everyone brought their instruments and played along — a raucous behavior that was most certainly forbidden in some of the region's churches, but embraced in others. Thus, despite the relatively infrequent mention of Ernest Stoneman's involvement with sacred music as a youth, singing and playing these hymns was a natural, de facto part of his musical experience as much as were house parties and dances, and his sacred and his secular repertoires apparently shared musical styles in some instances.

Example 12. Published version of "I Know My Name Is There," by Warner and Warren, in *The Revival No. 2.*

Portrait of the Musicians

Considered together, the sacred recordings — the six "hymns" recorded by the Dixie Mountaineers in Bristol the afternoon of July 25, 1927, and the "songs" recorded by the trio that morning — offer a rather full representation of the Stonemans' musical identities and performance styles. At that recording session, the musicians were simply performing a cross-section of the gospel repertoire that was an integral part of their existence. Ernest Stoneman and his musical collaborators were, in effect, putting down on records what was commonly being sung in their communities. At the same time, the musicians were making creative decisions about their musical arrangements when adapting hymns from published versions.

The revivalist gospel hymn repertoire was an integral, yet often unnoticed, part of Ernest Stoneman's life when he was a boy. Hence, when he assembled the Dixie Mountaineers to record the hymns from his youth, Stoneman included two church organists, one of whom had amassed a significant collection of treasured hymnals and was fluent in reading musical notation. When the Dixie Mountaineers walked into the recording studio, published hymnals in hand, they were able to perform a long list of hymns with a standard approach to their musical arrangements. It is possible that these attributes limited Ernest Stoneman's fame — such a professional procedure and attitude lacked the mystique of the singer-songwriter or the nostalgia of the folksong collector (the latter qualities, of course, were the approaches of the musicians who emerged from the Bristol sessions with superstar status).[42] The Stonemans and Ralph Peer could lay no publishing claim to the hymns they were recording in Bristol. The presence of the hymnals in the studio belied any notion that this repertoire was extracted from the old, untainted traditions of the hills, a myth that had been fueled by record companies seeking out what they perceived to be "authentic" and "pure" folk music.

Clearly, when Ernest Stoneman and the Dixie Mountaineers recorded for Peer in Bristol, it was entirely second nature for this small ensemble of friends and relatives who were working musicians to perform hymn after hymn out of a stack of hymnals.

Appendix

The following list provides bibliographical information on four hymnals from Irma Frost's collection that contained the eight sacred songs recorded by Ernest Stoneman and the Dixie Mountaineers on July 25, 1927.

Revival No. 2, published by Charlie Tillman

> No. 23: "I Am Resolved," by Palmer Hartsough and J. H. Fillmore, copyright 1896 Fillmore Bros., J. A. Lee, owner.
> No. 29: "Sweeping Through the Gates," by J. L. Moore, by per., arr. By J.L.M., copyright 1890 E. T. Pound.
> No. 91: "I Know My Name Is There," by D. S. Warner and B. E. Warren (no printed copyright information).
> No. 176: "The Resurrection," by G. R. Street, by per. of A. S. Kieffer (no printed copyright information).

Windows of Heaven No. 2, published by John B. Vaughan

> No. 29: "Tell Mother I Will Meet Her," by Ralph S. Tinsman, copy right 1902 T. M. Bowdish.

Windows of Heaven No. 6, published by John B. Vaughan

> No. 28: "The Dying Girl's Farewell," by J. D. Patton and G. W. Archer, copyright 1902 J. D. Patton.

No. 91: "No More Goodbyes," by E. R. Latta and J. H. Fillmore, copyright 1890 Fillmore Bros.

Waves of Glory, published by Robert E. Winsett

No. 93: "Are You Washed in the Blood," by E. A. Hoffman (no printed copyright information).

These eight selections are available on the following recordings:

Ernest Stoneman with Family and Friends, Volumes I and II (Old Homestead OHCD 4172 and 4173). Contains "The Resurrection," "Sweeping Through the Gate," "Are You Washed in the Blood," and "I Know My Name Is There." Also contains "The Dying Girl's Farewell," listed as "Dying Girl's Message."
The Bristol Sessions: Historic Recordings from Bristol, Tennessee (Country Music Foundation CMF-011-D). Contains "Are You Washed in the Blood," "Tell Mother I Will Meet Her," and "The Resurrection."
Ernest V. Stoneman and the Blue Ridge Corn Shuckers (Rounder 1008). Contains "The Dying Girl's Farewell," "Sweeping Through the Gates," "Are You Washed in the Blood," and "I Know My Name Is There."
Round the Heart of Old Galax (Old Time Tunes & Songs as Played Round the Heart of Old Galax: The Traditional Music of Grayson & Carroll Counties, Virginia) (County 533). Contains "No More Goodbyes" and "I Am Resolved."

Notes

1. The Center for Popular Music, Middle Tennessee State University, Murfreesboro, Tennessee, provided invaluable access to source materials for this topic. The Southern Folklife Collection, Wilson Library, University of North Carolina at Chapel Hill made recordings available for study. Dr. Charles Wolfe offered a wealth of information, and Ms. Patsy Stoneman made her extensive collection of original materials available to me. I express my gratitude to all of these people.
2. *The Baptist Hymnal* (Nashville:

Convention Press, 1991). "I Am Resolved," words by Palmer Hartsough (1844–1932), music by James Fillmore (1849–1936), c. 1896, Fillmore Bros.
3. The session took place at 408/410 East State Street, July 25, 1927.
4. Country music fans have embraced Nolan Porterfield's oft-quoted description of the Bristol sessions as the "Big Bang of country music evolution, the genesis of every shape and species of Pickin'-and-Singin' down through the years ... the place where it all started...." ("Hey, Hey, Tell 'Em 'Bout Us: Jimmie Rodgers Vis-

its the Carter Family," in *Country: The Music and the Musicians: From the Beginnings to the 90s* [Abbeville Press, 1994] p. 16). Stoneman returned on Wednesday, July 27, to contribute a total of 17 recordings to the sessions.

5. The multifaceted connotations of the term "hillbilly" must be acknowledged in reference to this music. As Bill Malone recounts, the term was applied to early country music recordings when Al Hopkins quipped "Call [our band] anything you want. We are nothing but a bunch of hillbillies from North Carolina and Virginia anyway." (*Country Music USA* [Austin: University of Texas Press, 1985], p. 40). While by the 1950s the country music industry took formal steps to distance itself from the term, in the late 1920s, the musicians tended to accept the moniker and even embrace it as a celebration of identity. Roni Stoneman tells a story of working a show in Washington, D.C. as a young girl, meeting Grandpa Jones while he was in his stage costume, and feeling a kinship to the man who was dressed "like a hillbilly, just like me" (told at the International Country Music Conference, June, 2002). In this context, the term identifies a pride in cultural origins, rather than any derogatory dismissal. It is in the most positive connotation that I adopt the description in this writing.

6. Ivan Tribe's biography of the Stonemans includes an excellent exposition of who all the family members are, their relationships, and the general information about the family's history. See *The Stonemans* (Urbana: University of Illinois Press, 1993).

7. Patsy Stoneman, Ernest Stoneman's fourth child, shared many family stories about her father with me in personal interviews, March and May, 2002, Manchester, Tennessee. All subsequent quotations from Patsy Stoneman are from these interviews unlesss otherwise identified.

8. Henry Wilder Foote, *Three Centuries of American Hymnody* (Archon Books, 1968), p. 270.

9. See, for instance, Tribe, pp. 22–24, for a tale of a house party with particularly lively fiddling and dancing.

10. Tribe mentions that Stoneman's affection for Hattie was probably strengthened by her musical abilities (*The Stonemans*, p. 32). Ernest was quick to encourage her performing.

11. Newspaper advertisements from the time period list parlor organs (reed organs) in the neighborhood of $5–$100, while upright pianos were several hundred dollars. Sources that mention the instruments abound; *The New Grove Dictionary of Music and Musicians* lists some of the major manufacturers of reed organs, and Robert Gellerman's *The American Reed Organ* (Vestal: The Vestal Press, 1973) discusses their history in some detail. The use of parlor organs in music-making of the day is well documented; even Bill C. Malone's *Country Music, U.S.A.* (Austin: University of Texas Press, 1985) mentions their commonplace role in folk music (p. 26).

12. Today the organ sits in Patsy Stoneman's parlor, but during Hattie and Ernest Stoneman's time in Virginia, it was frequently on loan to whatever local church needed it, further tying the family into their church-centered community. Ironically, the organ remained in the family even through their worst economic straits because it was often either on loan to the church or residing in a relative's home, thereby preventing repossession.

13. Those hymnals from her collection that contain the six gospel hymns recorded in Bristol are listed in the appendix.

14. This photograph, which has been published several times, serves as the prominent inside cover art of *Country: The Music and the Musicians from the Beginnings to the '90s: Country (The Music and the Musicians)* (New York: Abbeville Press, 1994), where it acts as an iconic representation of the string band and hillbilly tradition of the 1920s. The original currently hangs in Patsy Stoneman's house.

15. Telephone interview with Donna Stoneman, March, 2002.

16. That Ernest Stoneman drew upon published sources has been known for quite some time. Charles Wolfe has writ-

ten about it in several places, including the liner notes to *The Bristol Sessions: Historic Recordings from Bristol, Tennessee* (Country Music Foundation CMF 011, 1991), where he explains that "Tell Mother I Will Meet Her" comes from a 1902 John B. Vaughan songbook, and that "The Resurrection" comes from a "Pentecostal songbook of the same era." The relationship of Stoneman's music to published sources, however, goes far beyond merely learning a few songs from songbooks or common-knowledge church hymns. It is the depth of this connection that can help inform our understanding of his music.

17. Ernest Stoneman also had a typed set of lyrics for this song in his collection of lyric sheets, which included guitar tablature, the chord progression, and a signature claiming rights to the song at the bottom. His 1927 recording of the song matches the melodic transcription.

18. Tribe, p. 43.

19. The song was the work of G. W. Archer and J. D. Patton, composed from the "farewell words of Miss Anna Taylor, who died September 10, 1897," copyrighted in 1902 and available in several published sources from that era. Patton was a student of the renowned publisher and singing-school teacher A. J. Showalter.

20. This page was typed up even though the Dixie Mountaineers had a copy of it in the hymnal *His Voice in Song* when they recorded it in 1926. "The Hallelujah Side," by Rev. Johnson Oatman Jr., and J. Howard Entwisle, and written in the key of A major, is no. 156 in that Winsett hymnal.

21. One of the most insightful accounts of the sessions is Charles Wolfe's "The Legend that Peer Built: Reappraising the Bristol Sessions" (*Journal of Country Music* 12/2 [1989] 24–35). Wolfe includes some of the exaggerations and myths that have emerged about the session, then proceeds with a remarkable historical account.

22. *Bristol Herald Courier,* September 5, 1926, p. 13.

23. This aspect of community life has not yet diminished in the area. Even

though the city boasts a present-day population of only about 40,000, Sprint's yellow pages lists an impressive eight pages of churches in its tiny print.

24. Stoneman had recorded both of these songs at earlier sessions, "Tell Mother I Will Meet Her" for Edison in 1927, and "The Dying Girl's Farewell" for OKeh in 1925. The six hymns from the afternoon session were not numbers he had previously recorded, however.

25. In 1926, the Dixie Mountaineers (with only a few alterations in personnel) did a very similar recording session in Camden, New Jersey, where they recorded seven such numbers. Of the many ensembles that Ernest Stoneman put together, the name "Dixie Mountaineers" was used for the group that did the sacred tunes. Many of the same personnel comprised the Blue Ridge Corn Shuckers and various other ensembles — it was the nature of the repertoire, more than the members, that changed with the different ensemble names.

26. All eight songs, their publication information, and their location in the four hymnals used for this recording session are listed in the appendix. Available or relatively recently available recordings of all eight songs are also listed there, and the reader is encouraged to listen to the hymns in conjunction with reading this article. It is worth noting that two of these six hymns are still commonly sung in various worship traditions today — "I Am Resolved" and "Are You Washed in the Blood."

27. These hymnals do not include their publication dates, and as these publishers released multiple versions of each volume, the specific dates are not readily available. Of these four volumes, Charlie Tillman's *Revival No. 2* is the earliest, dating from 1896. John B. Vaughan's *Windows of Heaven No. 2* appeared in 1902, with *No. 6* following a few years later. Robert E. Winsett's *Waves of Glory* is the latest, appearing around 1920.

28. Charles Wolfe shared with me in personal correspondence that he had gathered much of the information about the

recording equipment's functionality from his own personal interviews with remastering experts Michael Brooks (CBS/Sony), NY, May 1983, and Bernado Cosachov (remastering lab, RCA/BMG), NY, June 1983.

29. In an equal tempered tuning system, the interval of a half step is defined by the frequency ratio 2½₂, or approximately 1.06. The frequency shift that occurs when playing back these recordings on modern equipment is equivalent to the ratio of 78/76.5, or approximately 1.02. Thus, if the Stonemans recorded a hymn in the key of A, we would hear it as a slightly sharp A, but not B-flat or A-sharp.

30. Microfilm copies of these session sheets are housed at the Country Music Foundation archives, Nashville, Tennessee.

31. Peer's notation fails to differentiate between the different volumes of *Windows of Heaven*.

32. Nolan Porterfield's account of Ralph Peer's early career details these business decisions and their impact on both Peer's success and the industry ("Mr. Victor and Mr. Peer," in *Jimmie Rodgers* [Urbana: University of Illinois Press, 1992], chapter 5).

33. Just how much Edna Brewer sang on these recordings is not clear. She likely joined Irma on the alto parts, although her contribution is not particularly bold.

34. This particular notation appears in "I Shall Meet Them Some Day," no. 170 in *Joyful Praise*, but similar notations are scattered throughout the hymnals.

35. The appendix lists the publication information, songwriters, and locations of these songs in their respective hymnals.

36. All of Irma's hymnals were shape note editions, but the illustrations of the published versions are shown here in round notes for convenience of reading.

37. This and all subsequent transcriptions are the author's.

38. For a detailed exploration of metric expansions and phrase alterations in early recorded country music, see this author's *Song Structure Determinants: Poetic Narrative, Phrase Structure, and Hypermeter in the Music of Jimmie Rodgers* (Ph.D. Dissertation, Eastman School of Music, University of Rochester, 2002, available through UMI).

39. "The Resurrection," by G. R. Street, by permission of A. S. Kieffer, appears as No. 176 in *The Revival No. 2*. No explicit copyright information is listed in the hymnal for this song, leading Ralph Peer to type "Non Copyr. R. S. Peer." in the session sheets.

40. The hymn is published in the key of E-flat major, but the performance is closest to E major. Such an adjustment would make it far easier for the fiddler players, and would offer no difficulties for the organist.

41. Stoneman's notes show that he performed this hymn in E-flat (as the recording reveals), but it is likely that he tuned his guitar so that he could finger the chords in D major.

42. Although Ernest Stoneman's earnings and success as a recording artist were the draw for the Bristol sessions, within a few months, the successes of Jimmie Rodgers and the Carter Family eclipsed his role in the burgeoning "hillbilly music" scene. A. P. Carter capitalized on the music industry's interest in "old-time folk music," and cultivated his image as a collector of traditional songs; Jimmie Rodgers drew on the autobiographical pathos of his blues tunes and claimed the persona of singer-songwriter to promote his own artistic success.

17. On the Vanguard of Change: Jimmie Rodgers and Alfred G. Karnes in Bristol, 1927

Thomas Townsend

Country music has trod a winding road since it first emerged as a distinct genre of American popular music, changing with each succeeding generation. The differences between the oldest and the newest country music recordings are so many and so profound that to call them by the same name seems almost inappropriate. Yet, somehow the simplicity of the early rural music was transformed into the urbane sound that dominates the country music charts today. How did today's commercial country music grow out of the old-time style? The genre's history is populated by innovators whose voices and hands continuously changed country music. This lineage can be traced back to some early "hillbilly" musicians whose eclecticism and invention distinguished country music from regional traditional music even at the very beginning of the recording industry. By comparing the old with the new, one might determine who among the earliest recorded country music performers foreshadowed later developments in country music. These distinctions can be found by exploring melody and song structure, two core attributes of music that give a musical genre its identity.

The recording sessions organized by Ralph Peer at Bristol, Tennessee, in July and August, 1927, provide a unique and valuable collection with which to undertake this exploration. Although not the first country music recording sessions, the Bristol sessions brought a wide range of rural musicians to one place, capturing a cross-section of the musical styles prevalent across the mountain region of the South at the time. The musicians who recorded at the sessions were on the brink of great cultural change. The influences that shaped these musicians' music came largely from other musicians who lived near them. In subsequent years, music would increasingly be transmitted over wide distances via recordings and radio. Peer documented rural Southern musical styles that existed before the widespread influence of the recording industry set commercial country music on a path of continuous reinvention.

Although most of the musicians involved in the 1927 Bristol sessions demonstrated solid allegiance to traditional musics, Jimmie Rodgers and Alfred G. Karnes stood out from the rest. What was it about their music that made them unusual? The short answer is that Rodgers and Karnes were more vocally inventive and expressive as well as more stylistically progressive than the others. To obtain the longer, more complete answer, one must take a closer look at the details of this expressiveness. In what respect were they expressive? In what way was their music both different from that of their peers and suggestive of future trends? A detailed comparison of early and contemporary country music may offer insight into how the genre has changed over the decades.

Some concepts of melody and some general perceptions about melody and rhythm will corroborate our intuitions about music. In *A Generative Theory of Tonal Music*, Fred Lerdahl and Ray Jackendoff address some of the issues at hand. Although the book focuses on classical music, many of its arguments apply to country music, which shares the use of a regular meter and diatonic melodic and harmonic structure with Western classical music. According to Lerdahl and Jackendoff, perceptions of musical meter are based on the "alternation of strong and weak beats.... In 4/4 meter, for example, the first and third beats are felt to be stronger than the second and fourth beats" (19). In 3/4 meter (waltz time), listeners tend to hear one strong beat followed by two weaker beats. Granted that stressed or accented beats should be interpreted as the strong beats in this strong/weak alternation, notes with longer duration suggest strong beats (79). Rules for unaccompanied song, though, are different than those for accompanied song. The metric "reading" of a song's melody is not very flexible when the song's accompaniment establishes a clear beat structure. When the voice performs alone, however, a song's melody must suggest its beat structure without any support, using techniques that can help the listener more easily recognize the meter.

One of the most noticeable melodic characteristics distinguishing newer country music from the early country vocal styles is the use of *melisma* as vocal ornamentation. Melisma refers to the embellishing of a plain melody line by adding turns and twists; melisma is, for many singers, a way to add personal expression to the performance of a song, and is characterized by the slurring together of more than one pitch per vocal syllable. The old-time singers represented in Bristol (with the exception of Rodgers and Karnes) typically did not employ this type of decorative expression in their singing, but it became more common after old-time music evolved into modern country. For example, Hank Williams Sr., who recorded in the late 1940s and early 1950s, used some melismatic ornamentation in his singing, but not usually to the point of obscuring the rhythm. By the 1960s, singers such as Patsy Cline and Dolly Parton were using melisma extensively; their expressive singing relied on instrumental accompaniment to keep a steady rhythm, allowing the singers rhythmic freedom.

LeAnn Rimes's 1997 recording of "Amazing Grace" offers an illustration of modern melismatic ornamentation (example 1). Rimes sang the song without accompaniment, and her nearly continuous use of vocal embellishment makes it hard to discern a steady rhythm. By frequently pausing and embellishing notes with complex vocal figures, Rimes created a sense of floating in free metrical space:

A - ma - zing grace, how - sweet the sound

Example 1: Leann Rimes, "Amazing Grace"*

Why is it hard to find the beat? The following passage from *Generative Theory* explains that listeners quickly determine the metric structure of the music they hear and are loath to accept contradictions. If regular metrical cues are lacking in a song, the listener finds it harder to find the rhythm:

> The moments of musical stress in the raw signal serve as "cues" from which the listener attempts to extrapolate a regular pattern of metrical accents. If there is little regularity to these cues, or if they conflict, the sense of metrical accent becomes attenuated or ambiguous. If on the other hand the cues are regular and mutually supporting, the sense of metrical accent becomes definite and multi-leveled. Once a clear metrical pattern has been established, the listener renounces it only in the face of strongly contradicting evidence. Syncopation takes place where cues are strongly contradictory yet not strong enough, or regular enough, to override the inferred pattern [17–18].

**All transcriptions in this paper are by the author, who assumes full responsibility for them.*

These explanations help explain why Rimes's "Amazing Grace" achieved the sense of floating in free time: so many irregular metrical cues were presented that there was little the listener could grasp. With this in mind, it is hard to imagine a modern country singer like LeAnn Rimes sing without instrumental accompaniment because so much of the sense of rhythm in the songs they would sing would be lost. In other words, the presence or absence of accompaniment influences the approach taken to the melody. A singer performing a cappella must provide regular and clearly articulated vocal cues if he or she wants the listener to find the rhythm easily. This was the case for most singers of traditional Appalachian songs even when performing with instrumental accompaniment. However, innovators such as Jimmie Rodgers and Alfred Karnes, capitalizing on the metrical freedom afforded by instrumentation, sang in a more complex, melismatic manner than their contemporaries, foreshadowing the vocal emancipation of Patsy Cline and LeAnn Rimes.

Blind Alfred Reed's recording of his own composition, "The Wreck of the Virginian," made at the Bristol sessions on July 28, 1927, is an example of the more common early country singing style (example 2). Reed recorded the song for Peer with only his own fiddle for accompaniment, playing the melody as an introduction and between verses. According to historical sources, Reed's son Arville would normally have played a guitar accompaniment to his father's song, but because of Peer's last-minute invitation of Reed to the Bristol sessions, Arville could not be there.[1] Blind Alfred Reed's solo recording of the song did not suffer from the lack of guitar accompaniment because the melody was clearly defined rhythmically and stood well on its own.

Reed's "The Wreck of the Virginian" and Rimes's "Amazing Grace" are two extreme examples of country singing that help point out a disparity between early and newer country music. Both performers sang their respective song without a rhythmic background, but Reed's clear rhythm and clean singing kept the song's pulse easily detectable, whereas Rimes's flexible style obscured a steady rhythm.

By their more pervasive use of vocal ornamentation, Alfred Karnes and Jimmie Rodgers set themselves apart from the other Bristol acts. When those two musicians sang, the rhythmic aspect of the melody was detailed and complex. The following musical abstraction (example 3) demonstrates the metric values for pitches found in the first few bars of four tunes recorded during the Bristol sessions. The first, taken from Ernest Phipps' "I Want to Go Where Jesus Is," shows a fairly simple metric contour, with few different note values used. The second, from the Tenneva Ramblers' recording of "The Longest Train I Ever Saw," has slightly more rhythmic diversity and incor-

Blind Alfred Reed, "The Wreck of the Virginian"[1]

porates triplets; it is, however, much simpler than the third sample, taken from Rodgers' "The Soldier's Sweetheart." In only a few measures, Rodgers employs a wide range of note values with little repetition from bar to bar. The last sample, taken from Karnes's "We Shall All Be Reunited," shows a high degree of metric variety and detail.

In "To the Work" (example 4), Karnes sings with melisma and melodic turns and other vocal embellishment to the point that accurate transcription of the rhythmic details becomes difficult. The transcription below, though, displays some of Karnes's vocal expressiveness, especially in measure 11, but the subtleties of his style result in fractional metric placement of notes, either just before or just after the precise beat to which they relate, and these notes do not translate easily into written notation.

This song was transcribed in Long Steel Rail: The Railroad in American Folksong *by Norm and David Cohen in the key of E major, with the additional comment that the original was in F♯ (250–253). I believe that the authors chose E because it is very common for guitarists to play songs in E and use a capo to change the pitch as necessary; it is certainly not usual for folk singers to play in F♯ without using a capo. The comment that the original key is F♯ is correct based on the sounding pitches in Reed's recording. However, it is my belief that it is much more likely that Reed, a fiddle player, would have performed the song in G, and that the discrepancy in pitch can be explained either by the tuning of his violin on that day or by the pitch of the recording equipment.*

[†]*I do not vouch for the correctness of the name P. T. Alridge*

Example 3: Metric contours

"We Shall All Be Reunited" is another Karnes song that demonstrates his unique melodic ornamentation. An examination of the notation for this song reveals that Karnes made use of a wide variety of metric values (example 5), which other old-time singers avoided.

Karnes's style seems to reflect African American influence, though the available biographical data offers no direct evidence for this.[2] Nevertheless, Karnes's approach is certainly unlike the singing styles of the other musicians who came to Bristol to record.

In modern popular music, especially in pop or rock music, melodic phrases often start on a metric location just after the downbeat, sometimes on a fractional value. This is so prevalent in much of the music of our time that it does not seem unusual. In the country group Alabama's "Song of the South," for example, the refrain melody begins metrically on the first upbeat of the first measure (example 6).

If the same melody were presented with no instrumental accompaniment, it is likely, given the aforementioned ideas of Lerdahl and Jackendoff, that the listener would be temporarily confused regarding the meter. Example 6a suggests how the same melodic fragment from "Song of the South" might sound without accompaniment or other rhythmic clues.

In traditional Appalachian music, melodies did not begin on fractional beats after the downbeat. Instead, they started on the downbeat or on an easily discernible upbeat. Of all the songs recorded in Bristol, only one does not adhere to this guideline. Such consistency among all the songs implies that this was likely a regional stylistic characteristic of traditional Appalachian music. In the lone exception, Karnes's recording of "I'm Bound for the Promised Land" (example 7), the first note of each phrase is consistently placed on fractional metric locations just *after* the measure's downbeat (either on the second sixteenth note or the second eighth note of the measure). The

Example 4: Alfred G. Karnes, "To the Work"

effect is not at all unusual to our modern ears, but in this context is quite remarkable and suggests one way in which Karnes foreshadowed future musical trends.

The rhythmic structure of Karnes's performance of "I'm Bound for the Promised Land" is clear because his own guitar accompaniment appears first and establishes the rhythm. It might be said that Karnes's vocal melody relies on this instrumental accompaniment to achieve and maintain rhythmic clarity. If there were no accompaniment, the listener might hear the melody of example 7a, with at least a few moments of uncertainty regarding the precise location of the beat.[3]

Example 5: Alfred G. Karnes, "We Shall All Be Reunited"

It seems unlikely that such a melody could exist. If Karnes had sung this song a cappella (that is, without his guitar accompaniment), he would have changed it a bit to make it easier to understand, or he would have found another way to establish the rhythm, such as by clapping hands. The metric simplicity of almost all old-time Appalachian melodies suggests that traditional Appalachian singing style was based upon a cappella performance. In addition, many old songs, particularly religious ones, were passed on from one generation to the next via printed music. In the American South, simple rhythms were favored in music intended for congregational singing.

Why do singers utilize vocal ornamentation? Perhaps the answer lies in the sense of drama and emotion that ornamentation can help create. In plays, events build to a climax before eventual resolution, and the same principle applies in music. Latter-day country musicians have created drama by adopting a linear structural design. Rather than repeating sections of songs without variation, recent country musicians have added new melodic and textural elements to songs as the songs unfold, changing a song enough to keep listener interest but keeping it predictable enough to maintain coherence.

Example 6: Alabama, "Song of the South"

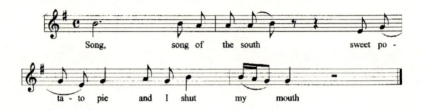

Example 6a: Alabama, "Song of the South" (hypothetical a cappella interpretation).

In contrast, early country musicians almost invariably sang songs bearing strictly repeated patterns. The vast majority of the acts that recorded at the Bristol sessions adhered to this principle, establishing a musical pattern in a given song and sticking with it through the whole song. A good example of this trait is evident in Blind Alfred Reed's recording of "The Wreck of the Virginian" (see example 2). Even though the song clearly has a dramatic text, Reed did not reflect a sense of drama in the vocal melody. Each cycle of the song is melodically nearly identical, even as the lyrics advance the story to its tragic conclusion.

However, in each of his two Bristol sessions recordings, Jimmie Rodgers incorporated a linear song structure that allowed him to reinforce musically the dramatic nature of the lyric. In "The Soldier's Sweetheart" (example 8), Rodgers communicates the sad tale of a young woman whose fiancé was called to serve in World War I and then was killed in action. Each verse of the song's lyrics brings the soldier's tragic fate closer, and the singer represents this dramatic situation in two ways. First, Rodgers sings with a considerable degree of vocal inflection and expressive ornamentation, both of which underscore the emotion of the song.[4]

In addition to employing an ornamented singing style, Rodgers incorporated drama into "The Soldier's Sweetheart" by altering the melody slightly as the song unfolded, overriding the predictable repetitions typical to the traditional old-time style so common in early country music. In fact, Rodgers

Example 7: Alfred G. Karnes, "I'm Bound for the Promised Land"

never sang any two verses of the song with exactly the same melodic line. The example below (example 8a) demonstrates the first few measures of each verse of "The Soldier's Sweetheart" stacked atop each other to reveal how completely he followed this principle in the song.

In "Sleep, Baby, Sleep," the other song he recorded at the Bristol sessions, Rodgers took a different approach to bringing dramatic tension to a song. Because "Sleep, Baby, Sleep" contained no drama in its lyric, Rodgers spent much of the song yodeling, a vocal technique that requires no lyric content per se but that does draw attention to the singer's vocal capabilities. While his contemporaries continued presenting their lyrics in the straight-forward manner of the traditional Appalachian singing style, Rodgers placed his presentation of the song's mood ahead of the lyrics.

Rodgers's structural arrangement of the tune (example 9a) frustrates expectations of a cyclic pattern. After hearing two verses (**A** and **A'**) followed by a yodel sequence (**B**), the listener is prepared for another round of the same. However, consistent with his approach to "The Soldier's Sweetheart,"

Example 7a: Alfred G. Karnes, "I'm Bound for the Promised Land" (hypothetical a cappella interpretation).

Example 8: Jimmie Rodgers, "The Soldier's Sweetheart"

in which he also avoided exact repetition, Rodgers introduces subtle changes in the melody of the third verse (**A"**), as shown in example 9b.

After the third verse of "Sleep, Baby, Sleep," Rodgers repeats the yodeled section (**B**) instead of going on to another verse. By yodeling ahead of schedule, he surprises the listener, increasing interest in the song. Then, as the yodel concluded, Rodgers stretched that section a little further with a new extension of yodeling (**B'**). By bringing in what amounted to a third melodic

Example 8a: Jimmie Rodgers, "The Soldier's Sweetheart" (first four measures of each verse).

passage, he again breaks new ground. By twice upsetting listener expectations in this tune, Rodgers created a linear design and generated real drama. Other traditional Appalachian and early country music singers would perform a dramatic lyric while not overtly emphasizing the drama in their singing style; Rodgers did just the opposite and in the process helped move country music vocals from the emotionally detached Appalachian traditional singing style toward a vocal approach that sanctioned an increased sense of melodrama. The non-cyclical structure of "Sleep, Baby, Sleep" does not seem at all out of place to our modern musical sensibilities, but when compared with the recordings of his contemporaries at the Bristol sessions, Rodgers was clearly trying something new. (Perhaps this explains why it took more takes for Rodgers to achieve finished recordings than anyone else on the Bristol roster.[5])

In recent years, many instrumental breaks in country songs literally "break" away from the melody. However, this was not the case in early country music, where in almost every recorded example that allowed both an instrumental and a vocal melody, the two were essentially identical. Early country musicians did not improvise much or diverge significantly from the established melody. There are many examples of this conservative approach among the songs recorded at the Bristol sessions. Similarly, fiddle tunes recorded in Bristol, such as "Skip to My Lou" and "Billy Grimes the Rover,"

Example 9: Jimmie Rodgers, "Sleep, Baby, Sleep"

verse 1 / verse 2 / yodel sequence / verse 2 / yodel / new yodel

or,

A — A' — B — A" — B — B'

Example 9a: Structural arrangement for "Sleep, Baby, Sleep"

Example 9b: "Sleep, Baby, Sleep" showing details of the subtle melodic change in the second repetition of verse 2.

alternate between sung and instrumental presentations of the melody, and both the vocal and the instrumental sections are essentially the same. Among the musicians who recorded at the 1927 Bristol sessions, Maybelle Carter of the Carter Family was innovative in her approach to performing instrumental melodic breaks on her guitar, but she still preserved the idea that the melody was the main point of the song.[6]

Two songs recorded by Alfred Karnes at Bristol, however, featured arrangements that departed from the old-time tradition of alternating within a given song a vocal melody with a nearly identical instrumental melody. In "The Land Where We'll Never Grow Old," Karnes began the song with a bass-note melodic riff on his guitar that was not related to the song's melody. Next, he proceeded through three verses, each one alternating with the chorus. After the third time through the chorus, Karnes played the introductory bass-note figure again as an instrumental break, then sang the chorus one last time. The arrangement is diagrammed below (example 10):

introductory bass line / verse 1 / chorus / verse 2 / chorus / verse 3 / chorus / introductory bass line returns / chorus (end)

Or,

A — B — C — B' — C — B' — C — A — C

Example 10: Arrangement pattern for "The Land Where We'll Never Grow Old"

"The Land Where We'll Never Grow Old" was fundamentally different from most of the country music songs of that era. First, the bass-note melody was not directly derived from the song's melody and was therefore an instrumental break of the type that became popular among country musicians many years later. Second, by singing a chorus after the break, Karnes departed from the traditional alternation of sections that was the norm in old-time and early country music.

"I'm Bound for the Promised Land" (transcribed earlier as example 7) was another Bristol sessions recording from Karnes containing an instrumental break not derived from the song's melody that acted to vary the song's structural pattern. The transcribed excerpt below represents the accented bass-note melody that Karnes played in that song (example 11). The subsequent diagram suggests how that instrumental melody fit into the song (example 11a).

Example 11: Alfred G. Karnes, "I'm Bound for the Promised Land" (guitar's bass notes from instrumental break).

introductory bass line / verse 1 / chorus / verse 2 / chorus / instrumental break / verse 3 / chorus / verse 4 / chorus / verse 5 / chorus

Or,

$$A - B - C - B' - C - A - B' - C - B' - C - B' - C$$

Example 11a: Arrangement pattern for "I'm Bound for the Promised Land."

A common misconception about Karnes's guitar playing bears reconsideration here. Historical sources indicate that Karnes brought a now-rare instrument known as a harp guitar to the Bristol sessions. His instrument was built by Gibson, which manufactured harp guitars from 1906 to the late 1920s (other luthiers and manufacturers made similar instruments at the time). The harp guitar had a larger body than most acoustic guitars, and the Gibson model featured either six or ten "harp" strings (or sub-bass strings) added to the guitar's usual six. These extra strings were stretched partly over an extension of the sound box and partly over open space rather than over the guitar's fingerboard. In this way, the instrument combined open strings, as used in a harp, with the fretted strings of the guitar. The harp strings were low bass strings and were placed so the player could pluck them in much the same way that he or she might have played the six strings of a standard guitar, although playing the harp strings did require a slightly wider reach.[7]

Awareness that Karnes brought a harp guitar to Bristol, combined with his prominent bass-note work on his Bristol sessions recordings, has usually led to the assumption that he must have used the harp strings to produce the bass notes. However, it might well have been that while Karnes did use the harp guitar, he played only the standard guitar strings and did not use the special features of the instrument. A careful study of Karnes's Bristol recordings suggests this to be the case.

First, the harp strings were intended to sound lower than the guitar's usual bass notes (see the tuning diagram in example 12 below). The bass notes identified in this study and indicated in the transcription of Karnes's recording of "I'm Bound for the Promised Land" (example 11) are not below the guitar's normal range (the reader needs to bear in mind that the guitar is notated an octave higher than it sounds).[8] Karnes likely used a capo on most of his tunes to bring the pitch up. In any event, the bass notes on "I'm Bound for the Promised Land" were not lower than what could be achieved on the usual guitar strings.

Example 12: Tuning for the 6- and 10-stringed Gibson harp guitar.

A second clue as to Karnes's preference for standard guitar strings over the harp strings for playing the bass notes is evidenced in the tone of the bass notes. In "I'm Bound for the Promised Land" and other Karnes songs, those notes have a snapping sound, likely caused by their vibration against the fingerboard of the guitar. Since the harp strings on the harp guitar stretch out over open space, they have nothing to snap against. It is possible to simulate Karnes's tone on the standard guitar, and the bass notes that he played land naturally on the fingerboard of a six-string guitar when one plays using chord voicings similar to those Karnes likely used.

A third clue emerges from the observation that to produce the bass notes of Karnes's guitar break on "I'm Bound for the Promised Land," eleven different pitches are required (example 11). To play such pitches, Karnes would have had to use an alternative tuning for the harp strings as well as different strings from the standard recommended set, since the bass strings would have to have been tuned quite a bit higher than the manufacturer's suggestion.[9] Perhaps he played some of those notes on the guitar's neck and some on the harp strings, but if this was the case, why are the tones of the bass notes so consistent?

Any of these arguments taken alone is not entirely convincing, but taken together they offer strong evidence that, while Karnes owned a harp guitar and played it at the Bristol sessions, he used only the standard guitar strings in these recordings.

Old-time music had a clearly defined approach to melody and rhythm, even though the genre incorporated a wider range of instrumental and vocal combinations than encouraged in modern country music. The old-time singer's job was to present the melody and lyrics with clarity and humility. When the lyrics communicated a dramatic story, old-time singers did not overtly express the drama; they let the words do it. The melody, built on a strong foundation of simple meter, could convey the song by itself; accompaniment was optional.

After the Bristol sessions, country music overturned almost all of the principles of the old-time music from which it evolved. Articulation of the melody in country music today assumes a high degree of rhythmic flexibility, and a steady rhythmic background is needed for preserving metric sense for the listener. Modern country music singers are free to treat rhythm as expressively as they wish; they may make themselves into dramatic characters, or choose songs that project their own persona to the world. Country music singing departed dramatically from its old-time music roots, and such innovators as Rodgers and Karnes helped pave the way for such continual evolution.

Old-time styles, though, are not forgotten. A large number of enthusiasts today try to keep the old tunes alive by playing them, sharing them, and writing about them. Ralph Peer was primarily trying to record songs that could earn a profit, yet he did Appalachian music an invaluable service in Bristol during those two weeks in 1927, producing recordings that honored its past and that continue to shape its future.

Notes

1. Rounder Collective, 114.
2. Donald Lee Nelson, pp. 31–36.

3. Lerdahl and Jackendoff, 79–80.
4. Porterfield, 51.

5. Porterfield, 109.
6. Townsend, 179.
7. John Doan, www.willamette.edu/ ~jdoan/instruments/harpguitar/article3.html.
8. John Doan, www.willamette.edu/

~jdoan/instruments/harpguitar/tuning. html.
9. John Doan, www.willamette.edu/ ~jdoan/instruments/harpguitar/tuning. html.

Bibliography

Cohen, Norm. *Long Steel Rail: The Railroad in American Folksong.* Music edited by David Cohen. 2nd Edition. Chicago: University of Illinois Press, 1981.
Doan, John. "The Harp Guitar in America." Dec. 9, 1998. http://johndoan.com/instruments/harpguitar/article3.html; http://www.willamette.edu/~jdoan/instruments/harpguitar/article3.html
Lerdahl, Fred, and Ray Jackendoff. *A Generative Theory of Tonal Music.* Cambridge: The MIT Press, 1996.
Nelson, Donald Lee. "The Life of Alfred G. Karnes." *John Edwards Memorial Foundation Quarterly* (Volume VIII, Part 1, No. 25) Spring 1972, 31–36.
Porterfield, Nolan. *Jimmie Rodgers: The Life and Times of America's Blue Yodeler.* Urbana and Chicago: University of Illinois Press, 1992.
The Rounder Collective. "The Life of Blind Alfred Reed." *John Edwards Memorial Foundation Quarterly* (Volume VII, Part 3, No. 23) Autumn 1971, 113–115.
Townsend, Thomas. "The Carter Family's Rhythmic Asymmetry." *Country Music Annual 2001.* Charles K. Wolfe and James E. Akenson, editors. Lexington: University Press of Kentucky, 161–187.
Wolfe, Charles K. "Event Songs." In *Reading Country Music,* edited by Cecelia Tichi. Durham, N.C.: Duke University Press, 1998.
_____. "Ralph Peer at Work: the Victor 1927 Bristol Sessions," *Old Time Music* 5 Summer 1972, 10–15.

PART V

After the Bristol Sessions

18. The Rest of the Story: Other Early Recording Sessions in the Tri-Cities Area

Charles K. Wolfe

I. Peer's 1928 Return to Bristol

By October 1928, little more than a year after his groundbreaking sessions at Bristol, Ralph Peer had watched two of his discoveries, Jimmie Rodgers and the Carter Family, become nationally known recording stars. Both acts had been brought north to record in the big Victor Talking Machine Company studios at Camden, New Jersey, where Rodgers recorded his "career" song, "Blue Yodel" ("T for Texas") in November 1927, and the Carters had recorded their theme song, "Keep on the Sunny Side" in May 1928. By now, in fact, Rodgers had recorded some twenty-three songs in addition to his two at Bristol, and the Carters had done twelve additional songs. Furthermore, Peer had been sufficiently impressed with other Bristol musicians to also bring them to Camden for additional sessions. Blind Alfred Reed came up in December 1927 to record four more songs, two topical ballads and the social commentary song "Why Do You Bob Your Hair, Girls?" In May 1928, the Johnson Brothers (Charles and Paul) came to Camden to do an additional eight songs, including the local murder ballad, "The Crime of the D'Autremont Brothers." The black harmonica player El Watson actually appeared in Victor's New York City studios, where he did an additional four pieces in May 1928. In February 1928, at a temporary studio in Atlanta,

Georgia, Peer summoned Bristol-based musicians the Tenneva Ramblers (featuring vocals by Claude Grant) for six additional sides, and the Stoneman Family for eleven more sides. All this activity reflected the commercial success and artistic quality of the musicians (including those lesser known than Rodgers or the Carters) who recorded at Victor's 1927 field sessions in Bristol.

In addition to supervising these and dozens of other sessions in Victor's main studios at Camden and New York City, Peer continued his field recording trips. In fact, when he left Bristol on August 5, 1927, he did not immediately head back to New York. His crew packed up their gear and by August 9 had set up their next field recording studio in Charlotte, North Carolina. There, Peer recorded sides by the string band known as the Carolina Tar Heels, the north Georgia band the Georgia Yellow Hammers, and a rarely recorded African American string band featuring Andrew and Jim Baxter. Leaving Charlotte on August 16, Peer moved on to Savannah, where beginning August 22, he recorded such acts as a local jazz band, the remarkable pianist Sugar Underwood, and the cowboy singer Carl Sprague. Peer's trip finally ended on August 27, over a month after it had begun.

Peer started 1928 with a field recording session trip to Memphis and then to Atlanta; in Memphis, he recorded mostly blues and gospel music, by the Memphis Jug Band, Jim Jackson, Tommy Johnson, Gus Cannon, and Frank Stokes, among others, while in Atlanta, he recorded mostly old-time acts, including the Tenneva Ramblers, the Stoneman Family, and the Georgia Yellow Hammers. In August 1928, Peer returned to Memphis; then he traveled to Nashville (for the only recording session held in that city prior to World War II), to Atlanta, and, in late October, back to Bristol.

Peer pulled into Bristol on Friday afternoon, October 26, 1928, with what the newspapers described as "half a carload full of equipment." He rented a different location for the 1928 sessions than for the 1927 sessions— the Peters Building, located behind the City Bank. Whereas in 1927 Peer deliberately utilized the media to attract new musical acts, for the 1928 sessions he emphasized in a local newspaper that "only seventy-five records would be made this year," and that "these had already been booked" (*Bristol Herald Courier*, Sunday, 10/28/28). For whatever reasons, though, Peer only recorded 65 sides during his weeklong stay, and of those only 47 were eventually released— certainly a disappointing outcome when compared to the previous year's harvest. Ten individuals or groups not present in 1927 were recorded at this new session.

Peer told the local reporters a version of what must be the first mythologizing of the Jimmie Rodgers story, which would become legend. "Last year when the same crew was working in Bristol, they ran across some very fortunate material which during the last year has been developed into leading characters." The story continues:

Referring to one of the characters which he ran into last year, Mr. Peer said that Jimmy Rogers [*sic*], one of his exceptions, had been running around in the mountains playing at most anyplace where music would be accepted, and that one day Jimmy happened to pick up one of the Bristol papers and saw where the recording crew was working in Bristol. Bumming his way here, he asked for a tryout to see what he could do. He was laughed at, but being an exceptional singer and yodeler, he was given a chance. He combined these two together and produced his first record, the "Blue Yodel." He was paid for his performance and went back into the mountains.

Later when the record was published, the public went wild over the piece, and Jimmy was called to the factory to work regularly for the company.

Now he is drawing over $15,000 a year, and is on a circuit booked for twelve weeks, making over half a thousand a week. He produces a record every month for the Victor Company and is Gene Austin's keenest rival.

A. G. Karnes

In late October 1928, Alfred G. Karnes returned to Bristol to participate in Ralph Peer's second round of field recording sessions, as did several of Karnes's fellow musicians from the 1927 Bristol sessions (specifically, Ernest Phipps, Uncle Eck Dunford, and the Stoneman Family). Courtesy JEMF Collection, in the Southern Folklife Collection, University of North Carolina at Chapel Hill.

Rodgers, of course, had not recorded his "Blue Yodel" in Bristol, but in Camden, New Jersey. Nor did he leave the recording session to go "back into the mountains." To the contrary, Rodgers' biographer Nolan Porterfield has verified that Rodgers and his wife left for Washington, D.C., the day after the session.

Table 1 provides the complete list of recordings made at the 1928 Bristol sessions, compiled from Victor's files.

Table 1. Victor's 1928 Bristol Sessions

October 27, 1928

| 47229 | Smyth County Ramblers | My Name Is Ticklish Reuben | V- 40144 |
| 47230 | Smyth County Ramblers | 'Way Down In Alabama | V-40144 |

October 28, 1928

47231	Alfred G. Karnes	The Sinner Sinks in Sad Despair	uniss.
47232	Alfred G. Karnes	Do Not Wait Til I'm Laid 'Neath the Clay	V-40327
47233	Alfred G. Karnes	Days of My Childhood Plays	V-40076
47234	Alfred G. Karnes	We Shall All Be Reunited	V-40076
47235	Alfred G. Karnes	That's Why the Boys Leave the Farm	uniss.
47236	Alfred G. Karnes	Clouds of Glory	uniss.

October 29, 1928

47237	Ernest Phipps & His Congreg.	If The Light Has Gone Out in Your Soul	V-40010
47238	Ernest Phipps & His Congreg.	Went Up in the Clouds of Heaven	V-40106
47239	Ernest Phipps & His Congreg.	The Firing Line	uniss.
47240	Ernest Phipps & His Congreg.	I Know That Jesus Set Me Free	V-40106
47241	Ernest Phipps & His Congreg.	Shine on Me	B-5540
47242	Alfred G. Karnes	The City of Gold	uniss.

October 30, 1928

47243	Ernest Phipps & His Congreg.	Bright Tomorrow	V-40010 B-5273
47244	Ernest Phipps & His Congreg.	Cloud and Fire	uniss.
47245	Ernest Phipps & His Congreg.	A Little Talk with Jesus	B-5275
47246	Howard and Peak, the Blind Musicians	I Cannot Be Your Sweetheart	V-40189
47247	Howard and Peak	Three Black Sheep	V-40189
47248	Stoneman Family	Beautiful Isle O'er the Sea	uniss.
47249	Stoneman Family	Willie, We Have Missed You	uniss.
47250	Clarence Greene	Goodnight, Darling	V-40141
47251	Clarence Greene	Little Bunch of Roses	V-40141
47252	Stoneman Family	The Fate of Shelly and Smith	uniss.
47253	Stoneman Family	Broken-Hearted Lover	V-40030
47254	Uncle Eck Dunford	Angeline the Baker	V-40060
47255	Uncle Eck Dunford	Old Shoes and Leggin's	V-40060

October 31, 1928

47256	Stoneman Family	Minnie Brown	uniss.
47257	Stoneman Family	We Parted by the Riverside	V-40030
47258	Stoneman Family	Down to Jordan and Be Saved	V-40078
47259	Stoneman Family	There's a Light Lit Up in Galilee	V-40078
47260	Stoneman Family	Going Up the Mountain After Liquor — Part 1	V-40116
47261	Stoneman Family	Going Up the Mountain After Liquor — Part 2	V-40116
47262	Stoneman Family	Spanish Merchant's Daughter	V-40206
47263	Stoneman Family	Twilight Is Stealing	uniss.

November 1, 1928

47264	Stoneman Family	Too Late	V-40206
47265	Stoneman Family	I Should Like to Marry	uniss.
47266	Smith Brothers	There's No One to Care for Me (William and Roosevelt)	uniss.
47267	Stamps Quartet	I'll Be Happy	V-40029

November 2, 1928

47268	Stamps Quartet	Like the Rainbow	V-40122
47269	Stamps Quartet	Because I Love Him	V-40090
47270	Stamps Quartet	Come to the Savior	V-40062
47271	Stamps Quartet	Do Your Best, Then Wear A Smile	V-40122
47272	Stamps Quartet	We Shall Reach Home	V-40062
47273	Smith Brothers	My Mother Is Waiting for Me in Heaven Above	V-40201
47274	Smith Brothers	She Has Climbed the Golden Stairs	V-40201
47275	Palmer Sisters	We Shall Sing on That Shore	V-40037
47276	Palmer Sisters	Singing the Story of Grace	C-1566
47277	Palmer Sisters	Help Me to Find the Way	C-1566
47278	Palmer Sisters	He Will Be with Me	V-40037
47279	Stephen Tartar — Harry Gay	Bonnie Blues	V-38017
47280	Stephen Tartar — Harry Gay	Unknown Blues	V-38017
47281	Carolina Twins	Where Is My Mama?	V-40044
47282	Carolina Twins	When You Go A-Courtin'	V-40044
47283	Carolina Twins	I Sat Upon the River Bank	V-40098

November 3, 1928

47284	Fred Pendleton –Clyde Meadows	The Last Farewell	uniss.
47285	Carolina Twins	New Orleans Is the Town I Like Best	V-40123
47286	Carolina Twins	She Tells Me That I Am Sweet	V-40123
47287	Carolina Twins	Mr. Brown, Here I Come	V-40098

November 4, 1928

47288	Shortbuckle Roark and Family	Broken-Hearted	uniss.

47289	Shortbuckle Roark and Family	I Truly Understand, You Love Another Man	V-40023
47290	Shortbuckle Roark and Family	Terrible Day	uniss.
47291	Shortbuckle Roark and Family	My Mother's Hands	V-40023
47292	George Roark	I Ain't a Bit Drunk	uniss.
47293	George Roark	Hook and Line	uniss.

Of the "new" ensembles that Peer recorded at the 1928 Bristol sessions, one of the most appealing was a string band called the Smyth County Ramblers; it was built around the considerable banjo-playing skills of Jack Reedy, as well as around two Bristol musicians, fiddler Jack Pierce (from the Tenneva Ramblers, who had recorded at the 1927 Bristol sessions) and guitarist Malcom Warley. They were joined by a second guitarist, Carl Cruise, from nearby Damascus, Virginia. Reedy, who would become one of the most recorded and publicized central Appalachian musicians, was born c. 1895 in the Grassy Creek community in North Carolina, near the Virginia line. As a boy, he had learned to play the banjo on a homemade instrument with a head made of stretched groundhog skin. He spent most of his life near Marion, Virginia, in Smyth County (hence the band's name).

Reedy had first recorded in 1927 with the popular vaudeville band from Galax, Virginia, known as the Hill Billies, using his finger-picking style to interpret such favorites as "Cluck Old Hen." In February 1928, he traveled to Ashland, Kentucky, to make records for the Brunswick label with his own band: Jack Reedy and His Walker Mountain String Band featuring two other well-known Bristol musicians, Fred and Henry Roe. When Peer scheduled the Reedy-Pierce band as his first recording act in the 1928 Bristol sessions, he was hardly experimenting with unproven talent. As in 1927, Peer began his sessions with acts he knew he could rely upon. "My Name Is Ticklish Reuben," featuring singing by Pierce and Warley, was an old 1902 vaudeville comic song popularized by Cal Stewart — the sort of song that was popular with young string bands in the 1920s. Likewise, "'Way Down in Alabama" was a sentimental song smoothly sung by Pierce; the song was later recorded by the Carter Family as "No More the Moon Shines on Lorena" (this is not the popular Civil War song "Lorena," but a song dating from c. 1889). In 1933, Reedy and Frank Bevins would win more fame at the White Top Folk Festival by playing for First Lady Eleanor Roosevelt and by making a Paramount newsreel. The Smyth County Ramblers (under the name the Southern Buccaneers) would later become a leading string band in southwest Virginia.

Another group that Peer had recorded earlier and that he recorded again at the 1928 Bristol sessions was a duo called the Carolina Twins, which recorded six sides, including the popular coupling of "Where Is My Mama" and "When You Go A-Courtin'." The Carolina Twins were Gwen Foster and David O. Fletcher; Foster had been a member of the well-known Carolina Tar Heels, whom Peer had recorded in Charlotte a few days after he had left Bristol in 1927. Few details are known about Foster's background other than that he was a mill worker from the Gastonia area in North Carolina; that his friend, fellow musician and songwriter Dave McCarn, remembered Foster as "dark-skinned"; and that he was nicknamed "Chinee" because of his oriental appearance. He was best known as a remarkable harmonica player, but he was also a good singer and guitarist. He and Fletcher had first recorded for Peer in Atlanta during February 1928 as the Carolina Twins. Both men probably came from the Piedmont region in North Carolina, both had a fondness for ragtime and jazz-flavored songs, and both, when playing guitar, revealed the influence of African American Piedmont-style guitarists. In the 1930s, Foster recorded with another East Tennessee singer, Clarence "Tom" Ashley. With the exception of "Where Is My Mama" and "When You Go A-Courtin'," the songs that the Carolina Twins recorded in Bristol were not traditional, being either originals or relatively new compositions.

Yet another group that Peer had already worked with was the Stamps Quartet, a gospel group whose vocal style was radically different from the ragged Pentecostal sounds of Ernest Phipps and his singers, the archaic "mountain" singing style of the Stoneman Family, or the country-tinged solo singing of Alfred Karnes. The Stamps Quartet represented the new movement in Southern gospel that had grown out of the singing schools of Texas, Arkansas, and Tennessee, where local singers were trained to sing with precision from shape note songbooks issued by companies like James D. Vaughan and Stamps-Baxter. By the end of World War I, these publishers, selling hundreds of thousands of their songbooks to rural churches and singing conventions, had developed the concept of having some of their best songwriters, editors, and singers form quartets and travel around the country performing samples of the new songs from the latest songbook. Gradually, rural churchgoers developed a preference for listening to the quartets over singing the songs themselves, and by the late 1920s, some quartets were becoming stars, appearing on radio as well as on commercial recordings.

The Stamps Quartet was led by bass vocalist Frank H. Stamps, who with his brother V. O. Stamps had recently founded in Dallas the Stamps-Baxter publishing company, which would emerge as one of the most influential music publishing firms of the twentieth century. Peer had recorded the quartet during October 1927 in Atlanta, after Stamps had talked him into recording one of the new songbook compositions, "Give the World a Smile Each Day." To Peer's surprise, the record became a strong seller; he recorded the group again in February 1928, and scheduled them for further sides at Bristol — including a follow-up to "Give the World a Smile Each Day" entitled "Do Your Best Then Wear a Smile." Peer scheduled the new Stamps Quartet songs for the first releases from the 1928 Bristol sessions, in March 1929. One of the releases by the Stamps Quartet, V-40062 ("Come to the Savior"/ "We Shall Reach Home"), became the best-selling record from the sessions, with sales of 13,700 copies.

There were fewer "discoveries" on Peer's second trip to Bristol. One of the more memorable acts was a black duo comprised of Stephen Tarter and Harry Gay. Tarter (c. 1893–c. 1935) was born near Knoxville, Tennessee, and, according to research by scholar Kip Lornell, learned to play fiddle, mandolin, guitar, and piano. Tarter met Harry Gay, a native of Gate City, Virginia, in Johnson City, Tennessee, in 1924, and the two performed together over the next decade. They often played for dances in both white and black communities, and regularly performed at coal camps. Peer only recorded two sides by Tarter and Gay, both blues, and released them on Victor's 38000 "race" series. Gay continued to live in Johnson City until his death in 1983.

Another of Peer's finds in 1928 was an eastern Kentucky banjoist and singer, George "Shortbuckle" Roark (1905–1990), who recorded two sides with his family singing along with him. A native of Pineville (near Middlesborough), Roark later gained further recognition as one of the "sources" pictured in a songbook published by Bradley Kincaid, and he also recorded for the Library of Congress. His best-known song was the hauntingly lyric "I Truly Understand You Love Another Man"; during the urban folk revival of the 1960s, that song became part of the repertoire of the New Lost City Ramblers, and was included in the group's popular songbook.

According to the surviving files of the Victor company, most of the releases from the 1928 Bristol sessions sold in the neighborhood of 4,000–5,000 copies — figures not so much a reflection of the quality of the recordings as of the fact that by now all the major companies were flooding the market with releases of old-time music. One of the popular recordings from the 1928 Bristol sessions seems to have been V-40010, Ernest Phipps's "Bright Tomorrow" backed with "If the Light Has Gone Out in Your Soul" (11,000 copies) and the Stamps Quartet recordings. (By comparison, at the same time records by the Carter Family and Jimmie Rodgers records were selling 50,000 copies or more.) Most of the 1928 Bristol recordings were released through 1929, and remained readily available for only a couple of years. A few of these recordings eventually were reissued. Ernest Phipps's "Shine on Me" was included by compiler Harry Smith in his *Anthology of American Folk Music,* a seminal collection that was first issued on LP on the

Folkways label in 1952 remained in print through its reissue on CD in 1997. This collection of recordings from the 1920s influenced several generations of musicians, and brought songs like "Bright Tomorrow" to a new and larger audience than that of the original 78s. Another recording included in Harry Smith's compilation was Uncle Eck Dunford's "Old Shoes and Leggins," a song dating back to 1730. That song was a favorite of the eccentric Dunford, who often wore overshoes even in the summer. Yet a third piece included in the *Anthology of American Folk Music* was "The Spanish Merchant's Daughter," recorded as a duet between Ernest Stoneman and his wife Hattie. Another song recorded by Dunford in Bristol in 1928, "Angeline the Baker" (which was either a garbled version of Stephen Foster's "Angelina Baker" or a deliberate parody of it), though not included in the Smith compilation, entered Appalachian tradition to become a standard. Even today, the song is commonly called "Angeline the Baker" among Southern fiddlers, and Dunford's was the first recording of it.

All told, the differences between the 1927 and 1928 Bristol sessions reflect the growing commercialization of the then-new country music industry. In the 1928 sessions, there were far fewer walk-ins who auditioned on the spot and were accepted; Peer was taking fewer chances, and had lined up the recording roster ahead of time. He recorded fewer traditional songs, and more newly composed or arranged songs. Nearly absent at the 1928 Bristol sessions were the freewheeling string bands like the West Virginia Coon Hunters or the Shelor Family; in their place were vocal groups and soloists, reflecting the emerging styles that would dominate country music in the 1930s. In the little over a year between the 1927 Bristol sessions and the 1928 Bristol sessions, hundreds of Southern musicians had trooped into makeshift studios across the South, hoping to achieve some of the success of the Carter Family and Jimmie Rodgers. Few did, but along the way across the South, these musicians left clear evidence of how fast the music was developing.

II. Columbia Records in Johnson City

Ralph Peer's biggest rival during the 1920s was his counterpart at Columbia Records, Frank B. Walker. A native of upstate New York, the soft-spoken Walker (1889–1963) was in later years best known as the man who first recognized the potential marketability of Hank Williams Sr. Long before that, Walker had emerged as an architect of Columbia's blues and old-time music series; joining the company as an A & R man in 1921, he "discovered" and signed such musicians as blues singer Bessie Smith and jazz pianist Clarence Williams. In 1924, Walker recorded his first white old-time musicians, north Georgia fiddler Gid Tanner and singer-guitarist Riley Puckett. Walker began making regular recording trips to Atlanta the following year, and in 1926, he built the most popular string band of the era, the Skillet Lickers around Tanner and Puckett.

Also in 1925, Walker created at Columbia a separate numerical series of what he called "Old Familiar Tunes and Novelties" featuring such groups as the Skillet Lickers, Charlie Poole and the North Carolina Ramblers, and the Blue Ridge Highballers. A year before Peer embarked on his trips for Victor, Walker had dozens of releases in his catalogue, and some of them, such as releases by the gospel group Smith's Sacred Singers and the Skillet Lickers, were selling over 250,000 copies. Although Walker had made Atlanta his main southern base, where he maintained a semi-permanent studio, he had also conducted field recording sessions in Dallas, New Orleans, and Memphis.

Walker and his crew arrived in Johnson City, Tennessee, during the second week of October 1928 — barely two weeks before Peer returned to nearby Bristol to begin the 1928 Bristol sessions. In addition to his engineers, Walker brought an assistant from Atlanta, Bill Brown, who had helped develop the Skillet Lickers and who had even appeared on some of their recordings. Making the John Sevier Hotel their headquarters, Walker did something for which Peer was credited but which the latter never actually did: Walker published an advertisement in the local newspaper. "Can you sing or play old-time music?" the ad asked. "Musicians of unusual ability — Small dance combinations — Singers — Novelty players, Etc. are invited to come to auditions on Saturday, October 13. This is an actual try-out for the purpose of making Columbia Records."

Can You Sing or Play Old-Time Music?

Musicians of Unusual Ability --- Small Dance Combinations--- Singers --- Novelty Players, Etc.

Are Invited

To call on Mr. Walker or Mr. Brown of the Columbia Phonograph Company at 334 East Main Street, Johnson City, on Saturday, October 13th, 1928—9 A. M. to 5. P. M.

This is an actual try-out for the purpose of making Columbia Records.

You may write in advance to 'E. B. Walker, Care of John Sevier Hotel, Johnson City, or call without appointment at address and on date mentioned above.

"Can you sing or play old-time music?" An announcement published in the local Johnson City newspaper attempting to draw in musicians for the 1928 Johnson City sessions for Columbia Records. Courtesy Columbia Records.

Downtown Johnson City, Tennessee, where producer Frank B. Walker held two different field recording sessions for the Columbia label in October 1928 and in October 1929. Collection of Charles K. Wolfe.

Walker worked faster in Johnson City than Peer had in Bristol. Over four days — Monday, October 15, through Thursday, October 18 — Walker managed to record some 67 masters, almost as many as Peer had made in two weeks during the 1927 Bristol sessions. Unlike with Victor's 1927 and 1928 Bristol sessions, we do not have preserved in the Columbia files any "session sheets" for the Johnson City sessions. On the first day of the latter sessions, Walker completed 16 masters, so he could not have had much time for auditions. Presumably, these had been held on the Saturday and Sunday of that week, or the acts had been approved in advance. The newspaper advertisement mentions that the sessions were held at "334 E. Main Street" in downtown Johnson City (a site later demolished for the construction of a highway ramp). One of the participants in the 1929 Johnson City sessions recalled that the recordings were held in a little building that had been a cream separating station.

In later years, Walker reflected on his temporary studios and how they helped break the ice with musicians who had little notion about what making records involved. "In many cases, they hadn't the slightest idea of what it was all about. So you had to give them an atmosphere that it was home, so you didn't pick a fancy place to record in. You usually took the upstairs of some old building where it looked pretty terrible. You hung some drapes and curtains and you also made it look and act a bit like home. You brought in a little mountain dew to take care of colds or any hoarseness that might happen, and also to remove their fear of strangers doing this kind of work. You tried to make them feel at home...."

Most of Walker's groups came to Johnson City from nearby Appalachian cities, town, and farms. The Grant Brothers — the same band that Peer recorded as the Tenneva Ramblers — were based in Bristol. The string band the Roane County Ramblers journeyed from just west of Knoxville, a little over a hundred miles distant. Fiddler Charlie Bowman and his daughters lived in or near Bristol, while the McCartt Brothers and Patterson came from just north of Knoxville. A large contingent traveled to Johnson City from Kentucky, especially from the area around Corbin. Richard Harold, Earl Shirkey, and Roy Harper (aka Roy Harvey) arrived from West Virginia, while Clarence Greene came from North Carolina. In contrast to Peer's 1928 sessions in Bristol, Walker's 1928 sessions in Johnson City still included a sizeable number of string bands, and a fair number of songs descended from the oral tradition. Where Peer pushed his acts to come up with more modern, original songs, Walker had a rather romantic attitude toward the Southern and Appalachian music of that era. As he explained in an interview with Mike Seeger, "You see, what is generally not understood, Mike, is that a songwriter in the South or in the hills is different than a songwriter in the north or in the cities. Primarily he's a poet. Up here, a man may be a musician. Down there they write the words first."

A complete list of the music recorded during the 1928 Johnson City sessions, as reconstructed from master numbers by the author, appears in table 2.

Table 2. Columbia's 1928 Johnson City Sessions

Monday, October 15

147176	Shell Creek Quartet	My Boyhood Days	15355
147177	Shell Creek Quartet	Back Where the Old Home Stands	15355
147178	Grant Brothers	When a Man Is Married	15322
147179	Grant Brothers	Good-Bye My Honey I'm Gone	15460
147180	Grant Brothers	Tell It to Me	15322
147181	Grant Brothers	Johnson Boys	15460
147182	Roane County Ramblers	Home Town Blues	15328
147183	Roane County Ramblers	Southern Number 111	15328
147184	Roane County Ramblers	Step High Waltz	15377
147185	Roane County Ramblers	Tennessee Waltz	15377
147186	Renus Rich & Carl Bradshaw	Goodbye Sweetheart	15341
147187	Renus Rich & Carl Bradshaw	Sleep Baby Sleep	15341
147188	Clarence Greene/Wise Bros.	Pride of the Ball	15679

147189	Clarence Greene/		
	Wise Bros.	Kitty Waltz	15679
147190	Clarence Greene	Johnson City Blues	15461
147191	Clarence Greene	Ninety-Nine Years in Jail	15461

Tuesday, October 16

147192	Ira Yates	You'll Never Get to Heaven with	uniss
		Your Powder and Paint	
147193	Ira Yates	The Weary Gambler	uniss.
147194	Uncle Nick Decker	Parody of Home Sweet Home	uniss
147195	Uncle Nick Decker	She Never Came Back	uniss
147196	Proximity String Quartet	Lindy	15533
147197	Proximity String Quartet	Louise	15533
147198	[untraced]		
147199	[untraced]		
147200	Hardin and Grindstaff	Single Girl — Married Girl	uniss
147201	Hardin and Grindstaff	Seven Years	uniss
147198	Greensboro Boys Quartet	Sing Me a Song of the Sunny South	15507
147199	Greensboro Boys Quartet	Sweet Little Girl of Mine	15507
147200	[untraced]		
147201	[untraced]		
147202	Richard Harold	The Battleship Maine	15586
147203	Richard Harold	The Fisher's Maid	15586
147204	Richard Harold	Sweet Bird	15426
147205	Richard Harold	Mary Dear	15426
147206	Bowman Sisters	My Old Kentucky Home	15473
147207	Bowman Sisters	Swanee River	15473
147208	Charlie Bowman	Roll on Buddy	15357
	and his Brothers		
147209	Charlie Bowman	Gonna Raise the Ruckus Tonight	15357
	and his Brothers		

Wednesday, October 17

147210	Bill and Belle Reed	You Shall Be Free	15336
147211	Bill and Belle Reed	Old Lady and the Devil	15336
147212	The Reed Children	I'll Be All Smiles Tonight	15525
147213	The Reed Children	I Once Did Have a Sweetheart	15525
147214	The Reed Family	A Few More Years	uniss
147215	The Reed Family	Bright and Golden Light	uniss
147216	Hodges Bros.	Dog-Gone Mule	uniss
147217	Hodges Bros.	What Are You Going to Do with Baby?	uniss
147218	Hodges Quartet	I'll Go Flipping Through the Pearly Gates	uniss
147219	Hodges Quartet	You Can't Make a Monkey Out of Me	uniss
147220	Bailey Briscoe	The Joke Song	uniss
147221	Bailey Briscoe	Times Are Gettin Hard	uniss
147222	Rbt Hoke/Vernal Vest	In the Shadow of the Pines	uniss
147223	Rbt Hoke/Vernal Vest	Bye and Bye You Will Forget Me	uniss
147224	McVay and Johnson	Aint Gonna Lay My Armor Down	15370
147225	McVay and Johnson	I'll Be Ready When the	15370
		Bridegroom Comes	

Thursday, October 18

147226	Earl Shirkey & Roy Harper	Steamboat Man	15326
147227	Earl Shirkey & Roy Harper	When Roses Bloom for the Bootlegger	15326
147228	Earl Shirkey & Roy Harper	Poor Little Joe	15376
147229	Earl Shirkey & Roy Harper	We Parted at the Gate	15376
147230	George Roark	I Ain't a Bit Drunk	15383
147231	George Roark	My Old Coon Dog	15383
147232	Ed Helton Singers	A Storm on the Sea	15327
147233	Ed Helton Singers	My Old Cottage Home	15327
147234	Garland Bros./Grindstaff	Just Over the River	15680
147235	Garland Bros./Grindstaff	Beautiful	15680
147236	Dewey Golden & His Kentucky Buzzards	Big Sandy Valley	uniss
147237	Dewey Golden & His Kentucky Buzzards	Going Down to Corbin	uniss
147238	The Holiness Singers	Mother Dear Has Gone Away	uniss
147239	The Holiness Singers	Mother Is Gone	uniss
147240	Frank Shelton	Someone Else May Be There	uniss
147241	Frank Shelton	Why Have You Left Me Lonely	uniss
147242	McCartt Bros/Patterson	Green Valley Waltz	15454
147243	McCartt Bros/Patterson	Over the Sea Waltz	15454

As with the releases from the 1928 Victor sessions at Bristol, company files actually preserved sales figures for all of the Columbia releases. Since the taste of the record-buying public in 1928 differed from the aesthetics of modern traditional music fans, it is interesting to identify and analyze the hits from those sessions. As with the 1928 Victor recording sessions, most Columbia releases from the 1928 Johnson City sessions sold between 4,000 and 5,000 copies — a far cry from Walker's first Skillet Lickers recordings, which often had sold more than 100,000 copies per individual release just two years earlier. But by far the best-seller from this session was Columbia 15326, coupling two songs — "Steamboat Man" and "When the Roses Bloom Again for the Bootlegger" — by the singing duo of Roy Harper and Earl Shirkey. This release sold some 72,500 copies — ten times the average sales figure for the sessions. Both songs were actually parodies of earlier old-time favorites: "Steamboat Man" was a rewriting of a blues-based song commonly called "K.C. Railroad," while "When The Roses Bloom Again for the Bootlegger" (apparently the hit side) was a clever rewriting of the popular Victorian parlor song "When the Roses Bloom Again."

"Roy Harper" was a pseudonym for Roy Harvey, a 36-year-old former railroad engineer from Monroe County, West Virginia. Harvey had developed into a talented guitar soloist and singer, and had been playing regu-

Columbia *"New Process"* Records
REG. U. S. PAT. OFF.

ROANE COUNTY RAMBLERS

LUTHER BRANDON, *Guitar*
HOWARD WYATT, *Banjo*

J. R. McCARROLL, *Fiddle*
JOHN L. KELLY, *Mandolin*

TAKE a good look, ladies and gentlemen, at this bright bunch of boys, with the smiles that put Rockwood, Tennessee, on the musical map.

The man with the fiddle is the famous McCarroll, of "McCarroll's Breakdown," the champion breakdown artist of the South.

ROANE COUNTY RAMBLERS

And yes, girls, Howard Wyatt is as good a catch as he looks. He sings, twigs a wicked banjo, and manages the tours of the other Ramblers on a wide and successful circuit.

McCARROLL'S BREAKDOWN GREEN RIVER MARCH—Instrumentals	} 15438-D
ROANE COUNTY RAG EVERYBODY TWO STEP—Dance Music	} 15398-D
TENNESSEE WALTZ STEP HIGH WALTZ	} 15377-D
SOUTHERN No. 111 HOME TOWN BLUES—Vocals and Instrumentals	} 15328-D

VIVA-TONAL RECORDING. THE RECORDS WITHOUT SCRATCH

[37]

An advertisement promoting records by the Roane County Ramblers, the most important act to be "discovered" at the 1928 Johnson City sessions. Based in the hills west of Knoxville, Tennessee, the Ramblers returned to Johnson City one year later to make additional recordings for Frank B. Walker and Columbia Records during the 1929 Johnson City sessions. Courtesy Guthrie T. Meade Collection, in the Southern Folklife Collection, University of North Carolina at Chapel Hill.

larly and recording with North Carolina's renowned old-time singer, Charlie Poole. Harvey also had started recording with Poole's band under his own name, and had just completed a session for Brunswick in Ashland, Kentucky, in February 1928 — a possible reason for the pseudonym. Of the musicians who recorded at the Johnson City sessions, Harvey was the closest to being a slick professional, and the success of a topical song involving prohibition and moonshine recalls Walker's earlier successes as a producer, having been responsible for such important "event" songs as "The Death of Floyd Collins."

The Johnson City sessions also resulted in several influential recordings by some of the greatest of the Tennessee string bands. Undoubtedly, the biggest discovery of the 1928 sessions in Johnson City was a group from the hills west of Knoxville, the Roane County Ramblers. The Ramblers — fiddler Uncle Jimmy McCarroll, guitarist Luke Brandon, mandolin player and manager John Kelly, and banjoist Howard Wyatt — were a strictly regional dance and contest string band, albeit a very accomplished one. Their fiddler, Jimmy McCarroll, had learned from his part–Cherokee grandmother, as well as from both his parents, and he played with a wild, driving abandon that calls to mind such north Georgia fiddlers as Earl Johnson and the Skillet Lickers. The group's most popular recording was "Southern No. 111," which McCarroll had written to celebrate a train that ran from Knoxville to Danville, Kenucky. Walker was impressed enough with the band's skills and record sales to invite them back for two more sessions in later years.

The second exceptional string band recorded in Johnson City in 1928 was the same group that had recorded as the Tenneva Ramblers at the 1927 Bristol sessions. During the year since those sessions, the Bristol-based group — by now known as the Grant Brothers — continued to work up new material, and in late 1928, the group was tighter and more cohesive. Of the four songs The Grant Brothers recorded in Johnson City, two became old-time classics. One was "Johnson Boys," a traditional East Tennessee Civil War song that had evolved from the old Irish song "Dorian's Ass." Later picked up by bluegrass bands (including Flatt and Scruggs), "Johnson Boys" became a favorite during the urban folk revival of the 1960s. The other popular record from the Grant Brothers was "Tell It to Me," a song about cocaine adapted by the Grants from an older African American song "Take a Whiff on Me."

Another side from the 1928 Johnson City sessions that attracted new generations of fans was Bill and Belle Reed's "Old Lady and the Devil." Where the Reeds came from is unclear, but some evidence suggests central Kentucky. Bill and Belle Reed recorded two sides, and their children made two sides by themselves — a rare instance of children being featured on commercial releases of old-time music. "The Old Lady and the Devil," sung by Bill Reed to his own guitar accompaniment, is one of the few traditional British ballads to be recorded by a commercial company during the 1920s. Known commonly as "The Farmer's Curst Wife," the ballad was widely known in Appalachia. In 1952, Reed's recording of the ballad was chosen for inclusion in Harry Smith's *Anthology of American Folk Music.*

Other noteworthy performances from these sessions included "Johnson City Blues" by Clarence Greene, a singer-guitarist from western North Carolina. A group called the Proximity String Quartet recorded two vaudeville songs, "Louise" and "Lindy"; while little is known about the band, notices in a trade publication from that period refer to a touring vaudeville act by the same name, composed of two white and two black musicians. If this was the same group, these two Johnson City recordings would mark one of the first times white and black country musicians recorded together.

One major failure in the 1928 Johnson City sessions came when a music store owner from Corbin, Kentucky, Dewey Golden, transported a group of local musicians to Johnson City. Golden promised Columbia he could sell a lot of records by these musicians, which included an excellent string band led by the Hodges brothers, as well as legendary banjoist Bailey Briscoe and singer Frank Shelton. (Indeed, one of the Hodges brothers, Ralph, moved to the West Coast and became a widely known bandleader for Decca Records in the mid–1930s; his brother Ernest moved to Atlanta, where he taught, played on the radio with Riley Puckett among other musicians, and eventually settled in Waynesville, North Carolina, where he established a reputation as one of the best contest fiddlers in the South.) Golden herded his musicians into several cattle trucks for the long drive to Johnson City, and he succeeded in insulting most of them. This conflict — or Golden's insistence on receiving a percentage of the payments made to his musicians — resulted in virtually none of the recordings by any of the group of Corbin-area musicians being released.

A little over a year after holding his 1928 sessions, Walker returned to Johnson City for a second series of recordings. By this time, Columbia had merged with its long-time rival OKeh, and though each individual firm continued to release material on its own label, by the middle of 1929 the newly merged company was sending out one field unit to record material for both labels. During the second week in October 1929, Walker and the others in the field unit set up a studio at Richmond, Virginia, where they made a large number of African American gospel and blues recordings, and also recorded a handful of country acts. Finishing in Richmond on October 18, the Columbia/OKeh people drove 350 miles southwest to Johnson City, where they set up a studio, probably in the same former cream separation station they had used before. In four days of intensive work, they recorded 65 sides (two less than in 1928) by 18 different acts, 13 of which had not been at the 1928 Johnson City sessions. Table 3 shows the complete session list.

Table 3. Columbia's 1929 Johnson City Sessions

Monday, October 21

149200	Blalock and Yates	Morning Star Waltz	15576
149201	Blalock and Yates	Pride of the Ball	15576
149202	Jack Jackson	Flat Tire Blues	15662
149203	Jack Jackson	My Alabama Home	15662
149204	George Wade / Francum Braswell	Think a Little	15515
149205	George Wade / Francum Braswell	When We Go A-Courtin'	15515
149206	Jack Jackson	In Our Little Home Sweet Home	15497
149207	Jack Jackson	I'm Just a Black Sheep	15497
149208	Roane County Ramblers	Free a Little Bird—1930 Model	15498
149209	Roane County Ramblers	Johnson City Rag	15498
149210	Roane County Ramblers	Callahan Rag	15570
149211	Roane County Ramblers	Alabama Trot	15570
149212	Roane County Ramblers	Big Footed Nigger	uniss
149213	Roane County Ramblers	Smoky Mountain Waltz	uniss
149214	Wyatt and Brandon	Evalina	15523
149215	Wyatt and Brandon	Lover's Farewell	15523

Tuesday, October 22

149216	Roy Harvey / Leonard Copeland	Just Pickin'	15514
149217	Roy Harvey / Leonard Copeland	Beckley Rag	15514
149218	Roy Harvey / Leonard Copeland	Underneath the Sugar Moon	15582
149219	Roy Harvey / Leonard Copeland	Lonesome Weary Blues	15582
149220	Spindale Quartet	Sweet Peace the Gift of God's Love	15541
149221	Spindale Quartet	God Will Take Care of You	15541
149222	Spindale Quartet	Face to Face	15488
149223	Spindale Quartet	Lift Him Up	15488
149224	Queen Trio	Sunday Morning Blues	uniss
149225	Queen Trio	The June Bug	uniss
149226	Earl Shirkey / Roy Harper	Virginian Strike of '23	15535
149227	Earl Shirkey / Roy Harper	Little Lost Child	15642
149228	Earl Shirkey / Roy Harper	My Yodeling Sweetheart	15490
149229	Earl Shirkey / Roy Harper	I'm Longing to Belong to Someone	15490

149230	Earl Shirkey/ Roy Harper	We Have Moonshine in the West Virginia Hills	15642
149231	Earl Shirkey/ Roy Harper	A Hobo's Pal	15535
149232	Moatsville String Ticklers	West Virginia Hills	15491
149233	Moatsville String Ticklers	Moatsville Blues	15491
149234	Moatsville String Ticklers	Lost Waltz	uniss
149235	Moatsville String Ticklers	Goodbye My Lover Goodbye	uniss
149236	Weaver Brothers	You Came Back to Me	15487
149237	Weaver Bothers	Prison Sorrows	15487
149238	Weaver Bros. String Band	Raleigh County Rag	uniss
149239	Weaver Bros. String Band	Homesick Boy	uniss

Wednesday, October 23

149240	Byrd Moore and His Hot Shots	Frankie Silvers	15536
149241	Byrd Moore and His Hot Shots	The Hills of Tennessee	15536
149242	Byrd Moore and His Hot Shots	Careless Love	15496
149243	Byrd Moore and His Hot Shots	Three Men Went A-Huntin'	15496
149244	Bateman Sacred Quartet	Nothing Like Old Time Religion	15608
149245	Bateman Sacred Quartet	Some Day	15608
149246	Fred Richards	My Katie	15483
149247	Fred Richards	Danville Blues	15483
149248	Fred Richards	Women Rule the World	uniss
149249	Fred Richards	Old Pal	uniss
149250	Clarence Ashley	Dark Holler Blues	15489
149251	Clarence Ashley	The Coo-Coo Bird	15489
149252	Clarence Ashley	Little Sadie	15522
149253	Clarence Ashley	Naomi Wise	15522
149254	The Bentley Boys	Down on Penny's Farm	15565
149255	The Bentley Boys	Henhouse Blues	15565
149256	Bowman Sisters	Railroad Take Me Back	15621
149357	Bowman Sisters	Old Lonesome Blues	15621

Thursday, October 24

149258	Fran Trappe	Wild Horse	uniss
149259	Fran Trappe / Charlie Bowman	Carolina Moonshine	uniss
149260	Eph Woodie / Henpecked Husbands	Last Gold Dollar	15564
149261	Eph Woodie / Henpecked Husbands	The Fatal Courtship	15564
149262	Ira and Eugene Yates	Powder and Paint	15581
149263	Ira and Eugene Yates	Sarah Jane	15581
149264	Ellis Williams	Buttermilk Blues	14482
149265	Ellis Williams	Smokey Blues	14482

In many ways, the highlight of the 1929 Johnson City sessions was a set of brilliant sides recorded by a well-known local singer and instrumentalist, Clarence "Tom" Ashley. Born in his grandfather's boarding house in Bristol, Tennessee, in 1895, Ashley was reared by his grandparents Enoch and Mattie. By 1900, they had relocated to run another boarding house near Mountain City, Tennessee. By the time he was eight, Tom was playing banjo and learning songs like "The Coo-Coo Bird" from his mother. "I had one aunt that was just a wizard on the banjo," he recalled in later years. "And the other one played fairly well." In 1911, when he was sixteen, Tom started playing with a traveling medicine show. Two horse-drawn wagons hauled tents and a portable stage, and Ashley was hired as an entertainer — and as a roustabout to help set up and break down the tents. Traveling with "Doctor" Hauer, a Knoxville resident who sold herbal remedies, and with White Cloud, an "Indian" who sold Native American remedies, Ashley criss-crossed western North Carolina, eastern Tennessee, Virginia, West Virginia, and Kentucky. He learned to sing many types of songs, from blues to ballads, and to perform blackface comedy to help draw crowds.

Ashley had actually started his recording career in early 1928 with a less-than-successful trip to the Gennett Company in Richmond, Indiana. In October 1928, Ralph Peer "discovered" Ashley and paired him with Dock Walsh and Garley Foster for a new edition of the Carolina Tar Heels, to record for Victor. Often singing with Walsh, Ashley made a number of popular records with the Tar Heels, including "My Home's Across the Blue Ridge Mountains," a song still popular today. None of these Victor sides, though, mentioned Ashley by name. In the meantime, he had begun working with another band on the medicine show circuit, this one composed of Byrd Moore (from Norton, Virginia) and Clarence Greene (from North Carolina); all three were seasoned professionals who had spent time in recording studios. They had no trouble making the cut at Johnson City, as Byrd Moore and His Hot Shots.

Ashley, keenly aware of the widespread interest in murder ballads, remembered such a ballad, "Frankie Silvers," about a woman who had been hanged in 1833 at Morganton, North Carolina, for the murder of her husband. The incident, which occurred beside the Toe River in the Blue Ridge Mountains, is chronicled in Muriel Earley Sheppard's 1935 book *Cabins in the Laurel* and served as the inspiration for a 1999 mystery novel by Sharyn McCrumb, *The Ballad of Frankie Silver*. Frankie allegedly recited the ballad herself as she stood on the scaffold just before her hanging. Although the song has been sung over generations, the 1929 Johnson City recording by Ashley and Moore was the first ever made.

Byrd Moore and His Hot Shots recorded another traditional song for

On Wednesday, October 23, 1929, at Columbia Records' second round of sessions in Johnson City, a group of professional musicians with considerable experience performing for medicine shows—Byrd Moore and His Hot Shots, featuring (from left-to-right) Byrd Moore, Clarence Green, and Clarence "Tom" Ashley—recorded several songs, including the first recording of the now nationally known Appalachian murder ballad "Frankie Silvers." Later that day, Ashley recorded four songs as a solo act; among them was "The Coo-Coo Bird," which during the urban folk revival would become one of the more famous of all 1920s era recordings of Southern white music. Courtesy Burton-Manning Collection, the Archives of Appalachia, East Tennessee State University.

the first time: the comic "Three Men Went A-Huntin'." Known in England as "Three Jolly Welshmen," it was in print as early as 1668. Ashley and Moore converted the old hunting song into a sprightly string band breakdown. They even customized the lyrics (it was common for Americans to substitute their own geographical references for the English ones mentioned in the Old World ballads) by adding some sarcastic references to Norton, Virginia, Moore's hometown.

The sides by Byrd Moore and His Hot Shots were the first on the schedule for Wednesday, October 23, and between takes, Ashley gathered courage to ask Walker if he would be interested in some "lassy-makin'" songs. So-called because of their association with molasses stir-offs in the mountains, these were old songs that Ashley had sung for years, accompanying the unusual melodies on banjo. Walker's curiosity was piqued, and Ashley then played a sample of some of them. Incorporating an odd modal tuning on his banjo (one he came to call "sawmill"), Ashley delivered one of the most evocative of all Appalachian lyric folk songs, "The Coo-Coo Bird."

Like most lyric folk songs, "The Coo-Coo Bird" contains a number of free-floating interchangeable verses, some of which may well date back to Elizabethan England. Ashley's version of the song did not sell that well for Columbia when released in 1930— barely 3,000 copies — but it was included on Harry Smith's *Anthology of American Folk Music*, reaching later generations of folk singers and music fans. Ashley himself, after being "rediscovered" by urban folk revivalists in the 1960s, came to regard "The Coo-Coo Bird" as his signature song.

The 1929 Johnson City sessions generated recordings of several traditional ballads, with guitar and string band accompaniment: Ashley's "Naomi Wise," Eph Woodie's version of the "The Butcher Boy" (which he called "The Fatal Courtship"), and a version of "Little Bunch of Roses" (under the title "Lover's Farewell") by the duo of Wyatt and Brandon (members of the Roane County Ramblers). Also recording in Johnson City was a Jimmie Rodgers imitator, Nashville singer Jack Jackson, who did a "white blues" ("Flat Tire Blues") and a prison song, "I'm Just a Black Sheep." Roy Harvey returned to Johnson City in 1929 with Leonard Copeland to record a couple of influential guitar duets ("Beckley Rag" and "Just Pickin'"), as well as a topical song, "The Virginian Strike of '23." The latter song was about a railroad workers' strike at Princeton, West Virginia, involving approximately 4,000 men, including Harvey himself, who wound up losing his job as an engineer. Another bitter protest song from the 1929 Johnson City sessions came from a group called the Bentley Boys, from North Carolina, who recorded a strong statement about sharecropping called "Down on Penny's Farm." This record, which did not sell well in 1930, was also selected for the Harry Smith anthology, and by the 1960s was one of the bestknown protest songs in the United States. Bob Dylan utilized the song as a template for his 1962 song "Hard Times in New York Town."

Although the Brunswick-Vocalion company conducted two recording sessions in nearby Knoxville in 1929 and 1930, the deepening Depression eventually curtailed field recording activity, and after the 1929 Columbia sessions in Johnson City, no more records would be made in the Tri-Cities area until after World War II. Yet, some Tri-Cities area performers, including the Carter Family, traveled to studios in New York City to make important recordings during the early years of the Depression; a complete list of such musicians would form a considerable discography, and would reflect one of the richest troves of American music history.

19. The Birthplace of Country Music, 75 Years Later: The Cradle Still Rocks

Ted Olson and Ajay Kalra

The 1927 Bristol sessions may indeed have been "the Big Bang of country music," as scholars (beginning with Nolan Porterfield) have claimed and as the U.S. Congress has recognized,[1] since those recording sessions launched the careers of two of country music's most influential acts — Jimmie Rodgers and the Carter Family. Yet, however "big" it was, that "bang" went largely unheard, especially locally, until half a century later. Beginning in the 1970s, country music enthusiasts and scholars — virtually none of whom were from anywhere near Bristol — began to draw attention to the singular significance and stature of the 1927 Bristol sessions among the multitude of 1920s-era field recording sessions.

Despite increased attention to the Bristol sessions among some "outsiders," most residents of the Tri-Cities area (Bristol, Tennessee/Virginia, and the nearby communities of Kingsport and Johnson City, Tennessee) until recently did not know the global influence of the musicians who started their careers here. Tim Stafford, singer and guitarist in the early 1990s for Alison Krauss & Union Station and currently for the bluegrass group Blue Highway, grew up in Kingsport, not far from the Carters' residence in Maces Spring, Virginia, but he had no knowledge of the recordings and the repertoire of country music's "first family" until he was a high school student in 1974.[2] Older people in the Tri-Cities remember the heyday of traditional country and bluegrass music on local radio in the 1930s and 1940s, and most of these people take for granted the practice of community members making music together, viewing it as nothing that outsiders need get excited about. Many locals remain bemused at the ever-increasing interest in their region's music among enthusiasts from across the United States and around the world.

Several factors have deepened awareness among Tri-Cities residents toward the lasting value of the Bristol sessions' legacy, including urban folk revivalists' discovery of the Carter Family's music; the broadening influence of Jimmie Rodgers' music on recording stars from disparate music genres; the published writings of scholars who collected and/or interpreted the area's music; and the dissemination of that music heritage to a new generation through music instruction programs at regional schools. During the last two decades, local organizations have brought wider acknowledgement of the Tri-Cities area's musical heritage and have helped foster a continuation of those traditions.

A 1998 resolution passed by the U.S. Congress, though, may have overstated the case when declaring that the community of Bristol made a "significant contribution ... to the development and commercial acceptance of country music."[3] It would be more accurate to assert that Bristol was strategically positioned and that the Victor Talking Machine Company's 1927 recording sessions in Bristol were serendipitously timed to attract the two acts that form the basis of the city's contention for the title of "the birthplace of country music." This latter assessment is not intended to diminish the importance of other musical talent that participated in the 1927 Bristol sessions, but only to qualify that some of the other recordings from Bristol would not be basking in reflected limelight had they not been associated with the sessions where "The First Family of Country Music" and "The Father of Country Music" were "discovered" and initially recorded. Yet, the depth of the musical talent that the area continued to produce over successive decades is an equally important factor in Bristol's claim to being the cradle of country music. As Stafford observed in a *Bluegrass Unlimited* article, the relatively small area within a 100-mile radius of the Tri-Cities — the same vicinity that yielded a majority of Bristol sessions acts — has produced more significant old-time, country, and bluegrass music notables than any other similar-sized region. The musicians born and raised in this geographical area include Ernest Stoneman, the Carter Family, the Stanley Brothers, Red Rector, Tennessee Ernie Ford, Jim and Jesse McReynolds, the Osborne Brothers, Reno and Smiley, Jimmy Martin, Wiley and Zeke Morris, the Blue Sky Boys, Carl Story, Doyle Lawson, Kenny Baker, Ricky Skaggs, Roy Acuff, Dolly Parton, Chet Atkins, the Sauceman Brothers, Raymond Fairchild, Tater Tate, Benny Sims, Jethro Burns, George Shuffler, Tommy Jarrell, Ralph Blizard, Dave Loggins, Adam Steffey, Barry Bales, and Kenny Chesney.[4]

Bristol sessions producer Ralph Peer — impressed with his August 1927 recordings of the Carter Family and especially of Jimmie Rodgers (who after his 1927 sessions in Bristol had become one of Victor's top stars with the success of his "Blue Yodel," recorded at that company's Camden, New Jersey, studios) — returned to Bristol in 1928 for another series of recordings in the Tri-Cities area. Rival companies Columbia and Brunswick likewise recorded in nearby Johnson City and Knoxville, respectively. Soon, however, with the onset of the Great Depression, the field recording frenzy tapered off.[5] Jimmie Rodgers and the Carter Family were the only rural hillbilly music stars who found steady success in the tough economic times of the early 1930s.[6] The Carters made annual recording forays to the North and found consistent sales, while Rodgers was the first star of country music, likewise making many best-selling records up North. However, for Southern musicians with unproven commercial potential — from the Tri-Cities area, as elsewhere — the primary outlet for their music during the 1930s and 1940s was radio. With powerful transmitters and large broadcasting areas, barn dance programs like WLS Chicago's *National Barn Dance* (established in 1924) and WSM Nashville's *Grand Ole Opry* (established in 1925, renamed in 1927) were already drawing Southern musicians to their folds. Some people have speculated that if Bristol had had a radio show with a transmitter to match the strong signal of Nashville's WSM, Bristol might have become the country music capital instead of Nashville.[7] Regional radio and country music programming did come to the Tri-Cities area in 1929 with the establishment of radio station WOPI in Bristol, Tennessee. Started by W. A. Wilson, the proprietor of a Bristol retail radio shop, the station (whose call letters stand for "Watch Our Population Increase") prominently featured country music in its programming, which in its early years also included a mix of news, drama, variety programs, commercials, and live local entertainment. In addition to playing the recordings of such established acts as Jimmie Rodgers, the Carter Family, the Tenneva Ramblers, and Charlie Bowman, WOPI in 1935 established *Saturday Night Jamboree*, one of the area's earliest live radio barn dance programs. That show boosted the early careers of Bristol-native Tennessee Ernie Ford and Archie Campbell, from nearby Bulls Gap, Tennessee, and the show even drew significant musicians from the Knoxville area, including Homer and Jethro and Chet Atkins.[8]

Other Tri-Cities area radio stations soon implemented live country music programming. In the late 1930s, radio station WJHL began operation, with studios in Johnson City and Elizabethton, Tennessee. The station featured a number of country music shows, with the most successful program being *Barrel of Fun*.[9] In 1942, that show, staged at the Bonnie Kate Theatre in Elizabethton, hosted the radio debut of the young Stanley Brothers from Coeburn, Virginia.[10] Another local station with a much lower power transmitter, WNVA, in Norton, Virginia, would feature Carter Stanley after his discharge from the U.S. Army in the spring of 1946.[11] In the fall of that same year, when Ralph Stanley also finished Army service, the brothers inaugurated the Stanley Brothers and the Clinch Mountain Boys; the now-legendary bluegrass group got their first regular radio job on WCYB Bristol, a station launched in December 1946.[12] That station's daily noontime live country music program, *Farm and Fun Time*, would play as vital a role in bluegrass music history as the 1927 Bristol sessions played in the history of commercial country music. In addition to launching the careers of the Stanley Brothers, the program — which started as a one-hour program but which soon was stretched to two hours to accommodate new sponsors — featured not only bluegrass acts (such as Mac Wiseman, Flatt & Scruggs and the Foggy Mountain Boys, the Sauceman Brothers, Jimmy Martin, Curly King and the Tennessee Hilltoppers, Carl Story, Bobby Osborne, and Jim and Jesse McReynolds), but soon drew other acts playing traditional country music, including Charlie Monroe, the Blue Sky Boys, and even A. P. Carter.[13] Other than Bill Monroe, virtually every important musician from the first generation of bluegrass played on the *Farm and Fun Time* program.[14] The Tri-Cities area, by offering a ready market for more traditional styles of country music, served as a comfortable base for traditional country and bluegrass musicians as they honed their skills and in some cases prepared to pursue a larger national market.

In 1945, Johnson City–based music enthusiast and entrepreneur James Hobart "Hobe" Stanton started the Rich-R-Tone recording company to capitalize on the area's country music scene.[15] Before moving on to record for bigger labels, the Stanley Brothers and Wilma Lee and Stoney Cooper made their first recordings for Rich-R-Tone, which recorded about 200 acts in all, mostly at the studios of local radio stations.[16] While the Stanleys and the Coopers went on to prominent careers in bluegrass and traditional country music, respectively, their early recordings, initially released on 78 rpm records by this small regional label, remained out of print for decades, before being reissued on long-play (33 1/3 rpm) records and compact discs. Several even smaller recording companies operated in the Tri-Cities area during this period, including the Folk Star (a subsidiary of Rich-R-Tone), Shadow (located in Bristol, Tennessee), and Twin-City (Bristol, Tennessee/Virginia) labels.

By the late 1940s and early 1950s, many alumni of WCYB Bristol and some from Rich-R-Tone had experienced commercial success by touring nationally and recording for major record labels. Although the word "bluegrass" was not yet used as a descriptor for their music, Flatt & Scruggs, the

The Stanley Brothers — Ralph Stanley on banjo, Carter Stanley on guitar — performing for the *Farm and Fun Time* radio show over station WCYB Bristol. Natives of nearby Stratton, Virginia, the Stanleys launched their renowned career in bluegrass by performing around the Tri-Cities area. Courtesy Birthplace of Country Music Alliance.

Stanley Brothers, Mac Wiseman, Jimmy Martin, and the Osborne Brothers would make some of the genre's classic recordings during this period. By the time the term "bluegrass" was first used to identify the genre around 1955 or 1956, the regional music styles that it incorporated, along with other tradition-based country music styles, were facing stiff competition for audiences' attentions, locally as well as nationally, from television and from rock and roll. Wider recognition of the Tri-Cities area's musical heritage, though, soon began with the urban folk revival of the late 1950s and the early 1960s.

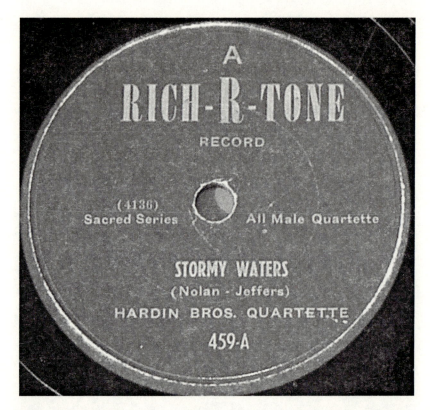

Rich-R-Tone Records was founded by James Stanton in 1946 and was based in Johnson City through the early 1960s. Despite being a regional label, Rich-R-Tone Records was important nationally in that it issued the initial recordings of two major musical acts, the Stanley Brothers and Wilma Lee and Stony Cooper. In all, Rich-R-Tone released recordings by approximately 200 different musical acts. Photograph by Bill Hartley. Courtesy Birthplace of Country Music Alliance.

Yet, well into the 1960s, traditional country music styles, including bluegrass, suffered commercially, locally as well as nationally.

By 1957, this folk revival was sparking interest in bluegrass music among people of urban backgrounds, including multi-instrumentalist and singer Mike Seeger and singer Bill Clifton. Such influential musicians viewed bluegrass as a form of Southern folk music (in 1959, folklorist and folk music collector Alan Lomax described bluegrass as "folk music in overdrive"). WCYB Bristol alumnus Earl Scruggs was the connecting link between the first two bluegrass albums released in the LP format, both released in 1957 — a compilation of banjo instrumentals produced by Mike Seeger entitled *American Banjo Three Finger and Scruggs Style* and Flatt & Scruggs and the

Foggy Mountain Boys' *Foggy Mountain Jamboree*. In 1960, the Osborne Brothers performed bluegrass on some college campuses, inaugurating the era of bluegrass acts finding success with audiences of urban youths.[17] Mother Maybelle and the Carter Sisters likewise toured campuses at this time, introducing many young city- and suburb-dwellers to country music. Despite growing recognition for specific musicians from the Tri-Cities area, there was little general perception of a local musical heritage through the 1960s — either among natives or among outside enthusiasts who moved to the area because they were attracted to its musical legacy.

In 1964, two professors in the English department at East Tennessee State University (ETSU), Thomas Burton and Ambrose Manning, started making field recordings of folk songs and ballads sung by people living in the mountains immediately to the east of the Tri-Cities.[18] This was the first effort by scholars based at the Tri-Cities' largest university, located in Johnson City, to preserve and study the area's musical heritage and to encourage wider appreciation of that music. Meanwhile, some Tri-Cities natives began to promote local traditional music and to attempt to clarify its position within country music history. In 1971, at the encouragement of local reporter Richard Boyle, Carl Pennington and the Odd Fellows Club collaborated with the Bristol Chamber of Commerce to oversee the installation of a memorial stone commemorating the Carter Family, Jimmie Rodgers, and the Bristol sessions in a downtown Bristol public park.[19] Pennington and his associates went on to form the Bristol Country Music Foundation, which, in an effort to memorialize the country music pioneers associated with the area, hosted the Appalachian Music Days festival and operated the Appalachian Music Museum.[20]

During the 1970s, equally significant attempts to celebrate Tri-Cities music traditions were occurring at ETSU, where several professors, especially Thomas Burton and Brooklyn, New York-raised ethnomusicologist and old-time fiddler and banjoist Richard Blaustein, not only collected and documented those traditions, but also preserved those traditions by donating their significant collections of regional music recordings to the Archives of Appalachia, founded at the university in 1978. These collections, later combined with other music collections from subsequent folklorists, collectors, and scholars, made ETSU an important center for the preservation, interpretation, and proliferation of the Tri-Cities' musical heritage.

Among the promoters of Appalachian music at ETSU was Jack Tottle. A bluegrass musician and songwriter raised in suburban Washington, D.C., Tottle moved to the Tri-Cities area in 1979, and in 1982 he started the Bluegrass and Country Music Program (now called the Bluegrass, Old-Time, and Country Music Program); initially administered in ETSU's music department, "the Bluegrass Program" has fostered increased pride among area residents toward their musical traditions. Before the introduction of this program, many young people from the Tri-Cities area were exposed to their musical heritage primarily through mainstream media productions such as *The Beverly Hillbillies*, as had been the case with Tim Stafford[21]; yet, today, local youths and adults have in "the Bluegrass Program" a forum through which to participate in and learn their own musical traditions. Multiplatinum-selling country music artist Kenny Chesney, from Luttrell, Tennessee, got his start in the program, having received his first guitar lesson from Jack Tottle.[22] Many students in the program have come to Johnson City from outside Appalachia, and a number of them from abroad. Tottle and the program's assistant director, multi-instrumentalist Raymond W. McLain, work with local organizations similarly concerned with preserving the Tri-Cities area's musical legacy, the most successful of which, founded in 1994, is the Bristol-based Birthplace of Country Music Alliance (BCMA).

While ETSU's Bluegrass, Old-Time, and Country Music Program has helped reinvigorate area musical traditions by providing instrument instruction workshops and performance opportunities for aspiring musicians, the program has long involved academic study of those traditions through courses offered as part of an Appalachian studies curriculum, co-sponsored by ETSU's Department of Sociology and Anthropology and that school's Center for Appalachian Studies and Services (CASS), a Tennessee Center for Excellence. In 2000, "the Bluegrass Program" was moved from ETSU's music department and made an official part of CASS. Including the B. Carroll Reece Museum and the Archives of Appalachia within its organization, CASS offers opportunities for scholars to better understand the Appalachian region and its cultural heritage, including its musical traditions. The Reece Museum not only features a substantial collection of musical instruments from the Tri-Cities area but also hosts diverse performances from area musicians.

Academic and civic efforts to reclaim the Tri-Cities' musical legacy and its place in the history of country music were in their relative infancy at the time of the Bristol sessions' 50th and 60th anniversaries. By 1997 — the 70th anniversary of the 1927 sessions and the 50th anniversary of WCYB Bristol's *Farm and Fun Time* show — the Birthplace of Country Music Alliance was taking significant strides in that direction. During the BCMA concert series that year, for example, members of the Carter and Stoneman families performed together on stage for the first time. Founded by Bristol native Tim White, a musician and visual artist, the BCMA had been instrumental in the passage of a proclamation by the State of Virginia recognizing Bristol and the surrounding vicinity as "the Birthplace of Country Music." In 1998, the U.S. Congress passed a resolution (U.S. Congressional Resolution H. R.

A sign outside the Carter Family Fold's main building commemorates the Fold's main mission: to honor the lives and music of A. P., Sara, and Maybelle Carter. Built on the site of A. P. Carter's former store in Maces Spring, Virginia, and situated beside a highway named after A. P., the Carter Family Fold honors the trio's musical legacy in a number of ways: maintaining the Carter Family Memorial Music Center (which features a collection of Carter Family-related memorabilia), hosting concerts of regional music every weekend, and offering the annual Carter Family Memorial Music Festival and Crafts Show. Photograph by John Maeder. Courtesy Birthplace of Country Music Alliance.

214) to affirm that claim. The BCMA became an affiliate of the Smithsonian Institution in 2000, entering a partnership that made the Bristol area's musical heritage a central focus of the 2003 Smithsonian Folklife Festival's "Appalachia: Heritage and Harmony" exhibition, held on the National Mall in Washington, D.C. In the summer of 2002, the BCMA hosted a widely publicized series of local events celebrating the Bristol sessions' 75th anniversary.[23]

Radio shows and live music venues have played a significant role in the resurgence of tradition-based music in the Tri-Cities since the mid–1970s. Among the best-known music venues in the area are the Carter Family Fold, located at the site of A. P. Carter's former store near Hiltons, Virginia; the Down Home, in Johnson City, Tennessee; and the Paramount Theatre, in

The late, great Johnny Cash was one of the many performers to grace the stage at the Carter Family Fold. After marrying Mother Maybelle Carter's daughter June, Cash often visited the Fold, and throughout his later years he publicly championed the important role of the Carters in American music history. In back of the Fold stage are framed portraits of Sara Carter and of A. P. Carter; seated beside Cash is the daughter of Sara and A. P., Janette Carter, who with her sister Gladys and her brother Joe founded the Fold. Photograph by John Maeder. Courtesy Birthplace of Country Music Alliance.

Bristol. The Carter Family Fold, a rustic barn-like performance venue with seating capacity for 1,000 people, was erected in 1976 by Gladys, Janette, and Joe Carter, daughters and son of Sara and A. P. Carter, when crowds attending live music performances at the A. P. Carter Store started to exceed the latter building's confines. Appearing on the National Register of Historic Places, the Fold hosts weekly Saturday evening shows featuring some of the most distinguished regional folk and country musicians. The Fold's small dance floor accommodates impromptu dances in which local audiences are often joined by visitors from afar. The Down Home has showcased many of the most prominent musicians in American "roots" music. That venue is co-owned by Johnson City–native Ed Snodderly, a multi-instrumentalist and singer-songwriter who made three internationally acclaimed albums in the 1990s as part of the revivalist brother duo, the Brother Boys (along with vocalist Eugene Wolf). An instructor in ETSU's Bluegrass, Old-Time, and Country Music Program, Snodderly wrote a song dedicated to the Carter Family entitled "The Diamond Stream," a verse from which is engraved on the wall at the Country Music Hall of Fame in Nashville.

Music-making was historically so popular in the Tri-Cities area that music gatherings held at a country store in Bristol's Hickory Tree community often drew up to a thousand musicians and enthusiasts. That tradition of informal music-making is currently experiencing a revival around the Tri-Cities area. Front porch jam sessions remain popular, and country stores and music shops regularly host gatherings for impromptu picking (and sometimes dancing). Musical acts from the area frequently perform in downtown Bristol at the site of a huge mural (this hard-to-miss landmark, commemorating the Bristol sessions, was painted by the BCMA's Tim White). National Heritage Fellowship recipient Ralph Blizard, a longbow fiddler, helped found the Traditional Appalachian Music Heritage Association (TAMHA), which sponsors a jam session every Friday in Blountville, Ten-

Born in Bristol, Tennessee, in 1919, country music star Ernest Jennings "Tennessee Ernie" Ford was residing in the city at the time of the Bristol sessions. Musically gifted from a young age, Ford worked as a disc jockey for radio station WOPI-Bristol while still a teenager, before leaving the city to study music at a conservatory. After his stint in the military during World War II, Tennessee Ernie Ford settled in California and soon attained stardom, yet he never forgot his roots in Bristol. Courtesy Birthplace of Country Music Alliance.

nessee. Country stores in the area — including Slagle's store in Elizabethton and a store in Rheatown, Tennessee — similarly host regular jams, as do many area music stores. One annual festival dedicated to celebrating the Tri-Cities area's musical heritage is the Rhythm and Roots Reunion, established in 2001 and sponsored by many local businesses and organizations, including the city governments of Bristol, Tennessee/Virginia. Further evidence of governmental interest in that heritage can be seen in downtown Bristol, where the Bristol sessions are commemorated through a monument, plaques, and city streets named after such Bristol sessions participants as Ralph Peer and Ernest Stoneman; not far from downtown Bristol are a Virginia highway dedicated to A. P. Carter and a Tennessee highway bearing the name of an important Bristol-born musician from a later generation, Tennessee Ernie Ford.

Despite the dominance of mainstream radio programming in the Tri-Cities, as across the nation, some area radio stations, including WOPI, WGOC, WJCW, WGAT, WMMT, WAXM, and WNCW, have worked with local music enthusiasts and experts to devote airtime to roots-based American music. For example, WETS-FM, located on the ETSU campus, offers extensive programming designed specifically to spotlight regional traditional music history and contemporary "roots music" talent, including the show *Studio One*, hosted by Dave Carter. WETS was the home of Jack Tottle's long-running show *Bluegrass Heartland*, which focused on contemporary regional bluegrass music. Jimmy Smith, Phil Leonard, Tim White, Mike Strickland, Dan Hirschi, and Wayne Winkler are among the music aficionados in the Tri-Cities who have hosted radio shows focusing on the area's musical legacy.

As in 1927, the Tri-Cities area remains a significant population center and a social hub for upper East Tennessee and parts of western North Carolina and southwestern Virginia. The various musical communities surrounding the Tri-Cities area have overlapping borders and a significant level of interaction due to shared traditions. Boone and Asheville, North Carolina, are known for their progressive-minded musical communities, but they are equally appreciative of acoustic-based musical styles. Legendary flatpick guitarist Doc Watson — born in Deep Gap, North Carolina, close to Boone — hosts the annual Doc Watson Music Festival in nearby Sugar Grove, North Carolina, as well as the largest festival of predominantly acoustic music in America, Merlefest, held in Wilkesboro, North Carolina. The latter festival, dedicated to the memory of Doc Watson's son and longtime musical partner Merle Watson, draws many thousands of devotees of traditional American musics. Asheville is the site each summer of the oldest extant folk festival in the United States, the Mountain Dance and Folk Festival, which was started in 1928 by folksinger and collector Bascom Lamar Lunsford. One of the more popular styles of music among the young audiences in this western section of North Carolina is the acoustic-based improvisatory style usually referred to as "jam band" music. Although many such musicians and their audiences are not from Appalachia and have come by their country and bluegrass music influences secondhand, through the influence of 1960s and 1970s roots music performers, the legacy of the Bristol sessions, often unbeknownst to them, underlies this seemingly "progressive" music.

The Tri-Cities area similarly hosts musical communities that favor more contemporary expressions of traditional acoustic music. On area radio stations, as well as at many performance venues, traditional country, old-time, and bluegrass music have been integrated with such later emerging styles as newgrass, progressive country, alternative country, Americana, and myriad subgenres of rock and jazz. While efforts by local organizations and institutions have certainly increased recognition of the area's country music legacy, the influence of the music itself continues to inform a variety of contemporary styles even without such assistance, forming the basis of a vital and vibrant musical culture. As in 1927, when Ralph Peer arrived in Bristol and produced "the Big Bang of country music," the Tri-Cities area's musical culture continues to successfully balance tradition and innovation.

Notes

1. Nolan Porterfield, "Hey, Hey, Tell 'Em About Us: Jimmie Rodgers Visits the Carter Family," in *Country: The Music and the Musicians* 2d ed., by the Country Music Foundation (New York: Abbeville Press, 1994); H. Con. Res. 214 available at http://www.birthplaceofcountrymusic.org /heritage/hr214.htm accessed on June 6, 2003.

2. Tim Stafford, "Rock Me in the Cradle of Bluegrass: Bluegrass Music in the Tri-Cities Region of Upper East Tennessee," *Bluegrass Unlimited* 22 no. 4 (1987): 18.

3. H. Con. Res. 214.

4. Stafford, "Rock Me in the Cradle," 20.

5. John Maeder, "Birthplace of Country Music Alliance's Celebration of Historic Bristol Sessions," *Bluegrass Unlimited* 37, July 2002, 37; Charles K. Wolfe, "The Discovery of Jimmie Rodgers: A Further Note," *Old Time Music* 5, 1972; Wolfe, "The Bristol Syndrome: Field Recordings of Early Country Music," *Country Music Annual 2002*, eds. Charles K. Wolfe and James Akenson.

6. Maeder, Ibid., 37.

7. Tim Stafford, "A View from Home: A Discussion With Doyle Lawson," *Bluegrass Unlimited* 22, no. 4 (1987): 43.

8. *Country Music in the Tri-Cities*, 30 min., Archives of Appalachia, East Tennessee State University, videocassette.

9. Ibid.

10. Jack Tottle, "The Stanley Brothers: For Most of Their First Decade, Bristol Was Home," *Bluegrass Unlimited* 22, no. 4 (1987): 27.

11. Ibid.

12. Ibid.

13. Ibid.

14. Ibid.

15. "Men Working to Preserve Label's History, 'Tree Streets' Role in Growth," *Johnson City Press*, 17 March, 2002.

16. Ibid.

17. Neil V. Rosenberg, *Bluegrass: A History* (Champaign-Urbana: University of Illinois Press, 1985).

18. Greg Powers, "Thomas Burton" *Now & Then* 11: 2, 1994, 39.

19. Jack Tottle, "The Bristol Country Music Foundation: Music, Memories and a Museum," *Bluegrass Unlimited* 15 (April 1981): 16–17.

20. Ibid.

21. Stafford, "Rock Me in the Cradle," 18.

22. Interview with Jack Tottle, June 3, 2003.

23. Birthplace of Country Music Alliance Homepage, www.birthplaceof-countrymusic.org/about/bcma%accomplishments.htm [Accessed on June 7, 2003]

Contributors

Richard Blaustein is a professor of sociology and anthropology and a senior research fellow of the Center for Appalachian Studies and Services (CASS) at East Tennessee State University. Between 1983 and 1992, he served as director of CASS. He has also served as president of the Tennessee Folklore Society and as a convener of the Music and Song Section of the American Folklore Society.

Tom Carter lived in Meadows of Dan, Virginia, during the summer of 1973, while working on a music collecting project sponsored by the National Endowment for the Humanities. There, he met Jesse and Clarice Shelor. Carter now teaches in the College of Architecture and Planning at the University of Utah.

Katie Doman is an assistant professor of English at Tusculum College in Greeneville, Tennessee. A singer and songwriter, Doman recently recorded a CD featuring her performances of her songs with student-musicians associated with the Bluegrass, Old-Time, and Country Music Program at East Tennessee State University.

Ajay Kalra, presently a doctoral student in ethnomusicology at the University of Texas at Austin, honed his editorial and writing skills while working as an assistant editor with the *Encyclopedia of Appalachia* at the Center for Appalachian Studies and Services at East Tennessee State University. In an earlier phase of his life, Kalra was a diagnostic radiologist, an artist, and a rock music trivia champion in New Delhi, India. He is also a bassist and a collector of country rock, folk rock, jazz rock, early world jazz, 1970s disco, soft rock, and Euro-pop music.

John Lilly is editor of *Goldenseal* magazine and serves as folklife director for the West Virginia Division of Culture and History in Charleston,
West Virginia. He is the editor of the book *Mountains of Music: West Virginia Traditional Music from Goldenseal*, and is a contributor to the *Encyclopedia of Appalachia*, *The West Virginia Encyclopedia*, and *The Encyclopedia of
Country Music*. Lilly is also an experienced old-time musician, singer, yodeler,
and songwriter.

The late **Gladys Carter Millard** was the oldest child of A. P. and Sara
Carter. In the mid–1970s, to commemorate and celebrate the music of her parents and her aunt Maybelle, Gladys co-founded (with her sister Janette Carter
and her brother Joe Carter) the Carter Family Memorial Music Center, Inc.
(also known as the Carter Family Fold), located near Hiltons, Virginia.

Mabel Phelps Morrell, who passed away shortly after the 75th anniversary of the 1927 Bristol Sessions, was one of the final surviving participants
in the 1927 sessions in Bristol, having recorded there when a child as a singer
with the group known as the Tennessee Mountaineers.

Eric Morritt is the owner of an information technology business in
Kingsport, Tennessee. He has studied and collected vintage recording technology since the age of 16, and has worked as technology consultant in several film and video projects, including recent work with the BBC on a
documentary. Morritt's sound recording collection consists of more than
2000 items, which include wax celluloid cylinders, commercial and instan-
taneous discs, and wire and radio transcriptions, dating from the 1880s
through the mid-1950s.

Jocelyn Neal is an assistant professor at the University of North Carolina at Chapel Hill, where she teaches courses in music theory and analy-
sis and popular music. Neal received the Ph.D. from the Eastman School of
Music. Her research has addressed topics ranging from the music of Jimmie
Rodgers to contemporary fan responses in country music.

Donald Lee Nelson lives in Los Angeles, California. In the 1970s and
1980s, he contributed numerous articles on American music and musicians
to the John Edwards Memorial Foundation's legendary publication *JEMF
Quarterly*.

Ted Olson is an associate professor at East Tennessee State University,
where he teaches Appalachian studies and English courses. Olson is the

author of *Blue Ridge Folklife*, the editor of James Still's *From the Mountain, From the Valley: New and Collected Poems*, and the editor of *CrossRoads: A Southern Culture Annual.*

Ralph Peer (1892–1960), a Kansas City native, was a major pioneer in several areas of the music business, including record production, music publishing, and managing performing acts.

Carrie Rodgers, who was married to Jimmie Rodgers from 1920 to the performer's death in 1933, was the author of *My Husband, Jimmie Rodgers* (1935). Carrie Rodgers continued to promote her late husband's musical legacy until her death in 1961.

The Rounder Collective features Ken Irwin, Marian Leighton-Levy, and Bill Nowlin, who together in 1970 founded Rounder Records, one of the most successful independent recording companies in the United States.

Brandon Story moved to Bristol, Virginia, when he was eight years old, but moved to Bristol, Tennessee, in the mid–1990s and has lived there, mostly, ever since. In his professional career, he has run heavy equipment, taught English composition classes, and played bass for the Tri-Cities–based old-time band the Reeltime Travelers. The chapter in this book on Ernest Phipps incorporates research conducted by Story for his M.A. thesis at East Tennessee State University.

Thomas Townsend lives in Bloomington, Indiana, with his wife, Julie Ann, and son, Gideon. Townsend works in information technology and compensates for the relentless futurism of high-tech employment by being an actively performing old-time musician, usually on the fiddle or banjo-ukulele. A recipient of a master's degree in music, he is particularly interested in applying music theory to old-time styles, and has published an article on this topic, concerning the music of the Carter Family, in the book *Country Music Annual 2001.*

Charles K. Wolfe, a professor at Middle Tennessee State University, is the author of more than twenty books on folk, country, and pop music, and he has been nominated for Grammy awards three times for his work in producing and annotating albums. Wolfe's book *A Good Natured Riot* won both the prestigious Ralph Gleason Award and the BMI award for the best book on American music. Most recently, he has written the script for the PBS television series *American Roots Music* and has completed, with scholar Neil Rosenberg, a definitive study called *The Music of Bill Monroe.*

Index

Numbers in **boldface** indicate photographs or song transcriptions